pasta
every day

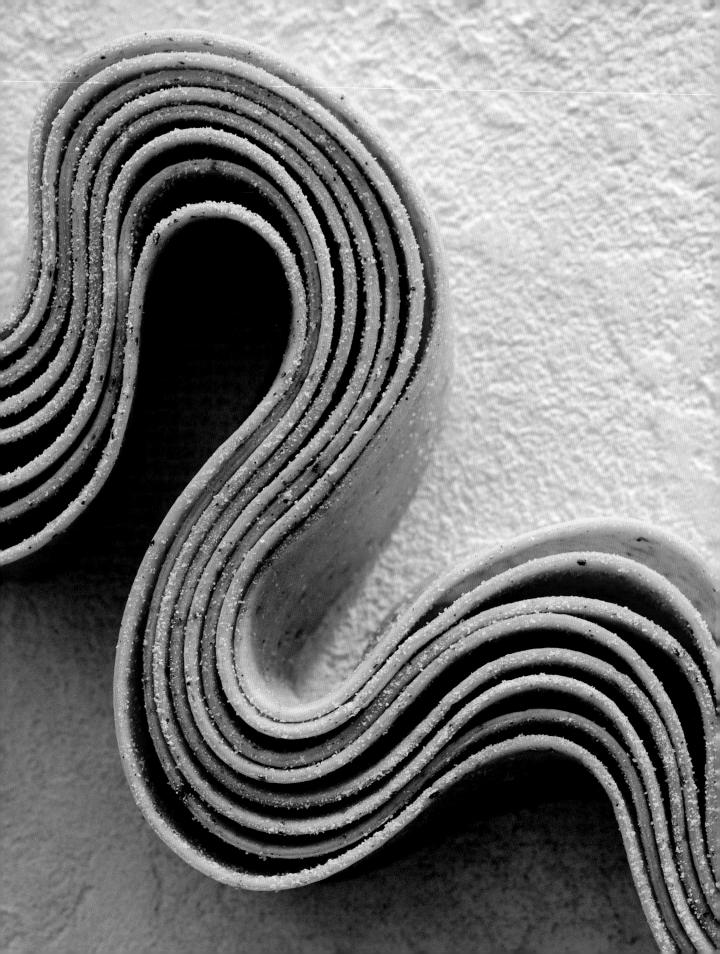

Make It,
Shape It,
Sauce It,
Eat It

pasta
every day

MERYL FEINSTEIN

Photographs by Nico Schinco

VORACIOUS

LITTLE, BROWN AND COMPANY
NEW YORK / BOSTON / LONDON

Voracious / Little, Brown and Company
Hachette Book Group
1290 Avenue of the Americas, New York, NY 10104
littlebrown.com

First Edition: September 2023

Voracious is an imprint of Little, Brown and
Company, a division of Hachette Book Group, Inc. The
Voracious name and logo are trademarks of Hachette
Book Group, Inc.

The publisher is not responsible for websites (or their
content) that are not owned by the publisher.

The Hachette Speakers Bureau provides a wide range
of authors for speaking events. To find out more, go to
hachettespeakersbureau.com or call (866) 376-6591.

Photographs by Nico Schinco, food styling by Judy Kim,
prop styling by Maeve Sheridan.

ISBN 978-0-316-36056-2
Library of Congress Control Number: 2023932356

2 4 6 8 7 5 3 1

LSC-C

Printed in China

INTRODUCTION   9

tools   13

pantry   16

PART ONE *doughs*   18

ingredients   23

techniques   27

flour & water pasta doughs   34
durum wheat & water pasta dough   37
soft wheat & water pasta dough   37
whole wheat & water pasta dough   38
basil pasta dough   38
saffron pasta dough   41

egg pasta doughs   42
standard egg pasta dough   45
whole wheat egg pasta dough   45
vegan "egg" pasta dough   45
almost all-yolk pasta dough   45
black pepper pasta dough   46
parsley-speckled pasta dough   46
sour cream & rye pasta dough   49
chestnut pasta dough   49
citrus-scented pasta dough   50
white wine pasta dough   50

colorful pasta doughs   52
colorful flour & water pasta dough   54
colorful egg pasta dough   54

gluten-free pasta doughs   56
gluten-free flour & water pasta dough   57
gluten-free egg pasta dough   57

gnocchi doughs   59
ricotta gnocchi dough   60
homemade ricotta   61
meyer lemon & herb ricotta gnocchi dough   64
pumpkin & ricotta gnocchi dough   65
potato gnocchi dough   66
ossola-style chestnut, squash & potato gnocchi dough   69
sweet potato gnocchi dough   70

PART TWO *shapes*   74

before we start   78

hand-formed pastas   80
pici   83
lagane   86
strozzapreti   88
corzetti della valpolcevera   92
cavatelli   96
capunti   100
malloreddus   102
spizzulus   104
busiate   106
orecchiette   108
foglie d'ulivo   110

how to roll pasta sheets (with a pasta machine)   114
rolling pasta by hand   117

playing with patterns & colors   118
herb-laminated pasta sheets   121
patterned pasta sheets   124

hand-cut pastas   128
tagliolini, tagliatelle, fettuccine & pappardelle   131

short-cut pastas   136
sorpresine   138
farfalle   140
garganelli   143
corzetti stampati   146
corzetti ravioli   147

stuffed pastas   150
"classic" ravioli   152
egg yolk ravioli (uovo in raviolo)   159
double-stuffed ravioli (ravioli doppi)   162
scarpinocc   166
cappelletti   168
tortelloni (& tortellini)   172
agnolotti & agnolotti del plin   177
caramelle   182

gnocchi   186
standard gnocchi method   188
delicate gnocchi method   192
stuffed gnocchi (gnocchi ripieni)   196

lasagne   198
besciamella   202
sorrento-style baked gnocchi (gnocchi alla sorrentina)   203

cooking & storing fresh pasta   204

SCAN THIS CODE
*for step-by-step videos of all the
pasta shapes to the right.*

PART THREE *fillings* 209

before we start 212

cheesy fillings

whipped ricotta filling 214
four-cheese filling 218
spinach & ricotta filling 218
black pepper & pecorino filling 219
honeymoon cheese & herb filling 221
roasted garlic & rosemary filling 222
alpine cheese fondue filling 225

vegetable fillings

any-greens filling 226
asparagus & spring pea filling with mint 229
summer corn & basil filling 230
mushroom, garlic & thyme filling 231
mashed potato & chive filling 232
eggplant & burrata filling 233
winter squash & brown butter filling 234
braised shallot & grana padano filling 236
smoky caramelized onion filling 239

meaty fillings

roasted salmon & mascarpone filling 240
sausage & spinach filling 242
braised beef & caramelized cabbage filling 243

PART FOUR 246
sauces & more

before we start 251

tomato sauces 254

all-purpose tomato sauce, three ways 256
no-cook tomato & basil sauce 259
tomato-cream sauce (no-vodka vodka sauce) 260
slow-roasted tomato & garlic sauce 263
tomato sauce with olives & fried capers 264
fiery calabrian chili sauce 267

vegetable & herb sauces 268

basil pesto 270
tomato & almond pesto (pesto alla trapanese) 274
citrus & pistachio pesto 275
red pesto (pesto rosso) 276

kale & arugula pesto 277
sage & hazelnut pesto 278
ligurian walnut sauce (salsa di noci) 279
broccoli sauce 281
fried zucchini sauce 282
wild mushroom sauce 285
sweet & sour eggplant sauce with burrata 286
braised onion ragù 289

butter, cream & cheese sauces 290

butter & sage sauce (burro e salvia) 293
butter & parmesan sauce (alfredo's alfredo) 294
compound butters 296
pecorino, pepper & lemon sauce 298
golden saffron sauce 301
roasted garlic & miso sauce 302
smoky pumpkin sauce 305
four-cheese sauce (quattro formaggi) 306
caramelized onion cheese sauce 308

meaty sauces 310

sausage, saffron & fennel ragù 312
the meatiest meatless ragù 315
casual bolognese 316
roasted red pepper & vegetarian sausage ragù 318
port-braised lamb ragù with shallots & rosemary 321

fish sauces 324

white fish ragù with lemon & capers 327
slow-roasted salmon & crème fraîche sauce with peas 328
anchovy & onion sauce with breadcrumbs 331
pantry tuna & tomato sauce 332
spicy garlic & anchovy sauce with broccoli 335

broths & soups 336

tomato broth 338
corn broth 341
parmesan broth 342
italian meat broth (brodo di carne) 345
grandma ruthe's chicken soup 346
chickpea soup with harissa & rosemary 349
white bean soup with parmesan & kale 350

toppings & condiments 352

toasted breadcrumbs (pangrattato) 354
garlic confit 355
balsamic reduction 356
salsa verde 357

ACKNOWLEDGMENTS 358

INDEX 360

introduction

ANYONE CAN MAKE FRESH PASTA
(EVEN YOU)

I fell in love with making pasta when I was twenty-eight. My husband and I had arrived in Modena—home of balsamic vinegar and Parmigiano-Reggiano, and the penultimate stop on our Italian honeymoon. It was April, crisp and sunny, and we found ourselves on the outskirts of town at a canary yellow house, blanketed in vines of newly bloomed wisteria. This was Acetaia Malagoli Daniele, a centuries-old, family-run balsamic vinegar producer, and an undeniably happy place to be. We were there to taste the vinegar, of course, but we were also there to make pasta.

Barbara was our host, and she was exactly the type of person you'd want to learn from—firm yet friendly, an expert from years of doing things over and over without pretension. We were making pasta in the sunroom, and everything we needed was laid out on a long wooden table: flour, eggs (from the hens out back), and a rolling pin—plus fresh ricotta to stuff inside.

She coached us as we cracked eggs into a heap of flour, kneaded the two into a smooth ball of dough, and rolled that dough into a thin, circular sheet. We made mistakes—a lot of them—but Barbara brushed them off: **Pasta is about pleasure, not perfection**, she assured us. Then she showed us how to cut pappardelle, pinch farfalle, and fashion oversized tortellini (called tortellacci) bursting with cheese.

Some of our shapes looked neat; others...let's call them abstract. But we didn't care. It was fun, soothing even, and we were proud of what we'd made. When we sat down to eat, it was the best pasta I'd ever tasted.

bringing pasta home

I'm telling you this story for a couple of reasons. The first is that fresh pasta is often misunderstood. It's a simple food with humble origins, long a staple of home cooks like Barbara. But over time it's become trapped by an intimidating reputation.

The first time my husband and I attempted fresh pasta was not in Modena but in Manhattan, a couple of years earlier when we lived in a 400-square-foot studio on the Upper West Side. It was an elaborate recipe for artichoke ravioli from The French Laundry (I know, I know). We started the dough at 4:00 p.m., took our first bite at 10:00 p.m., finished our plates at 10:05 p.m., and then ordered a pizza. This experience is not unique, but it should be. The idea that fresh pasta is a Michelin-level challenge, a minefield of fancy tools and complex techniques only fit for a restaurant chef, is a modern and American myth.

The truth is this: Anyone can make fresh pasta at home. What's more, **anyone can make *great* fresh pasta with what's already in their kitchen**.

The second purpose of this story is to assure you that it's never too late to try something new. I'm a descendant of Eastern European Jews; I was raised on matzah ball soup, not tortellini in brodo. But since that morning in Modena, not a day has gone by when I haven't made, eaten, or thought about pasta. By the time you're reading this, it'll be more than five years since I quit my corporate PR job, graduated culinary school, and started Pasta Social Club, a community of pasta lovers and makers; four years since I made hundreds of tortelli, corzetti, and cavatelli daily at one of New York's most popular pasta restaurants, Misi; and three years since I taught my first formal pasta class and started developing recipes for major food publications.

So although I'm now a trained chef who's made a lot of pasta, I haven't forgotten what it feels like to be nervous in the kitchen and start at the very beginning—because my own beginning was not so long ago. If I can do it, you can do it, too.

how to navigate this book

My goal is to empower you to make pasta at home with joy and confidence, and to inspire you to take risks in the kitchen. I have enormous respect for Italian cooking and tradition, both of which I study with fervor. But this is not a traditional cookbook or an Italian cookbook.

The recipes are organized not as complete dishes—say, cheese ravioli with butter and sage—but by pasta's core components: **doughs, shapes, fillings** (for stuffed pastas), and **sauces**. These can be mixed and matched to create endless combinations so, like generations of pasta makers before us, **you can make what you like with what you have**. (For the more straitlaced among us, don't worry—there are plenty of suggested pairings peppered throughout.)

Some of the methods might seem lengthy, but they are not difficult. After years of answering pasta-related questions, I write instructions as if we are cooking together, side by side, and any extra explanation is there to ensure you succeed the first time.

True to pasta's modest roots, all the ingredients in this book are available in major grocery stores and online. Of course, if you have access to exciting local and seasonal ingredients, use them. You might also notice that most of these recipes are vegetarian-friendly, and many can be made vegan. This is both altruistic and selfish—the former, to ensure people with dietary restrictions can enjoy them; the latter, because I am one of those people. I grew up in a kosher home, so in keeping with those customs, you won't find any pork or shellfish here. Finally, although this book is about fresh pasta, it will also come in handy for the box of dried noodles in your pantry, with dozens of sauces to choose from.

Even in Barbara's sunroom I knew that a plate of pasta was about more than good food. Likewise, this book is not just about pasta and how to make it, but also about luxuriating in the kitchen. Pasta can be made loudly in the company of others or peacefully alone. Either way, it nudges you to slow down and be present. Pasta reminds us to find joy in something simple. It values pleasure, not perfection (worst-case scenario: an ugly-delicious dinner); it has always been and should always be about connecting with the ones you love. So, whether it's your first time or your fiftieth, give the recipes and techniques in this book a try. You might just find yourself making pasta every day.

Serving Sizes and Ingredient Conversions

All doughs are designed to serve four for hand-formed, hand-cut, and short-cut pastas, and four to six for stuffed pastas. Gnocchi doughs serve two to four.

Water-based doughs can be scaled up or down using the base recipe of 2 parts flour to 1 part liquid in weight, and I generally recommend 100 to 120 grams flour (50 to 60 ml water) per person. Egg-based doughs can be scaled using 100 grams flour and 56 grams eggs (1 large egg, give or take) per person.

I strongly recommend weighing your ingredients. It's the most accurate way to ensure the correct ratio of flour to liquid in your dough. I do, however, include volume conversions for anyone who does not have a scale. Many cooking resources suggest that 1 cup flour weighs 120 or 125 grams—these numbers are based on sifted flour weight. In practice, my recipe testers and I continually dipped cups of flour weighing about 155 grams for 00 and all-purpose flours, and about 165 grams for semola and semolina flours. These measurements were taken straight out of the bag with no sifting. Volume measurements for other flours like rye, chestnut, and whole wheat have been converted similarly.

If you are using cups instead of grams, know that your doughs will vary more often, but also remember that everything is fixable.

All sauces are designed to coat 1 batch of fresh dough or 1 pound (454 grams) dried pasta unless noted otherwise.

tools

I treasure my collection of pasta tools, but **you don't need any special equipment to make pasta** at home. (Don't believe me? Try the pici on page 83.)

Pasta tools are a blessing and a curse. A blessing because hand-carved wooden boards and sparkling brass cutters are beautiful to look at and even more fun to use. A curse because a long list of often-expensive, single-purpose tools can drive would-be pasta makers away.

Now that we're clear, here's what you'll find in my collection, as well as some other kitchen items that I use regularly.

for doughs

DIGITAL KITCHEN SCALE: An accurate scale will ensure great-textured dough, not to mention you can use it for a whole host of other cooking and baking needs. I use the Escali brand, but any scale where you can toggle from grams to ounces and pounds is great.

WOODEN BOARD: A natural wooden work surface provides friction when kneading and shaping (which is especially helpful for hand-formed pastas), and its porous texture absorbs excess moisture, so it acts almost like a nonstick surface. In Italy, you'll find table-size pasta boards called spianatoia (sometimes referred to as tagliere); I used a ten-dollar bamboo cutting board the size of a coffee table book for years and only recently upgraded to a John Boos pastry board. (My point is that your board doesn't need to be big or expensive.) Pastry boards and spianatoia are outfitted with a lip on one edge to secure them in place; if you're using a gripless cutting board, lay a damp dishcloth underneath to keep it from sliding.

A digital scale is my favorite kitchen tool and should be yours, too

I know using a scale is a big ask. I know that it makes things look and feel more complicated. But hear me out: A scale will make all your pasta-making endeavors—and so many other cooking projects—a breeze.

Of course, you don't *need* a scale to make amazing pasta. For a long time, I made egg pasta dough by strictly following the "recipe" I learned in Modena: 1 egg for every 100 grams (about ⅔ cup) 00 flour. There's history and beauty in that approach, and it can, with practice, teach you a lot about how a dough should look and feel. But it can also lead to frustration, especially when getting started, because—surprise!—the eggs you used are really big or really small, and now you're left with a very sticky or very dry pasta dough. And the last thing I want is for you to walk away annoyed and vowing to never make pasta again.

So! Even if—actually, *especially if*—making pasta is an occasional cooking project, please consider a scale. Big or small, inexpensive or top-of-the-line, it'll be your pasta guardian angel. The precision of weighing your flour and, more importantly, your liquids will result in great pasta dough no matter the size of your eggs, saving you from stress that none of us needs right now.

METAL BENCH SCRAPER: A bench scraper can help bring flour and liquid together, but I mostly use it for shaping—it's just sharp enough to slice through dough without the risk of nicking a finger.

POTATO RICER: This handy press is the key to making smooth and airy potato gnocchi. Most are inexpensive; OXO sells a good one.

for shapes

SHEET PAN: I always have a sheet pan (lined with semolina, a dishcloth, or parchment paper) on hand to place my shaped pasta. Nordic Ware half- and quarter-sheet pans (18 x 13 inches and 13 x 9 inches, respectively) are my preference—I can easily slide the smaller sizes into my fridge and freezer if I'm storing the pasta for future use.

ROLLING PIN: This comes in handy when making pici, busiate, and some gnocchi variations (a wine bottle is a good substitute for these techniques), and you can, of course, use one to roll pasta dough into sheets. I use a French-style rolling pin, but I also have a hand-carved mattarello, an Italian rolling pin—usually straight instead of tapered at the ends and extremely long—for rolling traditional pasta sheets (sfoglie).

GNOCCHI OR CAVAROLA BOARD: These carved wooden boards give texture not only to potato gnocchi, but also cavatelli, capunti, malloreddus, and spizzulus. If you want to test the waters with one pasta tool, this is my pick—many are inexpensive and all make the process more enjoyable. Try the Eppicotispai gnocchi boards, which come with a garganelli dowel. If you want to get fancy, q.b. cucina sells a beautiful olive wood board, or check out Etsy for herringbone-textured cavarola boards.

MALLOREDDUS PADDLE: A gnocchi board will impart malloreddus' defined ridges, but specific malloreddus paddles with wider grooves are also available. Mine was kindly given to me by a friend; you can find them online at Fante's Kitchen Shop.

FERRETTO: This long metal rod, usually square-shaped, is used to make busiate and other twisted and hollow shapes. If you're in Italy, ask around for one of these;

otherwise, q.b. cucina's brass ferretto set is perfect. Or pick up a knitting needle or wooden skewer from your local crafts store.

PASTA MACHINE: To make hand-cut, short-cut, and stuffed pastas with ease, I strongly recommend investing in a pasta machine. There are plenty of models to choose from—some cranked manually and others electric—but I always opt for my manual Marcato Atlas 150 or KitchenAid pasta roller attachment. The Marcato churns out beautifully smooth and consistent pasta sheets every time; the KitchenAid is faster and can be easier to use, particularly for beginners.

SPRAY BOTTLE: A small spray bottle filled with water makes easy work of sealing stuffed pastas and hydrating dry dough.

FLOUR/SUGAR SHAKER: Like a spray bottle, I always keep a mug-shaped, fine-holed shaker filled with 00 or all-purpose flour on hand. It's great for evenly and easily dusting pasta sheets and gnocchi, especially when my hands are covered in dough. Mine is from my local restaurant supply store, but there are many options available online.

BICYCLE PASTRY CUTTER (BICICLETA): My first time making garganelli, I cut squares of pasta with a ruler and a paring knife. Then I got myself one of these—an accordion-style adjustable cutter with five wheels—and it changed my life. Use it to slice dough into uniform strips, squares, rectangles, and more in the blink of an eye. Know that some brands can be flimsy, so it's better to spend a little more here. The Ateco 5-wheel stainless steel cutter is my go-to.

PASTA WHEEL (ROTELLA): A rotella is one of the oldest pieces of pasta-making equipment, first depicted in an Etruscan tomb from the 4th century BCE, and later used to make pasta fit for Italy's elite. Used to cut sheets of pasta, you can find them fluted (ideal for farfalle wingtips and caramelle wrappers) and smooth, but whatever you choose, opt for brass or another sturdy metal. Brass is beautiful, sure, but it's also more precise. It can cut and seal your dough in one fell swoop, which is exactly what you need when making pastas like agnolotti and double-stuffed ravioli. Etsy and q.b. cucina both offer high-quality brass pasta wheels.

GARGANELLI BOARD/COMB (PETTINA): Today you'll find gnocchi boards that come with a wooden dowel used for making garganelli (like the one from Eppicotispai), but there are also traditional versions called pettine, made from old textile combs. If you're in Emilia-Romagna, look for Marco Galavotti (of Al Marangoun, meaning "carpenter" in local dialect), who restores century-old combs and sells his tools at markets throughout the region. Or, if a trip to Italy isn't on the horizon, q.b. cucina sells Galavotti's pettine online.

CORZETTI STAMP: This is perhaps my most niche suggestion, but one that makes a perfect gift. I have seven corzetti stamps (one will certainly suffice), all given to me by family over the years and all hand-carved in Tuscany by Filippo of Romagnoli Pasta Tools (available via Etsy). The Romagnoli family has been carving corzetti stamps since 1918, and they sell mattarelli (traditional pasta rolling pins), too.

COOKIE CUTTERS: A sturdy set of circular nesting cookie cutters (both fluted- and smooth-edged) is what I reach for when making stuffed pastas like ravioli, scarpinocc, and cappelletti because the various sizes offer the most flexibility. Both of my sets are made by Ateco.

for fillings

FOOD PROCESSOR: A food processor makes quick work of any pasta filling, not to mention you can also use it for sauces and dough (the Cuisinart 11- and 14-cup are my picks).

PASTRY BAGS: Pastry bags provide more control and precision when shaping any stuffed pasta, but they're especially helpful for agnolotti, caramelle, double-stuffed ravioli, and egg yolk ravioli. I use Ateco 21-inch bags, but you can opt for reusable ones instead—just be sure to clean them thoroughly.

for cooking & sauces

STOCKPOT: I use an 8-quart stainless steel stockpot for boiling pasta and making broths, though an Italian-style pasta pot with a colander insert is a great option for easy water-to-sauce transport. All my most-loved cookware is from Made In.

ENAMELED DUTCH OVEN: It might preclude a fancy pasta-toss, but an enameled 6-quart Dutch oven is often my preferred vessel for cooking sauces, particularly ragùs. Its deep, wide belly holds four to six servings of pasta comfortably, with plenty of room for mixing, not to mention it looks great on the table—just know that because Dutch ovens retain heat so well, they take longer to cool. Lodge, Le Creuset, and Staub are all good options.

PASTA PAN: In Italy you'll find a "padella per mantecare," a particular type of pan used for the final stages of cooking pasta—that is, marrying pasta and sauce (see page 252). These pans—lightweight (for easy tossing), high sides (for less sloshing), and a wide opening (to hold plenty)—are difficult to find stateside, but the Zwilling Ballarini 2800 frying pan and Winco aluminum stir fry pan are good dupes (a 3- or 5-quart saucier works as well). I use these for smaller portions, and particularly for swirling pasta in butter.

SPIDER SIEVE, SLOTTED SPOON, AND TONGS: A wide, basketlike spider sieve scoops up hand-formed, short-cut, and stuffed pastas effortlessly, though a smaller slotted spoon will do in a pinch. Tongs are helpful for transferring and tossing long strands, though I recommend using them to pull more delicate ribbons into the basket of a spider for gentler transport.

PASTA BASKET: For the more regular pasta makers and dinner party hosts among us, a pasta basket or two ensures you can lift all your pasta from the water at once and tip it into your sauce without stress.

LADLE: A 2-ounce (¼-cup) ladle is a good tool for scooping up pasta water to loosen sauces and bring dishes together.

BOX GRATER AND MICROPLANE: I prefer the smallest, star-shaped holes of a box grater when grating aged cheeses like Parmigiano-Reggiano and Pecorino Romano as an ingredient. The resulting powder melts quickly and easily into sauces, with less risk of clumping than cheese grated with a Microplane, which is especially helpful when making emulsified cheese sauces like cacio e pepe or the Butter & Parmesan Sauce on page 294. I *do* use a Microplane for zesting citrus and grating cheeses at the table.

pantry

Pasta's pantry staples—flour and eggs—will get their time in the spotlight soon enough, so I'll keep this section brief.

FLOUR
Head to page 23 for the full spiel; for quick reference, here are the brands I use:

- **SEMOLINA:** Bob's Red Mill, available in many grocery stores and online.

- **SEMOLA RIMACINATA:** Antimo Caputo, available online (in the yellow bag); Molino Pasini semola di grano duro if I can find it wholesale.

- **00 (DOUBLE ZERO):** Antimo Caputo "Chef's Flour," available in some stores and online (in the red bag); Molino Pasini "Pasta Fresca" flour, available selectively online and more widely in Europe (if you spot it, grab it—it's the softest flour I've ever come across, and by some mysterious magic also helps egg pasta doughs retain their color longer).

- **ALL-PURPOSE:** King Arthur, available widely.

- **ALTERNATIVE, FRESH, AND WHOLE-GRAIN:** Arrowhead Mills, available widely; Hayden Flour Mills, available in some stores and online; Flourist, available online. Store fresh and whole-grain flours in the freezer for up to 6 months to prevent them from spoiling.

EGGS
The recipes in this book were developed and tested with large eggs, weighing approximately 50 grams each (and yolks weighing approximately 18 grams each). Use whatever eggs you have but know that happy hens yield more colorful and flavorful results. Vital Farms, Happy Egg Co., Consider Pastures, and Carol's Eggs are good, widely available brands.

OLIVE OIL
Use a milder extra-virgin olive oil for cooking and save the flavorful stuff for finishing. For cooking, I recommend California Olive Ranch and Frantoia Barbera; for finishing, Bona Furtuna (from Sicily), Bono (also from Sicily), EXAU (from Calabria), Frantoio Muraglia (from Puglia), and Laudemio (from Tuscany) are some of my favorites. Look for dark bottles or tins with a harvest date and avoid anything more than a year old. Oh, and don't save it for a special occasion—olive oil spoils more quickly than you think, so enjoy it while it's fresh.

BUTTER
Some sauces are made with butter alone, so find one that you love. Mine are Vital Farms and Kerrygold, and I keep unsalted and salted on hand.

SALT
Diamond Crystal kosher salt is what I use exclusively in my kitchen—sometimes I see it in stores, but more often I'll order it online. Head to page 205 for more about the great wide world of salt.

TOMATOES

Keep canned whole peeled tomatoes, passata di pomodoro (also called strained tomatoes or tomato purée), and tomato paste on hand for sauces and ragùs. More on the ins and outs of canned tomatoes on page 254.

CALABRIAN CHILI PEPPERS

You'll see this ingredient pop up a few times in this book. If you're a spice lover like I am, a jar of crushed Calabrian chili pepper paste or whole Calabrian chili peppers in oil is worth seeking out. They're spicy, yes, but also fruity and salty, with plenty of leftover infused oil to drizzle on toast, eggs, and anything, really. My favorite brand is Tutto Calabria.

CHEESE

Deeply savory, salty, and a little sweet, **Parmigiano-Reggiano** is essential to Italian cooking and therefore the recipes in this book, with **Pecorino Romano** (saltier, tangier sheep's milk cheese) and **Grana Padano** (a milder alternative to Parmesan) quick to follow. Always buy wedges (never pre-grated) and look for the signature branding on the rind. Which reminds me: Don't forget to save that rind for soups and broths.

Another cheese that dominates these pages is **ricotta**. Good ricotta can be made at home (page 61), found fresh at some deli counters, or packed in tubs (if the latter, invest in a high-quality brand like Calabro). For especially creamy pasta fillings, pat store-bought ricotta dry or drain it in a colander lined with cheesecloth for an hour or overnight before using.

PART ONE

doughs

Great pasta starts with great dough, and anyone can make great dough.

I know for some this part can be scary. When I bake, I tend to hesitate, question myself, and ultimately pop whatever it is in the oven hoping for the best. But pasta dough is something else entirely: It's forgiving. With pasta, you're in control, and even the messiest doughs can be fixed every time.

The real key to pasta dough isn't technique, it's confidence—not just in your own abilities (did I mention that you can *absolutely* make great pasta?), but also in knowing it's all going to work out, no matter what happens along the way.

"Pasta" comes from the Italian word "impasto": a mixture of flour and liquid, a dough, a paste. Before I started making my own, I always assumed this liquid included eggs. But this couldn't be further from the truth. Pasta can take so many forms, and there's an enormous number of fresh doughs made with just flour and water. So bid any excuses farewell: You can make pasta right now, with what's already in your pantry and your tap.

Some pasta makers wax poetic about the structure of wheat and a dough's optimal hydration level, while others hold fast to tradition. Both approaches make it too easy to become rigid when pasta requires flexibility. Every Italian region, city, town, and home has its own pasta recipes, from dough to shape to sauce. Many evolved over centuries; all were made from ingredients readily available at the time. I got a taste of this resourcefulness firsthand when the pandemic hit in 2020. Grocery store shelves were bare, and shortages took away every last bag of the specialty flours I'd always used to make pasta. At first, there was panic: *What am I going to do?!* But then I began to experiment with new flours and flavors, and lo and behold, I still ended up with a delicious plate of pasta.

So as we delve into dough, I'm going to attempt a balancing act. I'm not an Italian nonna who can make pasta with her eyes closed, who shrugs when you ask about her methods and says "dipende", it depends. I'm also not a restaurant chef who needs to know the exact level of humidity in my kitchen to turn out consistent plates of pasta to hundreds of diners a night. I'm somewhere in between—and I bet you are, too. My approach is relaxed with a sprinkling of precision to set you up for success and nudge you in the right direction if you get lost along the way.

Don't worry: You've totally got this.

ingredients

flours

You can make pasta with any flour. Until the 20th century, bread and pasta were made from whatever Italian cooks could find. Grains like millet, barley, emmer, and rye; legumes like fava beans and chickpeas; and nuts and seeds like buckwheat, acorns, and chestnuts were all milled into flour. And when corn started to flourish in northern Italy in the 16th century, it made its way into pasta, too. So using what you have at home, whether it's bread flour because you ran out of all-purpose, or some whole wheat that was hiding in the back of the pantry, is entirely Italian in nature.

But let's start with the two flours you'll come across most often: **durum wheat** (grano duro) and **soft wheat** (grano tenero). Then we'll move on to alternative flours.

DURUM WHEAT

Durum wheat is a "hard" strain of wheat. It has a high protein content, the highest of all wheat varieties, which means it yields a strong, sturdy dough—so strong that all it needs is water to make satisfying, chewy pasta. Durum wheat is also an expert at holding its shape. It's more plastic than elastic, which means that although it's not as stretchy as other types of flour, it's easier to mold.

In Italy, durum wheat thrives in the warm, dry climate of the south. Puglia and Sardinia, among other regions, are home to durum wheat, and most of the pastas you'll find there reflect as much: Little nubs of eggless dough, pushed and pulled by hand into Sunday lunch. It's worth mentioning, too, that for a long time eggs were an unaffordable luxury in these poorer regions.

Mill durum wheat once and you're left with **semolina**, a coarse yellow flour that gives texture to cakes, breads, and puddings. Mill it twice and you have **semola rimacinata** (rimacinata means "twice milled"),

a much finer, pale-yellow flour that's softer and easier to manipulate. Semolina's texture and durability make it the perfect match for factory-produced dried pastas, and in Italy it must be used by law; the finer semola rimacinata is great for making pastas by hand.

I stock both in my pantry: semolina for dusting and storing already-shaped pasta because its grainy consistency prevents dough from sticking to surfaces and itself, and semola for smooth, pliable doughs. Bob's Red Mill makes a great semolina that's available in many grocery stores, but try whatever you can find. Antimo Caputo is my go-to brand for semola rimacinata (you can order it from several retailers online; it's in the yellow bag), but if you can't get your hands on it, coarse semolina will still work well for dough—I used it exclusively for many years.

SOFT WHEAT

Soft wheat is, well, a soft strain of wheat, and it's a different species entirely from durum wheat. Soft wheat is lower in protein and more elastic, meaning it yields a tender and stretchy dough that—usually with the support of protein-rich eggs—is ideal for rolling into thin sheets. Soft wheat is primarily cultivated in central-northern Italy, specifically Emilia-Romagna, Veneto, Lombardy, and Piedmont. For centuries, this powdery flour was expensive, just like the eggs used to strengthen it, which suited these wealthier regions just fine.

Italian soft wheat flour is milled into different grades, each with a number that refers to its grind, starting with 2 as the coarsest. Travel down the ladder and you'll find **00** (double zero; doppio zero)—the finest, the silkiest, and the one used to make fresh pasta. To spare you some confusion, today you'll find several flours that are labeled "00." Stateside, very finely ground pastry flour can be sold as 00, but it has a much lower protein content than what you're looking for in pasta. The easiest approach? Opt for Italian brands like Antimo Caputo, Anna Napoletana, and Molino Grassi, or bags that are labeled specifically for pasta-making. (If you end up with 00 pizza flour, you can totally use it; they're pretty much the same.)

You can also reach for the all-purpose flour you already have, which usually consists of a mix of hard and soft wheat. It has a similar protein content as 00 and, although marginally coarser in texture, will work great in any recipe calling for the traditional stuff. (Note: Durum wheat (semolina) is unique in its texture so all-purpose flour is not a comparable substitute for durum-wheat doughs.)

ALTERNATIVE FLOURS

What was once a necessity is now fashionable and thank goodness for that. Whole and heirloom grains can impart wonderful character and flavor to pasta. Einkorn, rye, and spelt are favorites of mine, as are nut flours, particularly chestnut, for adding warmth and depth to cold-weather comforts like gnocchi. There are farms everywhere that are milling exceptional flours, durum and soft wheat included. Some of my favorites are from Flourist in Vancouver, Canada, and Hayden Flour Mills in Arizona. I encourage you to find whatever's local to you.

Perhaps the most important thing to remember here is to **always use alternative flours in conjunction with durum or soft wheat.** Using 100 percent whole grains in any cooking or baking project can be challenging. Each type has a different protein content and level of elasticity, so cutting it with durum or soft wheat flour will make your dough easier to handle and help preserve the pasta's signature texture and bite. This is critical with nut and legume flours (chestnut, chickpea, buckwheat), which are naturally gluten-free and don't have elasticity at all. I recommend starting with 25 to 50 percent of an alternative flour, as reflected in the recipes in this book, but I also encourage you to experiment and find a mix that works for you. (Many whole-grain, freshly milled, and gluten-free flours absorb and retain more moisture than typical white flours, which means they'll probably need a little more hydration. The recipes here take this into account, but in general when using alternative flours, keep some extra water nearby.)

Gluten & Starch in Pasta Doughs

Grains like wheat are made up of fiber, vitamins, minerals, starch, proteins, and fats. But for our purposes, let's focus on two proteins, glutenin and gliadin—together known as gluten—which make up about 80 percent of the protein in wheat flour and contribute almost entirely to its functionality.

When mixed with water, these proteins work together to build a weblike network, each unfurling from their coiled cocoons into long strands to connect with their neighbors. This network creates a dough's structure, both its elasticity (how stretchy it is) and plasticity (how well it holds its shape). Kneading the dough evenly distributes the flour and water so the gluten network can develop more fully. And resting the dough after kneading gives it time to relax, allowing it to fully hydrate and release any moisture it no longer needs. This is why a well-rested dough will feel softer and tackier to the touch.

Another important component of wheat flour is starch. When starch comes into contact with water and heat, it gelatinizes—which means that when pasta is cooked, the starch in the flour melts into a paste. The higher a flour's starch content, the smoother and silkier the pasta will be. This is why pastas made with 00 flour, which has plenty of starch, melt in your mouth. Starch is also a useful tool when combining pasta with sauce, but more on that later (page 252).

Gluten-free flour blends rely on starches and other thickeners to form a dough, so you can skip the extended kneading and resting processes.

liquids (water, eggs & more)

The second part of our "impasto" is liquid, and in pasta-making it can take many forms—water, eggs, vegetables, and wine are all sources of liquid.

WATER & EGGS

The liquid a pasta dough uses can tell us a lot about its origins. If flour is mixed with water only, you're probably looking at a shape from the south—cavatelli, capunti, orecchiette, busiate—or the rural, mountain regions of central Italy. Its partner will usually be, as mentioned earlier, durum wheat, though not always: In Tuscany, pici (page 83) and strozzapreti (page 88) are examples of water-based pastas made with soft wheat flour (and, depending on who you ask, some durum wheat, too). These areas were extremely poor and water was cheap.

Introduce liquid in the form of eggs and you're dipping your toe into the vast ocean of central and northern Italian pastas. We already talked about eggs as a sign of affluence, and it's here that pasta was served among the Renaissance nobility and Catholic church. With eggs come the historically more-expensive soft wheat flour and also fillings: Delicate ravioli, tortellini, and cappelletti are all made with egg-based dough. Add a splash of white wine to the eggs and you're probably making pasta from Liguria, where it's a mainstay of many local dishes.

Aside from their historical import, eggs impact a dough's texture. The water- and protein-rich whites provide elasticity and structure and the fatty yolks not only impart color and flavor, they also make a dough more tender. In Italy there are eggs with sunset-colored yolks specifically marketed for making pasta called sfoglia gialla or pasta gialla ("yellow pasta"). To achieve a similar effect, opt for free-range eggs (the more varied the hens' diet, the more vibrant the yolks), or substitute about three large egg yolks for one large egg.

OTHER FORMS OF HYDRATION

You can make every pasta in this book with water or eggs, but sometimes it's fun to get creative and introduce other sources of hydration. Here are some ways to give your pasta a little extra flair.

Vegetables

If you're interested in colorful pasta, look no further than what nature has to offer. Vegetables—whether chopped, powdered, or, my preference, puréed—provide a rainbow of reds, oranges, greens, and purples. Although some colorful pastas are more modern novelties, others, like those made with tender and wild greens, are firmly rooted in Italian tradition. When it comes to greens, you can cook and finely mince them in honor of those traditions or reach for the blender like I do. Chopped greens (whether by hand or in a food processor) will yield a rustic, textured look;

blended greens—and any puréed vegetable, for that matter—will produce smooth, uniform color.

Use vegetables alongside water or eggs. In water-based doughs, the vegetable fibers will leave your dough craving more moisture, so using 50 percent vegetables and just over 50 percent water is a good guide to make sure the dough isn't too dry. For egg-based doughs, the added water from the vegetables will result in a softer, chewier dough that can be more difficult to shape. Combining them with eggs, and mostly yolks, will add fat and protein to balance this extra moisture and ensure your dough is both vibrant and structured.

Vegetable purées are all about the color, and they rarely impart much, if any, flavor. This is great news because 1) you don't have to plan your sauce around the vegetable you used; 2) you don't have to like beets to make pink pasta; 3) you're getting a serving of veggies while eating pasta; and 4) your kids won't have a clue they're getting a serving of veggies while eating pasta.

I should mention that as colorful pasta cooks, some of the pigment leaches out into the cooking water. Luckily, fresh pasta cooks quickly (more on this later), so most of the color will remain intact, just softer than in its raw form.

Oils & Other Fats

Fat isn't *technically* a form of hydration, but when used alongside water or eggs, it can make a significant impact. Fats like butter, oil, and shortening are tenderizers, meaning they coat and weaken gluten bonds. In baking, fat is key to airy cakes and pastries; in pasta, it's part of what makes ravioli so delicate. Egg yolks are the most common source of fat, but other options are useful and delicious, too. In Lombardy, butter is typically used to make shoe-shaped dumplings called scarpinocc (page 166); in Sardinia, lard was once a common addition to pasta dough, too. And everywhere you'll find recipes with a spoonful of olive oil.

The more fat you use, the less chewy and more tender your pasta will be—a characteristic particularly well-suited to filled pastas. Use oils for their flavor (olive oil, of course, but walnut and pistachio oils are fun, too) and dairy like melted butter and sour cream for an especially light texture.

Wine

White wine is the secret to several delicious pastas, particularly in Liguria. It's used to make Genoa's famous stamped corzetti (page 92), as well as stuffed pastas like pansotti (filled with wild herbs) and turle (filled with potatoes, cheese, and mint). According to my friend and Genoese food writer Enrica Monzani, adding a splash of white wine to pasta dough "gives flavor and elasticity, and masks the taste of eggs." I wholeheartedly agree: A white wine–infused dough taps into all your senses, perfuming your hands and your kitchen.

Red wine pasta is a more modern phenomenon, though occasionally you'll see it used in lesser-known shapes like spizzulus (page 104). The first time I tried it, I was disappointed: Deep ruby red in the bottle quickly became dusty pink (okay, gray) when mixed with flour and eggs. The solution? Simmer the wine (I prefer something medium-bodied like Chianti or Montepulciano) so some of the water evaporates and the color concentrates. The longer it simmers, the bolder the result, leaving you with a moody shade of purple.

herbs, spices & other inclusions

Like a good cookie dough, pasta can be transformed by a few last-minute flavorings. Herbs are a great place to start: Mince them, purée them, or laminate them between sheets of dough (see page 121) for a pop of color and a hint of flavor. Use tender herbs like parsley, mint, basil, and dill, or softer woody herbs like sage and thyme leaves. Remove any tough stems to avoid puncturing the pasta when shaping.

Vegetable and herb-infused doughs can range in potency, so if you're looking to really pack a punch, head over to the spice rack. Spices have a long history in pasta making: In Sardinia, clever cooks used saffron, which once grew wild across the region, to turn flour-and-water pasta dough deep gold, tricking the eye into thinking it was made with eggs. Heating spices will best coax out their flavor. Toast and grind peppercorns and other seeds like fennel and caraway; steep paprikas, ground chilies, saffron, and turmeric in hot water for color, then use some or all of the infused liquid as the dough's hydration.

The recipes in this book only scratch the surface. I've seen pasta made with cocoa, espresso, and butterfly pea powder (a violet flower that'll dye anything blue), too.

EVERYTHING WE JUST COVERED, IN BRIEF

What It Is	What It Does
Durum wheat *Semolina and semola rimacinata*	Helps a dough hold its shape (plasticity); provides bite and chew
Soft wheat *00 flour and, for our needs, all-purpose flour (a mix of hard and soft wheats)*	Helps a dough stretch (elasticity); makes a dough soft and tender
Whole grains *Einkorn, spelt, emmer, rye, etc.*	Depending on the flour and its freshness, can make a dough drier and require more hydration; imparts nuttiness and character
Gluten-free flours *Chestnut, chickpea, fava, buckwheat, rice, gluten-free blends*	Lacks elasticity and makes a dough more delicate; high in starch and requires more hydration to become pliable; affects flavor
Liquid *Water, eggs (also a source of fat), wine, milk (also a source of fat), vegetable purées*	Makes a dough elastic and springy; can impact color; water from vegetables can make egg-based doughs softer, while vegetable fibers can make water-based doughs drier
Fat *Egg yolks, olive and other oils, butter, shortening, lard, cream (also a source of liquid)*	Makes a dough delicate and tender; a high concentration of fat can make a dough firmer in its raw state (particularly egg yolks and butter)

techniques

There's something particularly refreshing about making pasta dough (or anything, really) with your own two hands, as if returning to a near-forgotten, simpler way of life. Making dough by hand is, of course, the most traditional technique, and the one that grandmothers and chefs alike swear by. It's often called the **"well method"**—referring to the process of gradually incorporating the liquid into a flour "well"—and I do think it yields dough with a marginally superior texture, mostly because you have total control. But we're also lucky enough to have access to all sorts of modern kitchen appliances, and they can get the job done, too. So for those short on time or with any wrist or joint pain, the food processor and stand mixer make great alternatives. All three methods can be used to make any of the dough recipes in this book, except gnocchi (we'll get to that later).

But First: What Should Pasta Dough Look and Feel Like?

Think of pasta dough like Play-Doh that spends a lot of time at the gym. It's smooth and pliable, but also firm and resilient. It's not soft or sticky like many bread doughs, nor is it dry and crumbly like pastry dough. Some might describe it as heavy and dense. It springs back to the touch.

While you're in the thick of it, making dough will feel messy and chaotic. But when you're done, look at the dough and make a mental checklist of these visual and textural cues. If the dough sticks to your hands or work surface, give it a few more dustings of flour; if it's tough and dry, a small amount of water should do the trick.

Still, environmental factors, particularly humidity, can affect a dough's texture. A hot and humid kitchen will encourage stickiness, so maybe hold back a little water at the start or know you might need to reach for more flour; a cold and dry kitchen will do the opposite, so keep extra water nearby. Trust your intuition and remember that if you make a wrong turn, you can always course-correct because pasta is forgiving. Accept that every dough you make will be a little different and love them all the same. The process only gets easier over time.

making pasta dough by hand

Weigh and combine the flour(s) in a wide mixing or serving bowl. Weigh the liquid(s) and, if applicable, whisk them together until smooth.

Keep the flour in the bowl (this prevents runaway liquids) or turn it out onto a work surface. Make a wide "well" in the center with your fist, forming a wall of flour tall enough on all sides to contain the liquid. Pour the liquid into the well.

Using a fork, gradually incorporate a portion of the flour, a couple of teaspoons or so at a time, from the inner rim of the well into the liquid in a circular motion (*à la* scrambled eggs) until a thick, custardy batter forms. You'll use only about a quarter of the flour at this point; the majority will remain loose.

Incorporate the remaining flour into the thickened liquid, either by 1) pulling, folding, and pressing the flour into the center with your hands until it becomes a shaggy ball; 2) vigorously whisking the liquid and loose flour together with the fork until all the liquid is evenly distributed (and it looks like little flaky pebbles); or 3) if you're working on a flat surface, cutting the flour into the

Making Egg Pasta Dough by Hand

5

6

7

8

liquid with the help of a bench scraper. If it looks like a total mess—sticky here, flaky there—you're doing it right.

If you've been using a bowl, transfer the mixture to a flat surface, along with any large flaky pieces. It's also totally normal to have some flour left behind.

Knead the dough vigorously however works best for you (don't be shy; you can't overwork it). I like to push it forward with the heel of my hand, then fold it over on itself about halfway. Do this a few times in one direction, then rotate the dough 90 degrees and repeat, shifting 90 degrees every few strokes. Once the dough starts to come together, brush away any remaining flaky pieces. Always give it time before adding flour or water—more often than not, it will sort itself out after a few minutes. Then, if the dough still feels dry, add a small amount of water with your fingers to the dry areas and knead until smooth, repeating as necessary; if it feels very soft and sticky, work in more flour until it firms up.

After about 5 minutes, cover the dough tightly and completely in plastic wrap or under an overturned bowl (you can also use a clean shower cap or snug Tupperware container). Let it rest for 5 to 10 minutes— have a cup of coffee, a snack, a glass of wine—then uncover and knead the dough until it's smooth and firm, pliable but not soft, 3 to 5 minutes more. (This two-part knead makes the dough smoother; if preferred, skip the first rest period and knead the dough for about 10 minutes.)

When it bounces back from a light touch to the surface, cover the dough tightly and completely once more. Let it rest at room temperature for about 30 minutes, depending on the pasta you're making (see page 32 for suggested rest times).

making pasta dough in a food processor

Add the flour(s) and liquid(s) to the bowl of a food processor. Pulse the ingredients together in short bursts, scraping down the sides of the bowl as needed, until evenly distributed and beads of dough form. It'll look like cooked couscous and should come together easily when pressed. If the mixture is dry and sandy, add a teaspoon of water and pulse again; repeat as needed. If it's sticky and gummy, sprinkle it with flour and pulse until you've reached the proper consistency.

Transfer to a work surface and knead by hand for 5 minutes, or until smooth and firm. If the dough is still rough on the surface, cover it tightly and completely,

either in plastic wrap or under an overturned bowl (you can also use a clean shower cap or snug Tupperware container), for 5 to 10 minutes. Then knead 1 to 2 minutes more and cover it again. Let it rest at room temperature for about 30 minutes, depending on the pasta you're making (see page 32 for suggested rest times).

making pasta dough in a stand mixer

Add the flour(s) and liquid(s) to the bowl of a stand mixer fitted with the dough hook. Mix on low speed, scraping down the sides of the bowl and hook as needed, until the dough comes together, 7 to 10 minutes. If the mixture seems very dry after the first few minutes, add a teaspoon of water.

Transfer to a work surface and knead by hand for 5 minutes, or until smooth and firm. If the dough is still rough on the surface, cover it tightly and completely, either in plastic wrap or under an overturned bowl (you can also use a clean shower cap or snug Tupperware container), for 5 to 10 minutes. Then knead 1 to 2 minutes more and cover it again. Let it rest at room temperature for about 30 minutes, depending on the pasta you're making (see page 32 for suggested rest times).

resting & storing pasta dough

Making pasta dough is a workout. I've done it thousands of times and I still get a little winded; when it's done, I need a moment to collect myself. So does the dough. For me, that might mean grabbing a glass of wine; for the dough, that rest time allows it to relax and the flour to fully hydrate. A just-kneaded dough is tense and jumpy, but as it rests, the gluten lets out a sigh of relief: It becomes softer, more pliable, and tacky to the touch.

Rest times depend on the type of pasta you're making, although **30 minutes is a good rule of thumb**. Durum wheat (semolina) pastas tend to benefit from a shorter rest period: Less rest yields a drier dough, which in turn encourages the rough texture that defines many southern shapes like orecchiette. On the other hand, egg-based pastas (and some water-based soft wheat pastas) need more recovery time so they can stretch into long strands or sheets. If you find yourself fighting with a dough, let it rest longer.

Making Durum Wheat & Water Pasta Dough in a Food Processor

PASTA DOUGH REST TIMES, MORE OR LESS

Dough Type	Suggested Rest Time
Durum wheat (semolina) & water IN THIS BOOK: *Busiate, capunti, cavatelli, foglie d'ulivo, malloreddus, orecchiette, spizzulus* EXCEPTION: *Lagane—rest for 30 minutes to 1 hour for easier rolling*	20 to 30 minutes
Soft wheat (00 or all-purpose flour) & water IN THIS BOOK: *Corzetti della Valpolcevera, pici, strozzapreti*	30 minutes to 1 hour
Egg IN THIS BOOK: *All hand-cut pastas, short-cut pastas, and stuffed pastas, as well as lasagne sheets*	30 minutes or up to 2 hours if rolling by machine; at least 1 hour if rolling by hand
Gluten-free and gnocchi	None

Pasta dough is best used immediately after resting, but sometimes life gets in the way. To store the dough overnight, wrap it tightly in plastic wrap or store it in a snug Tupperware container and refrigerate. Remove the dough from the refrigerator 30 minutes to 1 hour before use so it can come to room temperature. If the dough feels very soft and sticky, knead it for a minute to help it firm up. (Egg doughs tend to oxidize, so this process also redistributes and revitalizes the color.) Use all doughs within 48 hours if you can.

Freezing Pasta Dough

Pasta dough is best used fresh, and I find the texture changes after freezing and defrosting. You can try it and see how you like the results, but my advice is to either refrigerate the dough (for up to 2 days) or freeze the pasta once it's shaped (page 74).

FAQs

IS THERE A SUBSTITUTE FOR DURUM WHEAT (SEMOLINA) FLOUR?

There are other hard wheat flours with high protein content (bread flour, for example), but the texture of durum wheat stands alone. If you can't get your hands on semolina, try the corzetti della Valpolcevera soft wheat dough variation on page 37. The eggs strengthen the dough and give it more bite, so it'll work particularly well for small shapes like cavatelli and malloreddus.

WHY DON'T YOU ADD SALT TO YOUR DOUGH?

Gnocchi aside, I don't add salt to my doughs mostly because I was taught to make pasta without it, and because I rely on salty cooking water to season my pasta. Salt tightens a dough by strengthening its gluten network. Sometimes this can work in your favor: The stronger the dough, the better when it comes to, say, intricate Sardinian pastas like lorighittas (made by braiding ultra-thin strands of durum wheat dough into rings) and pleated ravioli called culurgiones. But in Emilia-Romagna, where tender egg pasta reigns, I've never seen the addition of salt.

CAN I KNEAD PASTA DOUGH TOO MUCH?

No, especially when making it by hand. Ten minutes or so will do the trick, but if you're ever in doubt, keep going.

WHAT IF THE SURFACE OF MY DOUGH ISN'T SMOOTH?

Pasta dough will always have a few creases where the dough is folded over on itself, and this is a good indication that it has the right texture (if the dough is an entirely smooth sphere and very malleable, it's too soft—add more flour). When I knead, I like to concentrate these folds in one area so the majority of the dough stays smooth.

If you find yourself with creases all over the dough and it's already well-hydrated, pick the largest crease and position the dough so the crease is facing upward toward you. Then knead the dough, pushing and folding, in one direction, making sure to relocate and reposition that crease each time so it stays in that same area. Turn the dough 90 degrees and repeat, always ensuring the creases face upward and the rest of the dough is flush with the work surface. When you're done, turn the dough over to reveal the smooth side. (In the very niche pasta-making community on social media, there's a running joke that no one posts about this craggy "underside" of the dough.)

MY DOUGH IS WAY TOO STICKY/DRY TO HANDLE. WHAT SHOULD I DO?

If a dough seems like it's beyond saving, don't panic. Break it into pieces and add them to a food processor. If the dough is too sticky, throw in a handful of flour and pulse until you're left with beads of dough that resemble cooked couscous; if it's too dry, add a teaspoon or two of water and do the same. The mixture should come together when pressed between your fingers. Turn it out onto a work surface and knead briefly until smooth, then let it rest a little longer than usual.

flour &
water
doughs

WHAT THEY TASTE LIKE: Durum wheat (semolina) dough is firm and pliable and produces pasta that has bite without being doughy; soft wheat dough (made with 00 or all-purpose flour) is springier and chewier, akin to the texture of Japanese udon noodles. Both are mild in flavor, so they're the perfect canvas for bold and hearty sauces.

WHAT THEY'RE USED FOR: Use durum wheat dough for southern Italian pastas, particularly small and short-cut shapes that are dragged or molded by hand like capunti, cavatelli, foglie d'ulivo, malloreddus, orecchiette, and spizzulus. Durum wheat also works well with twisted shapes like busiate. Use the more elastic soft wheat dough for long strands like pici, as well as strozzapreti, which are made by rolling out thin ribbons before twisting them into rustic spirals.

THE RECIPE: The recipe for most flour-and-water pastas by weight is a simple 2:1 ratio (two parts flour to one part water), which makes it especially easy to scale. Using warm or tepid water better hydrates the proteins in the dough and makes it easier to manipulate.

NOTE: Depending on the cook, some pastas, including pici and strozzapreti, are also made with a combination of durum and soft wheat flours, so if you have both on hand, try a fifty-fifty split (the amount of liquid stays the same). This will yield a dough that's stretchier and more tender than typical durum wheat dough, and stronger with more of a bite than typical soft wheat dough.

USE IT WITH

*Busiate (106) · Capunti (100) · Cavatelli (96) ·
Lagane (86) · Malloreddus (102) · Orecchiette
(108) · Spizzulus (104)*

durum wheat & water pasta dough

400 grams (a scant 2½ cups)
**semola rimacinata
or semolina flour**

200 ml (¾ cup plus 4 teaspoons)
warm or tepid water

Make the dough according to your preferred method (see pages 27–33).

VARIATION

Foglie d'Ulivo and Orecchiette Dough: Use 400 grams (a scant 2½ cups) semola or semolina and start with 190 ml (¾ cup plus 1 tablespoon) water, adding more as needed. A slightly drier dough will yield better texture and definition.

soft wheat & water pasta dough

400 grams (a generous 2½ cups)
00 or all-purpose flour

200 ml (¾ cup plus 4 teaspoons)
warm or tepid water

Make the dough according to your preferred method (see pages 27–33).

VARIATIONS

Pici Dough: Add 15 ml (1 tablespoon) extra-virgin olive oil to the water.

Corzetti della Valpolcevera Dough: Replace half of the water with 100 grams (about 2 large) eggs.

whole wheat & water pasta dough

150 grams (2⅓ cups) **einkorn,
spelt, emmer**, or other whole
wheat flour

250 grams (1½ cups) **semola
rimacinata or semolina flour**

200 ml (¾ cup plus 4 teaspoons)
warm or tepid water, plus more
as needed

If you're interested in exploring local and freshly milled flours (which I hope you are!), here's a great way to use them. I prefer the rustic taste and texture of varieties like einkorn and spelt, but grab whatever you prefer. Use this for any flour-and-water pasta in this book, and once you get a feel for it, run wild with the ratios and adjust the amount of whole wheat flour however you'd like.

Mix the flours together and make the dough according to your preferred method (see pages 27–33). Keep some extra water nearby since this dough can run on the drier side depending on the type of whole grain you use.

basil pasta dough

100 grams (3½ ounces; about
3 large bunches) **fresh basil,**
leaves and tender stems

120 ml (½ cup) **tepid water,** plus
more as needed

400 grams (a scant 2½ cups)
**semola rimacinata or semolina
flour**

Abundant summer basil gives this dough delicious flavor (and great color, of course), so keep the sauce light to accentuate its sweetness. For a real showstopper, use it to make leaf-shaped foglie d'ulivo.

Bring a medium pot of water to a boil. Stir in the basil and blanch until wilted and vibrant green, about 20 seconds. Immediately drain and run the basil under cold water to stop the cooking (or submerge it in ice water and drain).

Transfer the basil to a small blender and add the water. Purée until very smooth. Weigh out 210 grams (1 scant cup) of the purée—if you have only a small amount left, use it all; if you don't have enough, add some more water. Make the dough according to your preferred method (see pages 27–33) using the basil mixture as the liquid.

Whole Wheat Busiate

saffron pasta dough

A generous pinch (about
½ teaspoon) **saffron threads**

200 ml (¾ cup plus 4 teaspoons)
hot, but not boiling, water

400 grams (a scant 2½ cups)
**semola rimacinata or semolina
flour**

Saffron is a cook's Midas, turning everything in its path into sweet-scented gold. It's no surprise that it's now the world's most valuable spice by weight, but the purple bulbs that guard these precious crimson threads once grew wild and abundant in Italy, particularly Sardinia. For centuries, a touch of this "red gold" was added to some of the region's water-based pastas to emulate the eggs used in the wealthier north. Sardinian gnocchi (malloreddus, page 102) and a tiny chickpea-like pasta called ciciones are a few of the pastas still infused with saffron. Crushing and steeping the threads in hot water will bring out their color and flavor, so a pinch is all you need.

Gently crush the saffron threads into a powder using a mortar and pestle or break them up between your fingers and add them to a bowl. Pour the hot water over and steep for 15 minutes. Make the dough according to your preferred method (see pages 27–33) using the saffron-infused water as the liquid.

VARIATION

Swap out the saffron for 1 tablespoon of another pigmented spice like Aleppo pepper, paprika, or turmeric. Remember that the dough will take on the flavor of the spice you're using.

egg
pasta doughs

WHAT THEY TASTE LIKE: Egg doughs are rich in flavor and, when rolled into thin sheets, delicate in texture. Doughs with a higher concentration of egg yolks (more fat) will be especially tender, and those with more whole eggs (protein and water) will be chewier and more substantial.

WHAT THEY'RE USED FOR: Shapes made from thin sheets like most hand-cut pastas (fettuccine, pappardelle, tagliatelle, tagliolini), many short-cut pastas (farfalle, garganelli, sorpresine), almost all stuffed pastas (there are exceptions, of course), and lasagne.

A NOTE ABOUT FLOUR: Many of the most traditional egg pasta dough recipes, particularly those from Emilia-Romagna, are made with 00 flour and whole eggs. I personally add a small portion of semola to my egg doughs to give them more structure and bite. This helps the pasta hold its shape after cooking, which is especially useful for intricate filled pastas. But if you prefer a more tender result, or if you don't have semola on hand, replace it with the same weight of 00 or all-purpose flour.

A NOTE ABOUT EGGS: You can refer to my spiel about digital scales on page 13, but I'll reiterate it here: Since all eggs are different sizes, weighing them will give you the most consistent results. When weighing eggs, if you're a little short of the amount you need, add another yolk or some water to make up the difference; if you're over, scoop out some of the whites. And if you don't have a scale, it's helpful to know that large eggs generally weigh 50 grams and large yolks generally weigh 18 grams.

MAKES

about 22 ounces; serves 4

USE IT WITH

*All hand-cut pastas (128) · All stuffed pastas
(150) · Farfalle (140) · Garganelli (142) ·
Lasagne (198) · Sorpresine (138)*

standard egg pasta dough

350 grams (2¼ cups) **00 or
all-purpose flour**

50 grams (5 tablespoons) **semola
rimacinata or semolina flour**

225 grams **eggs** (about 4 large
eggs plus 1 to 2 yolks)

Make the dough according to your preferred method (see pages 27–33).

VARIATIONS

Whole Wheat Egg Pasta Dough: Omit the semola and use 50 percent
(200 grams; 1⅔ cups) whole wheat flour of choice and 50 percent (200
grams; 1⅓ cups) 00 or all-purpose flour. Use 200 grams (about 4 large)
eggs and 55 grams (about 3 large) egg yolks.

Vegan "Egg" Pasta Dough: For the most similar taste and texture, swap
out the eggs and yolks for 225 ml (1 cup) liquid egg replacement like JUST
Egg and 15 ml (1 tablespoon) extra-virgin olive oil. You can also use the pici
variation of the Soft Wheat & Water Pasta Dough on page 37, but the texture
will be chewier than typical egg dough.

MAKES

about 23 ounces; serves 4

USE IT WITH

*Agnolotti del Plin (177) · Caramelle (182) ·
Double-Stuffed Ravioli (162) ·
Egg Yolk Ravioli (159) · Pappardelle (131) ·
Tagliatelle (131)*

almost all-yolk pasta dough

350 grams (2¼ cups) **00 or
all-purpose flour**

50 grams (5 tablespoons) **semola
rimacinata or semolina flour**

100 grams (about 2 large) **eggs**

135 grams (about 8 large)
egg yolks

15 ml (1 tablespoon) **water**, plus
more as needed

Although delicate to eat, dough made with egg yolks alone can be tricky to
handle—without the water and protein from the whites, it's much firmer and less
elastic in its raw form. Adding a couple of whole eggs and a touch of water still
yields a very vibrant, very tender dough, but one that's easier on the wrists (plus,
you can save yourself opening another carton of eggs). Use the leftover whites
in meringues, cakes, frittatas, and cocktails. They can be stored in an airtight
container in the refrigerator for 2 to 3 days.

Make the dough according to your preferred method (see pages 27–33).

MAKES

about 22 ounces; serves 4

USE IT WITH

All hand-cut pastas (128) •
"Classic" Ravioli (152) • Farfalle (140) •
Scarpinocc (166) • Sorpresine (138)

black pepper pasta dough

10 grams (4 teaspoons) **whole black peppercorns or freshly ground black pepper**

350 grams (2¼ cups) **00 or all-purpose flour**

50 grams (5 tablespoons) **semola rimacinata or semolina flour**

225 grams **eggs** (about 4 large eggs plus 1 to 2 yolks)

Toasting whole peppercorns before grinding will best bring out their flavor, but if you prefer, use freshly ground black pepper instead. Seeds like poppy, fennel, and caraway are fair game, too, or try pink peppercorns for a fruitier, prettier finish. Grind peppercorns and large seeds finely—too coarse and they'll puncture the pasta when rolling.

If using whole peppercorns, toast them in a dry skillet over medium heat until fragrant, shaking the pan often, 3 to 5 minutes. Transfer to a mortar and pestle or a spice grinder and crush until fine. Sift the ground toasted pepper (or freshly ground pepper) to remove any large pieces, then mix it with the flours. Make the dough according to your preferred method (see pages 27–33).

MAKES

about 22 ounces; serves 4

USE IT WITH

All hand-cut pastas (128) •
"Classic" Ravioli (152) • Farfalle (140) •
Garganelli (142) • Sorpresine (138)

parsley-speckled pasta dough

15 grams (1 loosely packed cup) **fresh flat-leaf parsley leaves** (no stems), finely chopped

350 grams (2¼ cups) **00 or all-purpose flour**, plus more as needed

50 grams (5 tablespoons) **semola rimacinata or semolina flour**

225 grams **eggs** (about 4 large eggs plus 1 to 2 yolks)

A handful of chopped herbs is the simplest way to decorate any pasta. Parsley is a favorite because it retains its color no matter how finely minced, but any tender herb will work here. Get creative with chives, dill, thyme, or sage. Basil and mint are beautiful, too, just know that they're particularly prone to bruising and will lose some of their vivid color.

Combine the flours and eggs according to your preferred method (see pages 27–33). If making the dough by hand or in a stand mixer, sprinkle the parsley over the dough after the first few minutes of kneading and continue working until it's evenly distributed. If using a food processor, pulse the flours and eggs together, then add the parsley and pulse again until just combined. Transfer to a work surface and knead until smooth. The moisture from the parsley might make the dough a little stickier than usual, so keep some extra flour nearby.

Black Pepper and Parsley-Speckled Fettuccine

*Sour Cream & Rye
Pasta Dough*

MAKES
about 22 ounces; serves 4

USE IT WITH
*Cappelletti (168) • "Classic" Ravioli (152) •
Scarpinocc (166)*

sour cream & rye pasta dough

60 grams (¼ cup) **full-fat sour cream**

70 ml (¼ cup plus 1 tablespoon) **tepid water**

100 grams (about 2 large) **eggs**

150 grams (1¼ cups) **rye flour**

250 grams (1⅔ cups) **00 or all-purpose flour**

Rye bread and sour cream remind me of my childhood eating smoked fish, potato latkes, and blintzes (cheese- and fruit-stuffed crepes). Put them together and you have a nutty, malty dough made soft and tender by a little extra fat. I usually use it when making kreplach, a Jewish dumpling that's fried or served in soup, so I'd recommend it both for long ribbons and filled pastas, particularly those stuffed with potatoes and cheese if you're a pierogi fan like I am.

You can also make this dough with 50 percent rye flour, just know the result is more fragile.

Whisk the sour cream, water, and eggs together in a bowl until well combined. Make the pasta dough according to your preferred method (see pages 27–33) using this mixture as the liquid.

MAKES
about 22 ounces; serves 4

USE IT WITH
*"Classic" Ravioli (152) • Farfalle (140) •
Pappardelle (131) • Scarpinocc (166) •
Tagliatelle (131)*

chestnut pasta dough

150 grams (1 cup plus 2½ tablespoons) **chestnut flour**

250 grams (1⅔ cups) **00 or all-purpose flour**

220 grams **eggs** (about 4 large eggs plus 1 yolk)

Warm and nutty chestnut flour is particularly popular in northern Italy. It's a staple in Liguria, where it's used to make a variation of the region's famous trofie pasta; in Tuscany, where it's a hallmark of rural cooking and the base of thin, irregular sheets of dough called lasagne bastarde; and in Lombardy and Piedmont, where it's common in gnocchi. You can find chestnut flour in some specialty stores or order it online like I do—I'll be the first to admit it's pricey (you can also make your own!), but a little goes a long way and the cozy complexity it adds is totally worth it.

Chestnut flour is both naturally gluten-free and high in starch, so it absorbs moisture quickly and readily. This dough will feel tackier and more delicate, so be gentle when rolling and shaping.

Make the dough according to your preferred method (see pages 27–33).

citrus-scented pasta dough

2 large **navel oranges**

2 large or 3 small **lemons**

350 grams (2¼ cups) **00 or all-purpose flour**

50 grams (5 tablespoons) **semola rimacinata or semolina flour**

100 grams (about 2 large) **eggs**

75 grams (about 4 large) **egg yolks**

Fresh citrus zest adds flecks of color and bursts of flavor that complement lighter sauces like White Fish Ragù with Lemon & Capers (page 307) and Basil Pesto (page 270), while also providing welcome brightness that can cut through heavy cream sauces. Tailor the fruit to your liking: Add more lemon, or try Meyer lemons, limes, or blood oranges.

Zest the oranges and lemons with a Microplane or other fine zester—you should have about 18 grams (3 tablespoons). Juice the lemons until you have 50 ml (3 tablespoons plus 1 teaspoon) of liquid.

Add the flours and zest to a large bowl. With your fingers, massage the two together to bring out the citrus oils. Whisk the eggs, yolks, and lemon juice together and make the dough according to your preferred method (see pages 27–33).

MAKES

about 21 ounces; serves 4

USE IT WITH

Corzetti della Valpolcevera (92) ·
Corzetti Stampati (146) · "Classic" Ravioli
(152) · Spizzulus (104)

white wine pasta dough

400 grams (2⅔ cups) **00 or all-purpose flour**

100 grams (about 2 large) **eggs**

50 ml (a scant ¼ cup) **dry white wine** like Pinot Grigio

50 ml (a scant ¼ cup) **tepid water**

This recipe is an adaptation of Enrica Monzani's corzetti dough, which she so kindly shared with me when we first cooked together. I'd made corzetti many times before, but nothing was as satisfying as this—soft, chewy, and wonderfully fragrant. Use it for both corzetti stampati (page 146) and corzetti della Valpolcevera (page 92), of course, but also filled pastas to give them a dumpling-like texture.

Make the dough according to your preferred method (see pages 27–33).

White Wine Corzetti Stampati

colorful
pasta
doughs

There are many ways to make colorful pasta. You can, of course, use spices like saffron (see page 41), turmeric, and paprika for bright yellows and orangey reds. For the other half of the rainbow, some use powders like beet, spinach, and spirulina. I understand the appeal: Like spices, powders don't add or take away moisture, meaning the dough's texture is more predictable. But I still prefer to cook and blend whole vegetables (or herbs, like the basil dough on page 38), since I find the results to be a little brighter (plus, you get those nutrients!). Adding a touch more moisture to water-based doughs and a higher proportion of egg yolks (fat) to egg-based doughs is all you need to ensure proper texture.

colorful flour & water pasta dough

120 grams (½ cup) **Green, Pink, or Orange Vegetable Purée** (recipes follow)

95 ml (⅓ cup plus 1 tablespoon) **tepid water**

400 grams (2⅓ cups) **semola rimacinata or semolina flour** or 400 grams (2½ cups) **00 or all-purpose flour**, depending on the type of pasta you're making

Combine the purée with the water and make the dough according to your preferred method (see pages 27–33). Any leftover purée can be frozen in an airtight container and defrosted for future use.

MAKES

about 22 ounces; serves 4

USE IT WITH

Caramelle (182) · Farfalle (140) ·
Fettuccine (131) · Garganelli (142) · Lasagne
(200) · Tagliatelle (131) · Tortelloni (172)

colorful egg pasta dough

120 grams (½ cup) **Green, Pink, or Orange Vegetable Purée** (recipes below)

50 grams (about 1 large) **egg**

60 grams (about 3 large) **egg yolks**

350 grams (2¼ cups) **00 or all-purpose flour**

50 grams (5 tablespoons) **semola rimacinata or semolina flour**

Combine the purée with the egg and yolks and make the dough according to your preferred method (see pages 27–33). Any leftover purée can be frozen in an airtight container and defrosted for future use.

green vegetable purée

Makes about 1 cup (215 grams)

170 grams (6 ounces) **spinach or other leafy greens** like kale, arugula, chard, mustard or dandelion greens, or a mix, any ribs and tough stems removed

Bring a medium pot of water to a boil. Add the greens and blanch until vibrant and tender, about 20 seconds. Drain immediately and rinse under cold water to stop the cooking (or plunge the greens into a bowl of ice water and drain).

Transfer the greens and their residual water to a small blender and purée until very smooth. If needed, add splashes of water, 1 tablespoon at a time, until they blend easily.

pink vegetable purée

Makes about 1 cup (225 grams), depending on the size of the beets

2 medium **red beets**, cleaned

Heat the oven to 400°F/205°C. Cut the stems and roots off the beets so the flesh is exposed and they stand upright. Place them cut-side down in a small, deep baking dish (a loaf tin works well) and add enough water to cover the bottom by ¼ inch.

Cover tightly with foil, prick a few holes in the top, and roast until very tender and easily pierced with a knife, 45 to 60 minutes. Check the beets halfway through; if the bottom of the baking dish looks dry, add a bit more water.

When the beets are still warm but cool enough to handle, remove the skins with a paper towel— they should peel off easily—and roughly chop. Transfer to a small blender and purée until smooth. If needed, add splashes of water, 1 tablespoon at a time, until they blend easily.

orange vegetable purée

Makes about ½ cup (120 grams), depending on the size of the peppers

2 large **red bell peppers**

Set the oven broiler to high. Cut the peppers in half lengthwise. Remove the seeds and stems, then arrange the halves cut sides down on a foil-lined sheet pan. Broil the peppers for 25 minutes, rotating the pan halfway through, or until the skins are almost completely blackened. Alternatively, if you have a gas stovetop, char the whole peppers directly over the flame, using tongs to rotate them until blackened.

Transfer the peppers to a bowl and cover tightly with plastic wrap or a dish towel. Let them steam for 10 minutes. When the peppers are cool enough to handle, peel away the skins. Transfer to a small blender and purée until very smooth.

gluten-free
pasta doughs

I firmly believe that the joy of making pasta should be available to everyone. Gluten is the key to creating elastic, chewy pasta, and although naturally gluten-free flours have been used for centuries, making pasta entirely without gluten has its hurdles. Luckily, we're in the midst of a gluten-free renaissance, and some of the products on the market can do magical things.

Gluten-free pasta dough will always be...different. I've tinkered with many gluten-free flour blends over the years. A lot of them "work," but few of them excel in taste. Caputo, the brand I trust with so much of my pasta making, recently developed a gluten-free flour mix called Fioreglut that's specifically formulated for pizza (and, in turn, works well for pasta). This mix is my winner in texture and flavor; you can order it online through several retailers. I should note, however, that the Caputo blend includes wheat starch, so although it's gluten-free, anyone with a wheat allergy should steer clear. Bob's Red Mill 1-to-1 Baking Flour is another good choice and doesn't contain wheat starch. You can find it in grocery stores and online.

Like many whole-grain and freshly milled flours, gluten-free blends soak up water greedily and need far more of it. This extra moisture is what makes these doughs workable—here, you're aiming for something soft and very pliable instead of the typical firmness. For flour-and-water pastas, know that the fragility of gluten-free dough lends itself best to simpler shapes like cavatelli and capunti (dragged shapes like orecchiette and foglie d'ulivo don't quite work); for egg-based pastas, know that when rolling the dough into sheets you need a gentler touch, and they won't stretch as thin as their glutenous counterparts.

gluten-free flour & water pasta dough

400 grams (a scant 3 cups) **Caputo Fioreglut gluten-free flour or blend of choice**

100 grams (about 2 large) **eggs**

30 ml (2 tablespoons) **extra-virgin olive oil**

140 ml (⅔ cup minus 1 tablespoon) **tepid water**

Make the dough according to your preferred method (pages 27–33; I usually opt for the food processor here). Knead the dough until it's soft and pliable, 1 to 2 minutes—no need to work up a sweat since there's no gluten to develop. Wrap the dough tightly and completely. You can start using it immediately, but make sure any unused dough is covered to prevent it from drying out.

USE IT WITH

*Corzetti Stampati (146) · Farfalle (140)
· Fettuccine (131) · Pappardelle (131) ·
Sorpresine (138) · Tagliatelle (131)*

gluten-free egg pasta dough

400 grams (a scant 3 cups) **Caputo Fioreglut gluten-free flour or blend of choice**

240 grams **eggs** (about 4 large eggs plus 2 yolks)

30 ml (2 tablespoons) **extra-virgin olive oil**

Make the dough according to your preferred method (pages 27–33; I usually opt for the food processor here). Knead the dough until it's soft and pliable, 1 to 2 minutes—no need to work up a sweat since there's no gluten to develop. Wrap the dough tightly and completely. You can start using it immediately, but make sure any unused dough is covered to prevent it from drying out.

gnocchi doughs

In the beginning, there were gnocchi. Derived from the word "gnocco," referring to a knot or lump, these dumplings—what I like to call little pasta pillows—are the mother of all pasta, first recorded in writing in the 14th century, but surely made for centuries before.

You can make gnocchi out of potatoes, of course, but potato gnocchi are a much younger member of the gnocchi family. Dumplings made from all types of flour—chestnut, rice, rye—came first, as did those made from leftovers, particularly bread: stale bread, soaked bread, bread dough, and thick, bready batters. Only in the 18th century did potatoes wriggle their way into the gnocchi pedigree.

I've always liked eating gnocchi, but I did not always like making them. The methods for making other fresh pastas don't apply to gnocchi, so I've failed more than a few times, endlessly cycling between flour and potatoes until I was left with a sticky, gluey dough monster. As with all failures, though, I learned far more than I could by succeeding, and now gnocchi and I are good friends. I'm excited to share my findings with you, so you too can master gnocchi. Here are my biggest tips for delicious and delicate dumplings:

DRY INGREDIENTS ARE YOUR FRIENDS. Mixing ingredients that carry too much moisture will make for a gluey marriage with the flour that binds them together. For fluffy, tender gnocchi, keep your potatoes and ricotta from bringing too much water to the party:

- Bake potatoes if you have the time, and always keep the skins on during cooking.

- Use high-quality, full-fat ricotta that's dense and not watery. Anything fresh from the deli counter works great, or make your own, page 61.

- For water-logged vegetables like squash and sweet potatoes, roast them, mash them, and pat them dry many times over to soak up as much moisture as possible. The drier the ingredients, the less flour you'll need, which brings me to...

KEEP THE FLOUR TO A MINIMUM. Flour masks the flavor of gnocchi's star ingredients and weighs them down. For lighter, more flavorful gnocchi, use only as much as you need to hold the dough together. Gnocchi doughs are delicate by nature, much more so than other pastas, so expect something rough and ready, not super smooth or elastic.

USE A LIGHT TOUCH. While I can check off my daily arm workout when kneading other types of pasta dough, for gnocchi, I only work the dough until the ingredients are evenly incorporated—an overworked dough risks becoming gluey and dense. This lightness applies equally to shaping: If rolling the gnocchi across a fork or board, a little pressure goes a long way. Which reminds me—gnocchi are an excellent gluten-free option. A quick knead means there's no real gluten development here, so wheat flour can easily be swapped out for a gluten-free alternative (rice flour is not uncommon in Italy).

One of my favorite aspects of making gnocchi is its speed: Once you get the hang of it, fresh gnocchi can be on the table on a weeknight. If you do want to incorporate potato gnocchi and its variations into your regular rotation, **I strongly recommend getting a ricer**. This handy tool pushes potatoes, sweet potatoes, and squash through small holes—removing any unwanted stringiness and undercooked pieces in the process—to ensure smooth and airy dumplings. It'll pay for itself in great gnocchi a hundred times over.

ricotta gnocchi dough

454 grams (16 ounces) high-quality **full-fat ricotta** (or make your own, page 61)

55 grams (2 ounces) finely grated **Parmigiano-Reggiano or Grana Padano**

70 grams **eggs** (about 1 large egg plus 1 yolk), lightly beaten

3 grams (1 teaspoon) **kosher salt**

Whole nutmeg (optional)

150 grams (1 cup) **all-purpose flour**

If you're looking to make delicious pasta pillows in under 30 minutes, look no further. Ricotta gnocchi are particularly popular in Emilia-Romagna, and I love them for their ease and texture, which is more toothsome than their potato cousins. The key to ricotta gnocchi is, well, the ricotta: Thick, dense varieties are necessary, like the fresh ones at the deli counter or high-quality brands like Calabro. The fewer the ingredients, the better, so look for milk, salt, and (sometimes) acid on the container; avoid gums and stabilizers, which will leave you with a sticky mess. Or, if you have some extra time, make your own ricotta using the recipe on the next page. It doesn't take long and it's more than worth it.

IF USING STORE-BOUGHT RICOTTA Line a plate with paper towels. Drain off any surface liquid from the ricotta, then dump it onto the paper towels and spread it out a little bit with a spatula. Pat the cheese with more paper towels to absorb as much liquid as possible. (If your ricotta sticks to the paper towels, use a silicone spatula to scrape off as much as you can.)

In a large mixing bowl, combine the ricotta, Parmigiano-Reggiano, eggs, salt, and a few gratings of nutmeg (if using) and mix thoroughly until smooth. Fold in the flour with a spatula until well combined. The mixture should hold together but still be a bit tacky. If needed, add another tablespoon of flour.

Turn the dough out onto a floured work surface and knead for a few moments, with a light touch, until the mixture is homogeneous and there are no visible streaks of flour. Shape using either the Standard or Delicate Gnocchi Method on page 188 and page 192, respectively. You do not need to rest the dough before shaping.

homemade ricotta

1.9 liters (½ gallon) **whole milk** (not ultra-pasteurized)

180 ml (¾ cup) **heavy cream**

5 grams (1½ teaspoons) **kosher salt**

45 ml (3 tablespoons) **distilled white vinegar**

Okay, so this isn't *technically* ricotta. Ricotta means "recooked" and is made from the whey left behind from mozzarella (another ode to Italian resourcefulness!). For our purposes, though, using milk instead of whey still creates a delicious, creamy cheese that will suit all your ricotta needs, from gnocchi to pasta fillings to slathering on toast. I prefer the neutral flavor delivered by white vinegar, but you can use lemon juice instead. Avoid ultra-pasteurized milk (pasteurized is fine) since it is designed to separate with difficulty and yields much less cheese.

The cheese will keep in the refrigerator in an airtight container for up to 3 days. Strain the leftover whey through a fine sieve and reserve the liquid to make especially smooth and tender pasta doughs (in place of water) and breads.

In a Dutch oven or heavy-bottomed pot, stir together the milk, cream, and salt. Gradually warm the mixture over medium-high heat, stirring occasionally to prevent the milk from scorching, until it reaches 195 to 200°F/90°C (just below a boil), about 15 to 25 minutes depending on your burner. If you don't have a thermometer, look for lots of steam and a layer of frothy bubbles on the surface. Do not boil.

Stirring constantly, add the vinegar. Stir for a few more seconds, then remove from the heat and let the mixture stand undisturbed until the curds separate, 5 minutes. If the curds aren't separating and/or the mixture still looks milky, return the pot to medium heat until large curds begin to form, then remove from the heat and let stand another 5 minutes. The liquid whey will be pale yellow in color.

Meanwhile, set a strainer over a large, heatproof bowl and line it with a few layers of cheesecloth, making sure there's some overhang around the edges.

With a spider sieve or slotted spoon, scoop the curds into the cheesecloth. Let drain until it's reached your desired consistency, anywhere between 15 and 45 minutes.

For the Ricotta Gnocchi Dough (page 60), Meyer Lemon & Herb Ricotta Gnocchi Dough (page 64), and Pumpkin & Ricotta Gnocchi Dough (page 65), drain the cheese for about 30 minutes, then briefly whizz it in a food processor until thick and creamy (this is optional but yields especially smooth dumplings). For pasta fillings, drain the cheese for 20 to 30 minutes and chill before use. If enjoying on its own, drain for 15 minutes, whip it in a food processor if you'd like (see page 214) and season to taste with salt.

Ricotta Gnocchi Dough

5

6

7

8

meyer lemon & herb ricotta gnocchi dough

454 grams (16 ounces) high-quality **full-fat ricotta** (or make your own, page 61)

55 grams (2 ounces) finely grated **Parmigiano-Reggiano or Grana Padano**

70 grams **eggs** (about 1 large egg plus 1 yolk), lightly beaten

3 grams (1 teaspoon) **kosher salt**

Grated zest of 2 **Meyer lemons**

10 grams (¼ cup) finely chopped **tender fresh herbs** like flat-leaf parsley, chives, dill, basil, and/or mint

150 grams (1 cup) **all-purpose flour**

If there were ever summery gnocchi, these would be it. Fresh parsley, chives, and dill work particularly well here since they maintain their color beautifully. Basil and mint are delicious, too, though they tend to bruise and brown. I don't mind a little discoloration, but if you do, blanch these herbs for a few seconds in boiling water, shock them in cold water or an ice bath, and dry them thoroughly before chopping and incorporating into the dough. The sweetness and orangey hue of Meyer lemons give these gnocchi a little something extra special, but if you can't find them, use a couple of regular lemons instead.

Make the dough as directed for the Ricotta Gnocchi Dough on page 60, adding the lemon zest and herbs to the cheese mixture before folding in the flour. Shape the gnocchi using either the Standard or Delicate Gnocchi Method on page 188 and page 192, respectively. You do not need to rest the dough before shaping.

pumpkin & ricotta gnocchi dough

225 grams (8 ounces) high-quality **full-fat ricotta** (or make your own, page 61)

225 grams (8 ounces) **pumpkin purée**

55 grams (2 ounces) finely grated **Parmigiano-Reggiano or Grana Padano**

70 grams **eggs** (about 1 large egg plus 1 yolk), lightly beaten

3 grams (1 teaspoon) **kosher salt**

Whole nutmeg

150 grams (1 cup) **all-purpose flour**

Canned pumpkin never looked so good! This dough is the festive shade of orange that I crave when the leaves shed their green for ruby, amber, and gold. While the dough is soft, the cooked dumplings are on the firm side, so if you're a fan of pasta with bite, these are for you.

Thoroughly pat the ricotta dry with paper towels, and do the same with the pumpkin purée (it's essential to sop up the pumpkin's moisture; use a few changes of paper towels!). Make the dough as directed for the Ricotta Gnocchi Dough on page 60, combining the ricotta, pumpkin, Parmigiano-Reggiano, eggs, salt, and a generous grating of fresh nutmeg until smooth before folding in the flour. The dough will be soft and slightly tacky, and you might need a little more flour than usual.

Shape the gnocchi using the Delicate Gnocchi Method on page 192. You do not need to rest the dough before shaping. Note: The pumpkin imparts more color than flavor.

— ✺ —

potato gnocchi dough

1.4 kg (3 pounds; about 4 large) **baking potatoes**, scrubbed

250 grams (1⅔ cups) **all-purpose flour**

5 grams (1½ teaspoons) **kosher salt**

35 grams (2 large) **egg yolks**, lightly beaten

MAKE IT VEGAN
Omit the egg yolks.

Despite such a short ingredient list, there are countless potato gnocchi dough variations, each marked by the preferences of the people who make them. Some use potatoes and flour alone, others prefer rice flour to wheat (reminder: gnocchi, potato and otherwise, are a great gluten-free option), and still others mix in flavorings like Parmigiano-Reggiano and nutmeg—something I'd highly recommend if you're serving these with a rich, creamy sauce like the Four-Cheese Sauce on page 306. This recipe is a simple one, so it's easy to tweak as you like.

Fresh from the pot, these gnocchi are delicate, and as someone who prefers a bit of bite, I often go one step further and pan-fry them. The crisp exterior contrasts nicely against the pillowy inside and, I think, accentuates the flavor of the potatoes. You can use any starchy baking potato here (russet, Idaho, or even Yukon Gold), though avoid very waxy varieties like Red Bliss and other red potatoes.

Both boiling and baking the potatoes will result in delicious gnocchi. I generally bake my potatoes not only because the dry heat draws out more moisture, but also because I can throw them in the oven and forget about them for an hour. The process is the same as making Sweet Potato Gnocchi Dough; see pages 72–73 for step-by-step photos.

TO BOIL THE POTATOES Submerge the unpeeled potatoes in a large pot of cold, salted water. Bring to a boil, reduce to a lively simmer, and cook until the potatoes are tender and easily pierced with a knife, about 40 minutes. Drain thoroughly and let them dry for a moment.

TO BAKE THE POTATOES Heat the oven to 425°F/220°C. Prick the potatoes with a fork and place directly on the oven's middle rack. Bake until tender and easily pierced with a knife, 60 to 70 minutes.

When the potatoes are cool enough to handle but still warm, peel off the skins. Pass them through a ricer onto a paper towel–lined sheet pan or gently mash them with a potato masher or fork (if using a masher/fork, remove any large undercooked pieces, then spread out on paper towels). Allow to cool for about 30 minutes and pat dry with paper towels before using. You should have about 1 kg (2.2 pounds) of riced potatoes; if you have significantly more or less, scale the amount of flour in the recipe accordingly.

continues

Ricing Potatoes

Mix the flour and salt together in a large mixing bowl. With your fist, make a wide hole (or well) in the center, pushing the flour up and around the sides of the bowl. Add half of the potatoes to the center of the well and drizzle with half of the egg yolks. Bring some of the flour from around the bowl on top and press it into the potatoes a bit, so everything is roughly covered in a layer of flour. Add the remaining potatoes and egg yolks on top.

Fold and press the rest of the flour from the sides and bottom of the bowl into the potato mixture from all directions until everything comes together into a rough, shaggy dough. It's okay if the dough is crumbly—press the mixture firmly until it holds together.

Transfer to a flat surface and knead gently until evenly incorporated, 1½ to 2 minutes (the longer you knead, the more bite the gnocchi will have). If the dough is very sticky (tacky is normal), work in a handful more flour. You're not looking for a super smooth dough; it should be rough around the edges. Clear your work surface with a bench scraper and dust with fresh flour, then shape according to the Standard Gnocchi Method on page 188. You do not need to rest the dough before shaping.

VARIATION

Gluten-Free Potato Gnocchi Dough: Swap out the flour for rice flour or your favorite gluten-free blend. Keep an extra 100 grams (⅔ cup) gluten-free flour on hand and add more, a little at a time, as needed until the dough is workable and no longer sticky.

ossola-style chestnut, squash & potato dough

800 grams (1¾ pounds; about 1 small) **butternut squash**

Extra-virgin olive oil

700 grams (1½ pounds; about 2 large) **baking potatoes,** scrubbed

120 grams (¾ cup) **all-purpose flour**

120 grams (1 scant cup) **chestnut flour**

5 grams (1½ teaspoons) **kosher salt**

85 grams (3 ounces) finely grated **Grana Padano or Parmigiano-Reggiano**

35 grams (2 large) **egg yolks,** lightly beaten

Whole nutmeg

MAKE IT VEGAN
Omit the egg yolks.

Gnocchi all'Ossolana are hearty cold-weather dumplings from the Ossola Valley in northern Piedmont, only a few miles from the Swiss border. In addition to the potatoes we know and love, these gnocchi are packed with winter squash and chestnut flour, which not only amplifies their warm flavor, but also gives them a rich, caramel color—think a crackling fire and cozy blanket in pasta form.

Heat the oven to 425°F/220°C.

On a slip-free cutting board, cut the top and bottom ends off the squash, then cut it in half crosswise where the neck meets the base. Stand each piece upright on its widest flat side and carefully slice from top to bottom, making sure your free hand is holding the squash in place above the knife. Scoop out the seeds and coat the squash in olive oil and kosher salt.

Place the squash cut sides down on a parchment-lined sheet pan. Prick the potatoes all over with a fork and place them alongside the squash. Roast until the squash is browned and easily pierced with a knife, and the potatoes are tender with a crisp skin, 50 to 60 minutes, rotating the pan halfway through. If the potatoes don't feel quite done, return them to the oven and bake, directly on the middle rack, for another 10 minutes.

When the potatoes are cool enough to handle, scoop out the flesh and pass it through a ricer or gently mash with a potato masher—you should have about 400 grams (14 ounces). Spread the potatoes on a paper towel–lined sheet pan and let cool for about 30 minutes. Pat dry with more paper towels before using.

When the squash is cool, scoop out the flesh and mash until smooth—you should have about 400 grams (14 ounces). Spread it on a paper towel–lined sheet pan and thoroughly pat dry to remove as much moisture as possible (use a few changes of paper towels to really sop it up!).

Combine the flours and salt in a large mixing bowl. Make the dough as directed for the Potato Gnocchi Dough on page 67, adding half of the squash, half of the potatoes, half of the cheese, half of the egg yolks, and a dash of freshly grated nutmeg to the well, then folding in some of the flour. Repeat with the remaining squash, potatoes, cheese, and a little more nutmeg. Shape the gnocchi using either the Standard or Delicate Gnocchi Method on page 188 and page 192, respectively. You do not need to rest the dough before shaping.

sweet potato gnocchi dough

1 kg (2½ pounds; about 3 large) **sweet potatoes**, scrubbed and halved lengthwise

360 grams (12.75 ounces; about 1 large) **baking potato**, scrubbed

35 grams (2 large) **egg yolks**, lightly beaten

5 grams (1½ teaspoons) **kosher salt**

250 grams (1⅔ cups) **all-purpose flour**

Whole nutmeg

MAKE IT VEGAN
Omit the egg yolks.

These gnocchi are an ode to my mom's sweet potato casserole—fluffy, buttery, and piled high with marshmallows—which she drives across three states every year to proudly place on our family's Thanksgiving table. They're also inspired by gnocchi di zucca, an Italian staple that celebrates autumn's bounty, particularly the dense, sweet, and vibrant orange Mantua pumpkin from the north.

Heat the oven to 425°F/220°C. Arrange the sweet potatoes cut sides down on a parchment-lined sheet pan. Roast until tender and easily pierced with a knife, 40 to 45 minutes.

Boil or bake the baking potato according to the directions for the Potato Gnocchi Dough on page 67.

While the sweet potatoes are still warm, remove the skins and peel away the tough outer layer on the cut sides. Pass the sweet potatoes through a ricer or mash with a potato masher or fork, removing any stringy and undercooked pieces. Spread them on a paper towel–lined sheet pan and let cool for about 30 minutes. Thoroughly pat dry with paper towels before using (really sop up all that moisture!).

Weigh out 450 grams (16 ounces) of the sweet potatoes (or, if you're just under or over, use however much you have).

Repeat the process with the baking potato—you should be left with roughly 250 grams (8.8 ounces) of riced/mashed potato but use however much you have.

Make the dough as directed for the Potato Gnocchi Dough on page 67, seasoning the mixture with freshly grated nutmeg and kneading the dough gently until it comes together. Shape the gnocchi using the Delicate Gnocchi Method on page 192. You do not need to rest the dough before shaping.

Sweet Potato Gnocchi Dough

PART TWO

shapes

The world of pasta shapes is an endless playground, and like a kid on her first day of school, I began with the letter A.

The first pasta book I owned was Oretta Zanini De Vita's *Encyclopedia of Pasta*, perhaps the most comprehensive compilation of Italian pasta shapes and their origins. Photo-less and bound in red, it could easily be mistaken for a presidential biography. The book begins with a lozenge-shaped pasta from Abruzzo called abbotta pezziende and, always having been a diligent student, I thought I should start there, too.

Over time, I learned about shapes I'd seen before, like agnolotti and orecchiette, and many more that I'd known nothing about. Traveling through the Italian peninsula and the alphabet, with only a few notes and the rare illustration as a guide, I welcomed the challenge of creating each shape. Occasionally a technique would come naturally, requiring only a few tries to get into a groove; other times, when the process was more interesting than the eating, my fingers would bruise from trying. This is a collection of some of the shapes I've grown to love most, my closest friends on the playground, if you will. Know this is only a beginning.

Making pasta is making art you can eat. It can be a solo endeavor, providing stillness and tactility in a noisy digital world. It can also be shared with others—family and friends gathered around the table, scraps of dough and bits of flour strewn about, half-filled glasses of wine, hands reaching over hands. And as with all creative endeavors, perfection is personal and never the goal: **Handmade pasta should look handmade.**

In this section you'll find what you expect when you think of fresh pasta (fettuccine, ravioli) and, I hope, you'll discover something new. We'll begin with shapes made mostly from flour and water, the ones you can make right now and without any special equipment, because nothing is more important to me than every reader knowing that **you can make fresh pasta with what you already have**. I call these shapes "hand-formed" pastas, even though every shape here is made by hand. Next we'll move on to "hand-cut" pastas—ribbons long and short, thick and thin—and from there to unfilled "short-cut" pastas like farfalle and garganelli. Stuffed pastas come next and, finally, gnocchi and lasagne.

Every shape can be made by a beginner and more seasoned pasta maker alike. They are ordered within each subsection by difficulty, starting with the simplest (or, in some cases, what requires the least equipment). I have, however, seen novices make perfect tortellini on the first try, so saying one shape is better suited to a certain level of experience is based entirely on *my* experience. Take it with a grain of salt.

This section is also where you'll find a sprinkling of pasta folklore. The stories will start to sound familiar—ingenuity is a common theme because Italian cooks have always been clever and resourceful. I hope you'll take these lessons into your own homes, take inspiration from your own surroundings, and experiment with what's in your own kitchen.

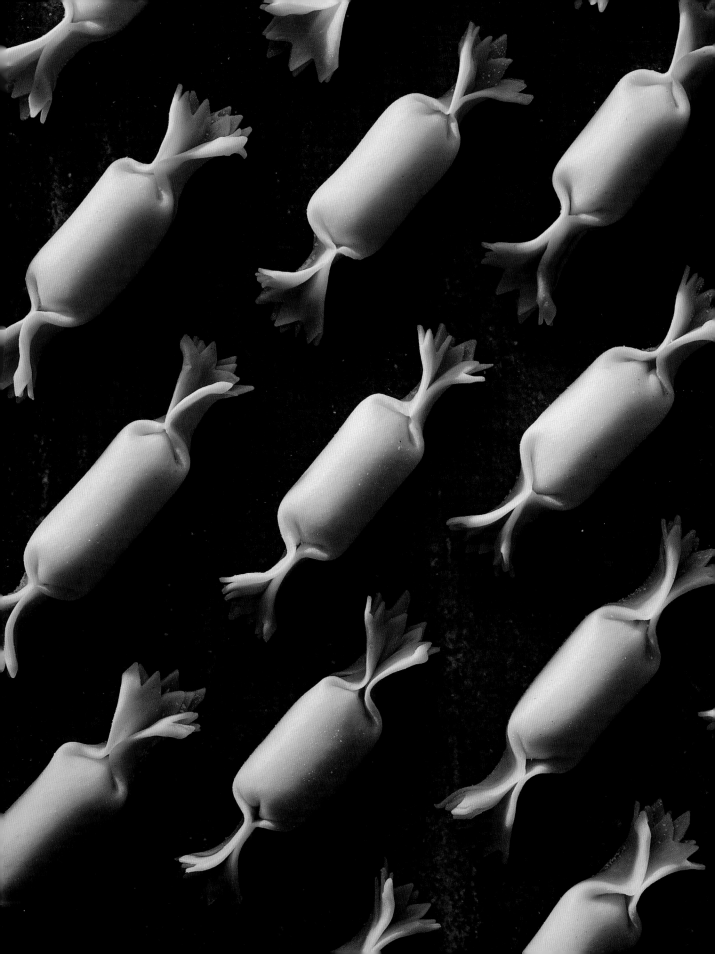

before we start

Making fresh pasta takes time. It's a steady process, and a rewarding one, but no one likes being forced to eat at 10 o'clock at night. The first time you try a new shape, set aside a couple of hours to make it (and rest assured that it'll only get easier and faster with practice). Beyond that, here are some things you can do to stay organized and efficient.

prep smart

The order in which you assemble the components of a dish can save you time, depending on what you're making. If it's cavatelli (page 96) with tomato sauce (page 254), first prepare the dough and, while it's resting, make your sauce, then the pasta; if it's pappardelle (page 131) with a long-cooking lamb ragù (page 321), get your meat in the oven before starting the dough, and roll and cut your ribbons once the meat is done and you're waiting for the water to boil. For stuffed pastas, the order of preparation depends on the filling: Cooked fillings need time to chill, so make them first, then the dough; fillings made with already-cold ingredients can be thrown together quickly while the dough rests.

Preparing the elements over a couple of days is always an option, too. Fillings can be made a day or two ahead, as can many sauces, particularly ragùs. Doughs can be refrigerated overnight and shaped pasta can be frozen for up to 3 months (more on that soon). You can tailor the process to your schedule.

have everything within reach

This includes tools, fillings, and the following:

- **A PLACE TO PUT FINISHED PIECES OF PASTA.** I use a sheet pan dusted with just enough coarse semolina (not fine semola) to cover the bottom. Semolina alternatives include cornmeal, polenta, a clean cotton (not terrycloth) dishcloth, or a wooden work surface—something that will absorb excess moisture. The semolina can be reused: Sift out any pieces of dried dough and store it in a bag or container for the next time you make pasta. Parchment paper is also an option, particularly for stuffed shapes.

- **EXTRA FLOUR.** I keep 00 or all-purpose on hand for egg pastas and gnocchi, and coarse semolina for hand-cut pastas to prevent the strands from sticking together.

- **A DAMP DISHCLOTH OR PLASTIC WRAP** to cover pasta sheets, particularly for stuffed and patterned shapes. These techniques are the most time-consuming and covering rolled pasta you aren't immediately using will prevent it from drying out.

- **A SPRAY BOTTLE WITH WATER** to seal stuffed pastas and add a little extra hydration to dry dough when you need it.

start small

Pasta dough can dry out quickly, especially on cold winter days. For most hand-formed pastas, work with only a small portion of dough at a time, a slice the width of one or two fingers (you'll be surprised by how much pasta it can make). For pastas made from thin sheets, cut the dough into quarters and roll one at a time. For individually sealed stuffed pastas like cappelletti, caramelle, scarpinocc, and tortelloni, start by filling a few at a time. This way you can keep the unfilled dough covered and adjust the amount of filling as you go.

FAQs

WHAT SHOULD I DO IF MY DOUGH IS STICKING TO THE PLASTIC WRAP?

A rested dough, having had time to relax and hydrate, will always be tackier to the touch than just after kneading. This can be particularly noticeable with durum wheat doughs, since it takes more time for the harder flour to absorb moisture. (That's why, when kneading a durum dough, it'll feel dry, flaky, dry, flaky, and suddenly hello! Smooth and pliable.)

If your dough sticks to the plastic after resting, especially if it's a hot and/or humid day, here are a few things you can do:

- Leave the dough uncovered as you work to help dry it out. Check occasionally—if it's starting to form a skin, cover it again with an overturned bowl or dishcloth.

- Once cut, let the individual pieces of dough dry for a few minutes before shaping. This is particularly helpful for orecchiette and foglie d'ulivo (drier dough = rougher surface = good for sauce), as well as busiate and garganelli (drier dough = no sticking to the rod/dowel).

- If it's a sticky mess and completely unmanageable, head to the food processor (see page 30).

I'M STRUGGLING TO ROLL MY DOUGH INTO A ROPE. WHAT AM I DOING WRONG?

Absolutely nothing! This probably means your dough is a little dry, which is preferred for many hand-formed pastas. If the dough is sliding around on your board and you can't get a good grip, rub or spray your hands with a little water and try again. The moisture will help with the friction.

If the dough is so dry that it's tough and unmanageable—it breaks instead of bends—the food processor can help (see page 30).

HOW MUCH FLOUR SHOULD I USE WHEN SHAPING MY PASTA?

Only as much as you need. A lot of excess flour will not only make dough difficult to fold and seal, but it can also make cooked pasta gummy. The dough recipes in this book should yield sheets that feel almost leathery, so you shouldn't need much, if any, extra flour.

There are, of course, exceptions: a humid day, doughs with a higher water content, and gnocchi, to name a few. And it's worth mentioning that the KitchenAid attachment can tear the surface of the dough the thinner it gets, so adding flour will help it glide through smoothly. Trust your instincts: If the dough is sticky or your sheets start to wrinkle or tear, dust both sides with 00 or all-purpose flour (not semolina), spread it around evenly, and wipe away any excess.

WHAT SHOULD I DO WITH MY SCRAPS?

Flour-and-water-based scraps can be rewrapped and reused like Play-Doh. Fresh egg-based scraps that feel pliable and well hydrated can be reused, too—smush them into a ball and rewrap in plastic so they can relax and rehydrate. Then, once you've finished shaping the fresh dough, roll the accumulated scrap ball through the machine once more. Any dry and brittle, herb-laminated, or patterned pasta scraps can be made into another pasta altogether: maltagliati.

Maltagliati are a pasta maker's secret snack, the irregular offcuts of rolled dough that make way for prettier shapes. The name means "badly cut," and these scraps can be frozen and saved for soups (pages 336–350) or tossed with sauce for a quick meal. Cut the trimmings into small squares and you have **quadrucci** or **quadrettini**, an ethereal addition to broths (page 336) or chicken soup (page 346) that cooks in the time it takes to gather the bowls.

hand-formed pastas

When asked where to start, I always say here. In these next pages you'll find chewy little hollows, ears, leaves, and spirals, first conjured by poor yet savvy cooks and often from Italy's south. Some are considered strascinati, meaning "dragged," referring to the push-and-pulls used to make them. Beyond this book there are hundreds more, some so intricate or so old that only a single town still makes them—which means there's always something new to discover.

A Note on Shaping Gluten-Free Pasta

Because gluten-free dough lacks elasticity, stick with shapes that require less stretching. Cavatelli, capunti, malloreddus, and spizzulus all work well with the gluten-free flour-and-water dough on page 57; orecchiette and foglie d'ulivo break easily, but by all means give them a try.

PAIR THEM WITH

Anchovy & Onion Sauce with Breadcrumbs (331) •
Parmesan-Garlic Butter (297) • *Pecorino, Pepper & Lemon*
Sauce (298) • *Slow-Roasted Tomato & Garlic Sauce (263)*

pici

What they are

Rustic, hand-rolled spaghetti from Siena, but also found elsewhere in Tuscany by a dozen other names. Pici are springy and toothsome—made with just flour (usually 00, but sometimes semola and sometimes both), water, olive oil, and a little elbow grease—more akin to Japanese udon than the spaghetti from the box. This one's for the kids, too; the soft dough and long noodles welcome little helping hands.

How they're traditionally served

With fried breadcrumbs (con le briciole); ragù, particularly duck (con la nana) or wild boar (al cinghiale); cacio e pepe; garlic-spiked tomato sauce (all'aglione).

What you need

- A work surface, preferably wooden;
- metal bench scraper or sharp knife;
- rolling pin or wine bottle;
- extra-virgin olive oil;
- pastry brush (optional).

MAKE THE DOUGH Make your dough of choice and let it rest, tightly covered, at room temperature for 1 hour—a completely relaxed dough will make for easier rolling.

SET UP YOUR WORKSPACE Dust a sheet pan with semolina or line it with a dry dishcloth. Gather your tools. Pour a little olive oil into a small bowl.

ROLL, OIL, AND CUT THE DOUGH Cut off a quarter of the dough and keep the rest covered. Flatten the dough with the palm of your hand into a rough oval. With a rolling pin (or wine bottle), roll the dough into a ¼-inch (6-mm) thick slab, about the thickness of pita bread.

With a pastry brush or your fingers, coat the dough completely in a thin layer of olive oil—get the front, back, and edges. This will prevent the surface from drying out and cracking.

Use a bench scraper or sharp knife to slice the dough into strips roughly ¼ inch (6 mm) wide. They will all be different lengths.

MAKE THE PICI Position one of the strips horizontally on your work surface and move the other pieces to the side. Pinch the sides of the strip upward so it's more cylindrical. Then, starting in the center, use your fingers to roll the strip of dough into a thin strand—first back and forth, until the surface is smooth, and then outward in opposite directions, eventually making your way toward the ends. The goal is a strand that's 2 to 3 mm thick.

Repeat the process with the remaining strips, and then the remaining dough. If the pieces start to dry and crack on the surface as you roll, add a touch more olive oil. If any of them break, don't sweat it—now you have two!

COOK OR STORE THE PASTA If cooking the pasta shortly after shaping, coil the finished strand into a loose spiral, making sure there's a little space between the concentric circles, and place it on the prepared sheet pan (you can also line them up in a row). If storing for future use, dust each strand in semolina on the sheet pan before coiling and freeze the pasta as directed on page 207.

Cook the pici according to the instructions on page 205 until tender but with some bite, 3 to 5 minutes, depending on their thickness.

Soft Wheat & Water Pici

MAKE THEM WITH
Durum Wheat & Water Dough (37)
Soft Wheat & Water Dough (37)
Whole Wheat & Water Dough (38)

PAIR THEM WITH
Chickpea Soup with Harissa & Rosemary (349) · Grandma Ruthe's Chicken Soup (346) · White Bean Soup with Parmesan & Kale (350)

lagane

What they are

An ancient pasta, perhaps the most ancient, even referenced by the Roman poet Horace himself. Wide and rustic, lagane have bite, which makes them a welcome accompaniment to thick, hearty sauces and soups. Durum wheat and water-based, you'll find them in the south, particularly around Calabria, Basilicata, Puglia, and Campania. Their robustness means they're easy to roll with a pin, though you can, of course, use a pasta machine, too.

How they're traditionally served

With hearty sauces and soups, particularly chickpeas and other legumes.

What you need

- A work surface, preferably wooden;
- rolling pin or pasta machine;
- sharp knife.

MAKE THE DOUGH Make your dough of choice and let it rest, tightly covered, at room temperature for 30 minutes to 1 hour—a more relaxed dough will make for easier rolling.

SET UP YOUR WORKSPACE Dust a sheet pan with semolina or line it with a dry dishcloth. Gather your tools. Set up your pasta machine if you plan to use one.

ROLL THE DOUGH INTO A SHEET Cut off a quarter of the dough and keep the rest covered.

Roll the dough by hand: With a rolling pin, roll the dough into a thin rectangle—it doesn't matter if the shape is uneven. You're aiming for 2 mm thick, but do the best you can. It's helpful to do this on a wooden surface to keep the pasta from sticking; if you don't have one, dust the sheet with 00, all-purpose, or semola flour as needed.

Or, roll the dough with a pasta machine: Follow the instructions on page 114 to roll the dough into a semi-thin sheet, stopping at setting 4 for both the Marcato Atlas 150 and KitchenAid machines. If the dough is at all sticky, or the sheet starts to tear on the surface, dust both sides with a little flour.

If you have the space, roll out the remaining sections of dough—the finished sheets can dry a bit; no need to cover.

CUT THE LAGANE Cut the sheets into stout strips, 1 inch (2.5 cm) wide and 3 inches (7.5 cm) long. Arrange the pieces on the prepared sheet pan in a single layer or, if you need to stack or freeze them (see page 207), sprinkle semolina between each layer and shake it off before cooking.

COOK OR STORE THE PASTA Cook the lagane either in boiling water or soup according to the instructions on page 205 until tender but with some bite, 2 to 4 minutes.

Durum Wheat & Water Lagane

MAKE THEM WITH
Soft Wheat & Water Dough (37) • Soft Wheat & Water Dough (Corzetti della Valpolcevera variation) (37) • Durum Wheat & Water Dough (37) • Whole Wheat & Water Dough (38)

PAIR THEM WITH
No-Cook Tomato & Basil Sauce (259) • Pantry Tuna & Tomato Sauce (332) • Red Pesto (276) • Tomato Sauce with Olives & Fried Capers (264)

strozzapreti

What they are

A medieval-era pasta from central Italy that always makes me smile. The name means "priest stranglers" and they take many forms, from the short twists here to gnocchi-like dumplings made with spinach and other greens.

Strozzapreti have several origin stories. One tells of a priest gone hunting without food or supplies. Ravenous upon returning home for dinner, he swallowed his pasta whole and started to choke, saved only when a merciful servant struck him in the back. Another is a story of spite: In centuries past, the Catholic church rented much of its land to farmers, and as a form of payment, the priests demanded the farmers' wives prepare pasta for them. Angered by their greed, the farmers wished the priests would choke on their wives' creations! Whatever the truth may be, this pasta—brought to life by loose, spontaneous movement—reminds me of the beauty of imperfection.

How they're traditionally served

With various local sauces depending on the form, and particularly tomato and seafood sauces.

What you need

- A work surface, preferably wooden;
- rolling pin or pasta machine;
- sharp knife.

MAKE THE DOUGH Make your dough of choice and let it rest, tightly covered, at room temperature for 1 hour—a completely relaxed dough will make for easier rolling.

SET UP YOUR WORKSPACE Dust a sheet pan with semolina or line it with a dry dishcloth. Gather your tools. Set up your pasta machine if you plan to use one.

ROLL THE DOUGH INTO A SHEET Cut off a quarter of the dough and keep the rest covered.

Roll the dough by hand: With a rolling pin, roll the dough into a thin disc or rectangle—it doesn't matter if the shape is uneven. You're aiming for about 1.5 mm thick but do the best you can. It's helpful to do this on a wooden surface to keep the pasta from sticking; if you don't have one, dust the sheet with 00, all-purpose, or semola flour as needed.

Or, roll the dough with a pasta machine: Follow the instructions on page 114 to roll the dough into a semi-thin sheet, stopping at setting 5 for both the Marcato Atlas 150 and KitchenAid machines. If the dough is at all sticky as it goes through the machine, or the sheet starts to tear on the surface, dust both sides with a little flour.

CUT THE SHEET INTO STRIPS   Cut the pasta sheet into 1-inch (2.5-cm) wide ribbons; it's totally fine if they're different lengths.

MAKE THE STROZZAPRETI   Position one end of each ribbon in the center of your non-dominant palm. Pinch the top a little to help get a grip and then, starting with the fingertips of your free hand, roll the dough upward quickly and lightly until your fingertips meet and the ribbon twists on itself to form a rustic spiral (the motion is like rubbing your hands together when they're cold). To make longer strozzapreti, reposition your hands at the end of the twist and repeat the motion once more.

Pinch off the twisted portion and continue the motion until the strip is gone. The length of the strozzapreti will depend on the size of your hand, but in general they'll be 2 to 4 inches (5 to 10 cm) long. They'll all look different, and that's the beauty of it!

Arrange the finished strozzapreti in a single layer on the prepared sheet pan. Repeat with the remaining ribbons, and then the remaining dough.

COOK OR STORE THE PASTA   Cook the strozzapreti according to the instructions on page 205 until tender but with some bite, 3 to 5 minutes, depending on their thickness. For storage options, see page 206.

Soft Wheat & Water Strozzapreti

MAKE THEM WITH

Soft Wheat & Water Dough (Corzetti della Valpolcevera variation) (37) · Durum Wheat & Water Dough (37) · White Wine Dough (50)

PAIR THEM WITH

Broccoli Sauce (281) · Port-Braised Lamb Ragù (321) · Red Pesto (276) · Citrus & Pistachio Pesto (275) · Wild Mushroom Sauce (285)

corzetti della valpolcevera

What they are

I had to include this lesser-known pasta shape because 1) it's very beginner- (and kid-) friendly, and 2) it's just that fun to make. Like corzetti stampati, their more popular medallion-shaped cousins (page 146), these corzetti hail from Genoa, and particularly the Val Polcevera area, where they're served during holidays and special occasions. I was introduced to this pasta by my friend and food historian Karima Moyer-Nocchi, who showed me the variations described here. I encourage you to try them all and pick your favorite.

How they're traditionally served

With a slow-cooked meat sauce called tuccu or with mushrooms.

What you need

- A work surface, preferably wooden;
- metal bench scraper or sharp knife.

MAKE THE DOUGH   Make your dough of choice and let it rest, tightly covered, at room temperature for 30 minutes to 1 hour.

SET UP YOUR WORKSPACE   Dust a sheet pan with semolina or line it with a dry dishcloth. Gather your tools.

ROLL THE DOUGH INTO A ROPE   Cut off a slice of dough, about the width of one or two fingers. Keep the rest covered.

Roll the dough into a rope, a generous ½ inch (1.25 cm) thick (about the thickness of a Sharpie marker): Start in the center and use your fingers or the palms of your hands to roll the dough, first back and forth, until the surface is smooth, and then outward in opposite directions, eventually making your way toward the ends. If the dough slides and it's difficult to get a grip, wet your hands a little and try again. The rope does not need to be perfectly even.

CUT THE ROPE INTO PIECES   Cut the rope into scant ½-inch (1.25-cm) pieces, so they're slightly narrower than they are tall.

MAKE THE CORZETTI   Shape the corzetti using one or a mix of the following methods:

Method 1: Position a nugget of dough so the longer sides run horizontally on your work surface and the cut sides are top and bottom. Line up your two index fingers so they're touching in the center of the dough. Press down and pull your fingers outward in opposite directions until the center is thinner than the ends. It'll look like a figure 8.

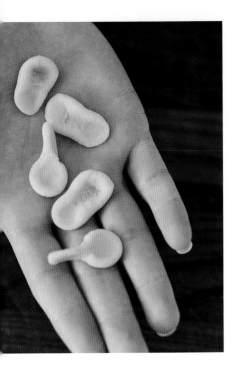

Method 2: Position a nugget of dough so the longer sides run horizontally on your work surface and the cut sides are top and bottom. Press one index finger into half of the dough's surface to anchor it. Then, with the other index finger, press down and stretch the other half of the dough outward until it looks like a figure 8.

Method 3 (my personal favorite): In the same horizontal orientation, hold half of the nugget between one thumb and index finger positioned front and back. Hold the other half of the nugget between the other thumb and index finger positioned top and bottom. It should remind you of a chain link. Simultaneously press the dough firmly between your fingers on each side so one half is flattened horizontally, like a pancake, and the other half is flattened upright. It'll look like a twisted figure 8.

Arrange the finished corzetti in a single layer on the prepared sheet pan. Repeat with the remaining pieces, and then the remaining dough. You can leave the pasta uncovered at room temperature until you're done and for up to 5 hours.

COOK OR STORE THE PASTA   Cook the corzetti according to the instructions on page 205 until tender but with some bite, 3 to 5 minutes, depending on size and drying time. For storage options, see page 206.

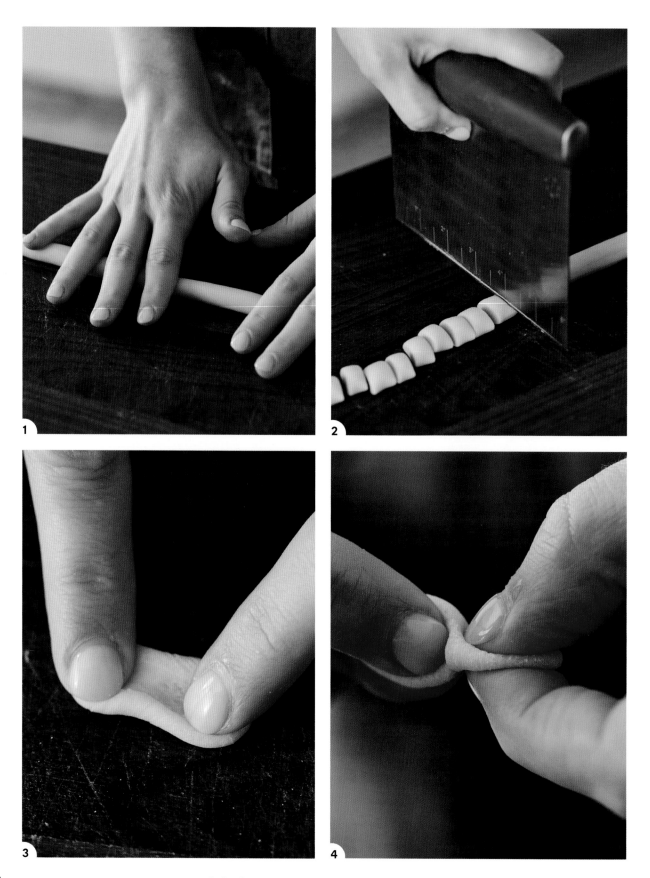

Soft Wheat & Water Corzetti della Valpolcevera

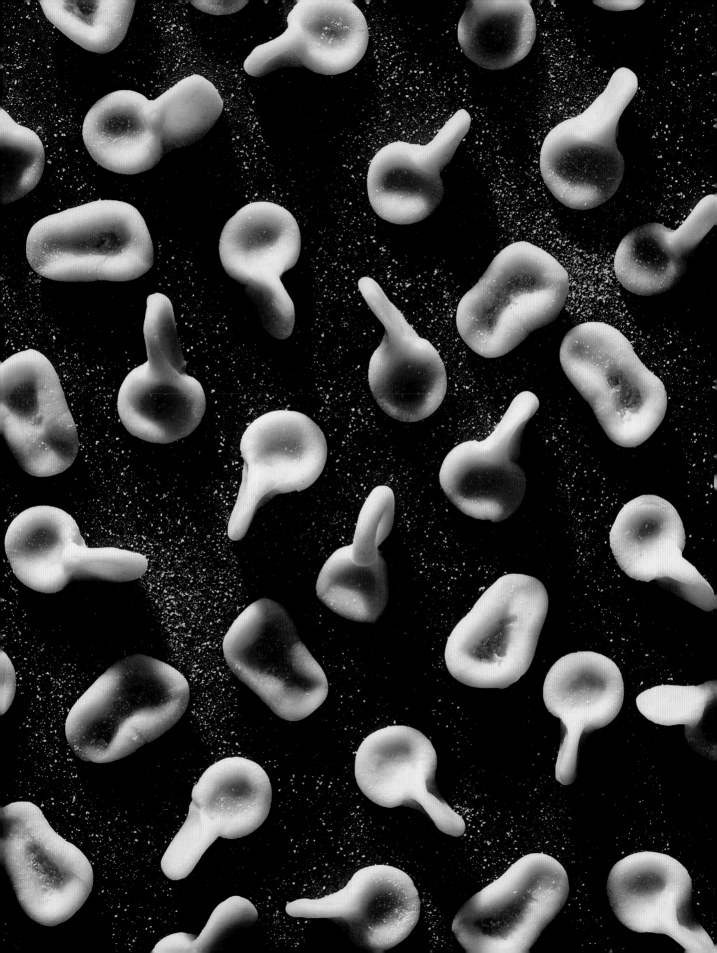

MAKE THEM WITH
Durum Wheat & Water Dough (37) ·
Whole Wheat & Water Dough (38) · Basil Dough (38)
· Saffron Dough (41)

PAIR THEM WITH
All-Purpose Tomato Sauce (256) · Basil Pesto (270) ·
Caramelized Onion Cheese Sauce (308) · Fried Zucchini
Sauce (282) · Roasted Red Pepper & Sausage Ragù (318)

cavatelli

What they are

Widely considered one of the oldest pastas, cavatelli and their many iterations appear throughout southern Italy. The name means "little hollows," and their seashell-like caves, made by dragging a nugget of dough with one, two, or even ten fingers, are excellent sauce-grabbers. Some are smooth on the outside, others are rolled across carved surfaces for texture, and all invite creativity—a zester, cheese grater, or sushi mat are all potential cavatelli makers. As with anything new, the first try might be tricky, but I assure you the technique quickly becomes familiar and you'll wonder how you never knew making pasta could be so simple.

How they're traditionally served

With everything from turnip greens, broccoli, or arugula and fresh tomatoes (Puglia), to pork sausage ragù (Molise), to broccoli rabe or king trumpet mushrooms (Basilicata), to 'nduja and Tropea onions (Calabria), to eggplant, tomatoes, and ricotta salata (Sicily).

What you need

- A work surface, preferably wooden;
- metal bench scraper or sharp knife;
- table knife (optional);
- gnocchi board (optional);
- zester, sushi mat, wicker basket, or whatever sturdy textured surface you have (all optional).

MAKE THE DOUGH Make your dough of choice and let it rest, tightly covered, at room temperature for 20 to 30 minutes.

SET UP YOUR WORKSPACE Dust a sheet pan with semolina or line it with a dry dishcloth. Gather your tools.

ROLL THE DOUGH INTO A ROPE Cut off a slice of dough, about the width of one or two fingers. Keep the rest covered.

Roll the dough into a rope, a scant ½ inch (1.25 cm) thick (about the thickness of a Sharpie marker): Start in the center and use your fingers or the palms of your hands to roll the dough, first back and forth, until the surface is smooth, and then outward in opposite directions, eventually making your way toward the ends. If the dough slides and it's difficult to get a grip, wet your hands a little and try again. The rope does not need to be perfectly even.

CUT THE ROPE INTO PIECES Cut the rope into ½-inch (1.25-cm) pieces, about the size of chickpeas.

MAKE THE CAVATELLI For smooth cavatelli, place your index and middle fingers at the top edge of one of the dough nuggets (the orientation of the dough doesn't matter, though I usually position the cut sides horizontally). Firmly press down, then drag the dough toward you, with generous pressure, until it curls over and forms a little cave. Don't be shy; you want to feel tension between your fingers and the dough. The more pressure you use, the hollower it will be, and the more sauce the pasta can grab.

That's it—you've just made a cavatello!

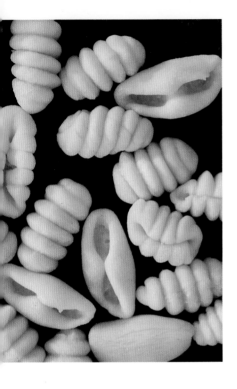

If you're unhappy with the results (perhaps it's very thick, or smeared across the board), smush it into a little ball and try again. But don't get bogged down in the details because each piece is meant to be unique.

To use a gnocchi board or other textured surface, position a nugget of dough near the edge of the board closest to you (near the handle, if it has one). Then press the side of your thumb into the near edge of the dough and push it away from you, with firm pressure, until it curls over once and is deeply imprinted with ridges on the outside. If you prefer, use the serrated edge of a table knife or the blade of a bench scraper to drag the dough across the board instead, like spreading butter on bread (some find this option easier, and more satisfying).

Note: The most obvious choice is to roll the dough across the back of a fork. You can absolutely do this, but in my house a fork doesn't provide a long enough "runway" to fully roll the pasta, resulting in denser dumplings.

Arrange the finished cavatelli in a single layer on the prepared sheet pan. Repeat with the remaining pieces, and then the remaining dough. You can leave the pasta uncovered at room temperature until you're done, for up to 5 hours.

COOK OR STORE THE PASTA   Cook the cavatelli according to the instructions on page 205 until tender but with some bite, 3 to 5 minutes, depending on their thickness and drying time. For storage options, see page 206.

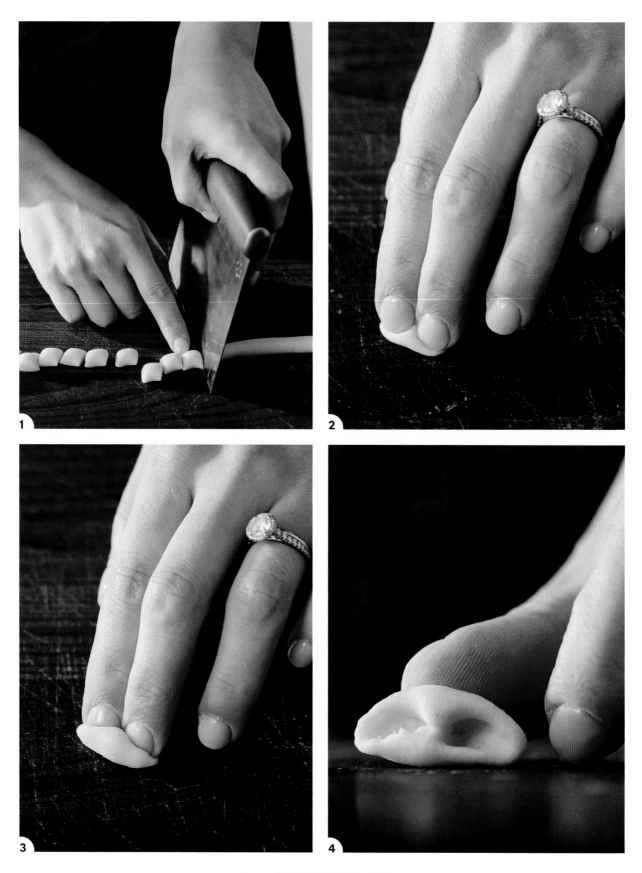

Durum Wheat & Water Cavatelli

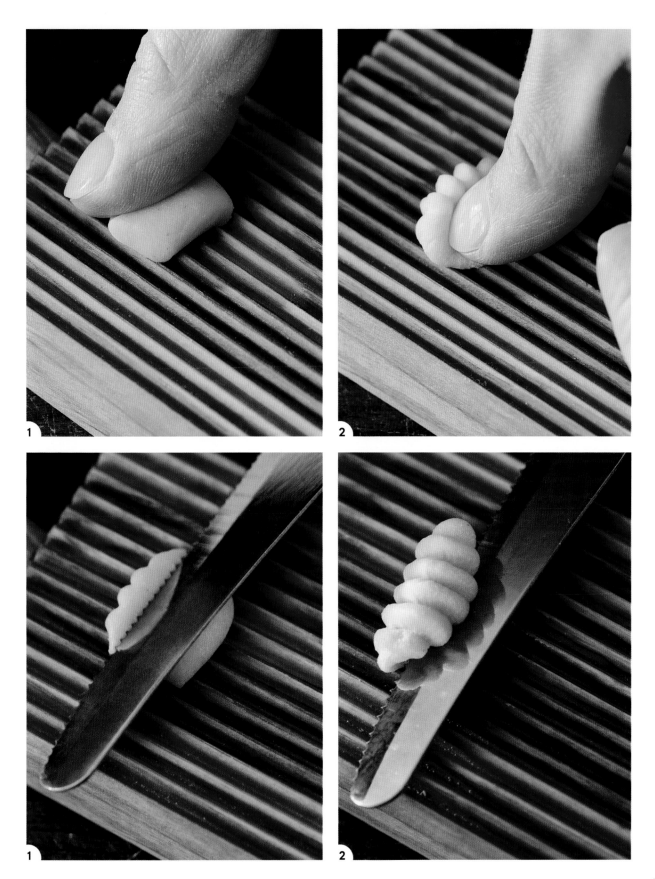

Making Cavatelli with a Gnocchi Board, Two Ways

MAKE THEM WITH
Durum Wheat & Water Dough (37) · *Whole Wheat
& Water Dough (38)* · *Basil Dough (38)* · *Saffron Dough (41)* ·
Green Flour & Water Dough (54)

PAIR THEM WITH
Roasted Garlic & Miso Sauce (302) · *Sweet & Sour
Eggplant Sauce with Burrata (286)* · *The Meatiest Meatless
Ragù (317)* · *Tomato-Cream Sauce (260)*

capunti

What they are

Pasta peapods that hail from the south, particularly Puglia and Basilicata. The name means "dug into," referring to the deep dimples your fingers leave behind for sauce to pool. Identical in technique to smooth-surfaced cavatelli, capunti similarly range from small segments called capuntini to long, eight-fingered canoes. They're sometimes infused with saffron or whole wheat flour, though a green dough really brings the peapod look to life.

How they're traditionally served

With king trumpet mushrooms and sausage, or with tomato and meat sauces.

What you need

- A work surface, preferably wooden;
- metal bench scraper or sharp knife;
- gnocchi board or cavarola board (optional).

MAKE THE DOUGH Make your dough of choice and let it rest, tightly covered, at room temperature for 20 to 30 minutes.

SET UP YOUR WORKSPACE Dust a sheet pan with semolina or line it with a dry dishcloth. Gather your tools.

ROLL THE DOUGH INTO A ROPE Cut off a slice of dough, about the width of one or two fingers. Keep the rest covered.

Roll the dough into a rope, a generous ¼ inch (6mm) thick (a little thicker than a pencil): Start in the center and use your fingers or the palms of your hands to roll the dough, first back and forth, until the surface is smooth, and then outward in opposite directions, eventually making your way towards the ends. If the dough slides and it's difficult to get a grip, wet your hands a little and try again. The rope does not need to be perfectly even.

CUT THE ROPE INTO PIECES Cut the rope into roughly 1½-inch (4-cm) pieces, or just long enough to fit your three middle fingers across.

MAKE THE CAPUNTI Position a piece of dough horizontally on your work surface and place your three middle fingers across its length. Firmly press down, digging your fingertips into the dough, then drag it toward you with firm pressure in a single, confident motion. The dough might flip over or it might not, but either way you should leave behind three deep dimples.

If you'd like, drag the dough across a gnocchi board, cavarola board, or other textured surface (as described in the cavatelli instructions, page 97).

Arrange the finished capunti in a single layer on the prepared sheet pan. Repeat with the remaining pieces, and then the remaining dough. You can leave the pasta uncovered at room temperature until you're done, up to 5 hours.

COOK OR STORE THE PASTA Cook the capunti according to the instructions on page 205 until tender but with some bite, 3 to 5 minutes, depending on their thickness and drying time. For storage options, see page 206.

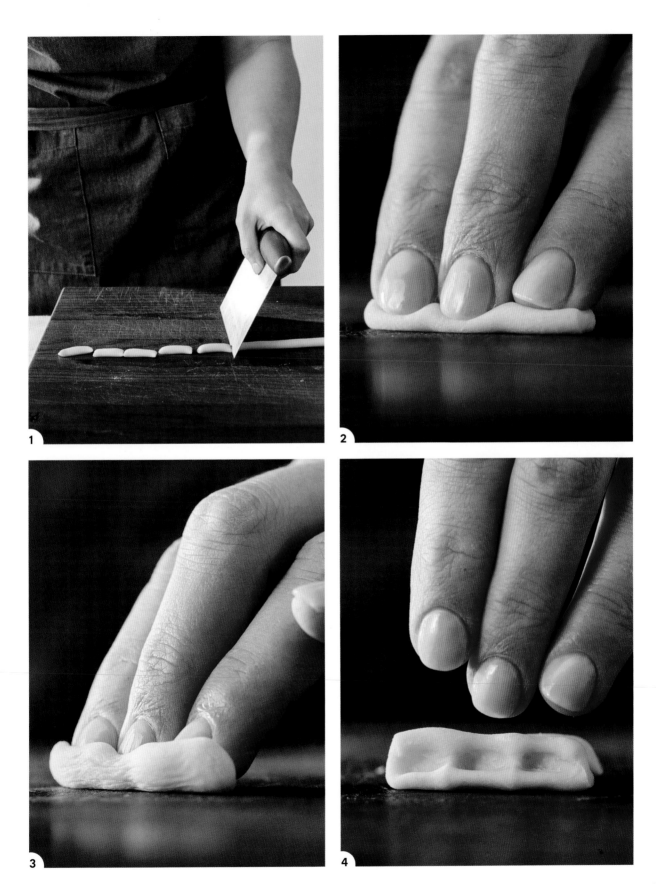

Durum Wheat & Water Capunti

MAKE THEM WITH
Saffron Dough (41)
Durum Wheat & Water Dough (37)

PAIR THEM WITH
All-Purpose Tomato Sauce (256) · Sausage,
Saffron & Fennel Ragù (314) · Spicy Garlic & Anchovy
Sauce with Broccoli (335) · Sweet & Sour Eggplant
Sauce with Burrata (286)

malloreddus

What they are

Also called gnocchetti sardi ("little Sardinian gnocchi"), malloreddus have much more in common with cavatelli than any potato dumpling. The technique is almost the same as the "little hollows," though they run smaller and the dough is often turned gold with a pinch of saffron. In centuries past, the signature ribbed exterior was made by rolling the pasta across a wicker basket or textured glass; today, specific paddles with wide wavy ridges are also sold, though a gnocchi board or any of the household items mentioned for cavatelli can be used here, too.

How they're traditionally served

With a tomatoey sausage ragù (alla campidanese); bottarga (cured fish roe) and clams; fresh tomatoes and basil; and often with local sheep's milk cheeses.

What you need

- A work surface, preferably wooden;
- metal bench scraper or sharp knife;
- table knife (optional);
- malloreddus paddle or gnocchi board.

MAKE THE DOUGH Make your dough of choice and let it rest, tightly covered, at room temperature for 20 to 30 minutes.

SET UP YOUR WORKSPACE Dust a sheet pan with semolina or line it with a dry dishcloth. Gather your tools.

ROLL THE DOUGH INTO A ROPE Cut off a slice of dough, about the width of one or two fingers. Keep the rest covered.

Roll the dough into a rope, about ¼ inch (6 mm) thick, or the thickness of a pencil. Start in the center and use your fingers or the palms of your hands to roll the dough, first back and forth, until the surface is smooth, and then outward in opposite directions, eventually making your way toward the ends. If the dough slides and it's difficult to get a grip, wet your hands a little and try again. The rope does not need to be perfectly even.

CUT THE ROPE INTO PIECES Cut the rope into ¾-inch (2-cm) pellets.

MAKE THE MALLOREDDUS If using a gnocchi board, follow the cavatelli dough-rolling step on page 96 using your thumb, a table knife, or a bench scraper.

If using a malloreddus paddle, hold the handle in your non-dominant hand with the face of the paddle tilting downward—the grooves should face you and travel north to south. Use the thumb of your other hand to roll a nugget of dough across the ridges, with generous pressure, starting at the area closest to you and pushing it away from you, until it curls over once and the grooves are deeply imprinted.

Arrange the finished malloreddus in a single layer on the prepared sheet pan. Repeat with the remaining pieces, and then the remaining dough. You can leave the pasta uncovered at room temperature until you're done, up to 5 hours.

COOK OR STORE THE PASTA Cook the malloreddus according to the instructions on page 205 until tender but with some bite, 3 to 5 minutes, depending on their thickness and drying time. For storage options, see page 206.

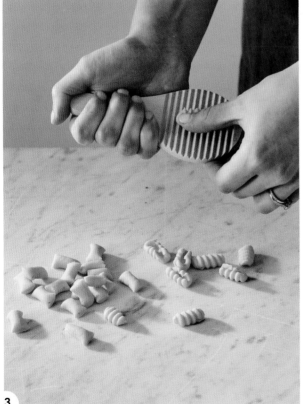

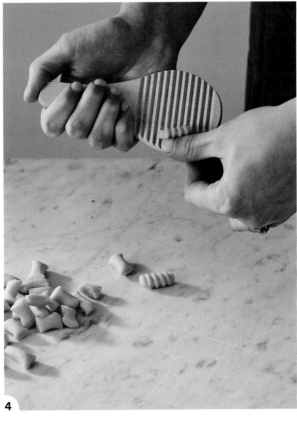

Saffron Malloreddus

MAKE THEM WITH
Durum Wheat & Water Dough (37) •
Whole Wheat & Water Dough (38) • Saffron Dough (41) •
Basil Dough (38)

PAIR THEM WITH
All-Purpose Tomato Sauce (256) • Braised Onion
Ragù (289) • Fiery Calabrian Chili Sauce (267) •
Kale & Arugula Pesto (277) • Roasted Garlic & Miso
Sauce (302) • Roasted Red Pepper & Sausage Ragù (318) •
Sausage, Saffron & Fennel Ragù (314)

spizzulus

What they are

A well-kept secret from the small southern town of Orroli in Sardinia. The name likely derives from the local word for "pinch" (pizzicare, in Italian), echoing the motion used to seal these little loops. The shape reminds me of my favorite Italian cracker, Puglian taralli, and, like taralli, the dough is traditionally infused with wine—in this case, red rather than white, coloring the pasta dusty rose. For me, they're another excuse to play around with my gnocchi board, not to mention the teardrop shape is like a bear hug for any sauce.

How they're traditionally served

With meat and tomato sauces; in this book, with anything you'd enjoy with cavatelli, capunti, or malloreddus.

What you need

- A work surface, preferably wooden;
- metal bench scraper or table knife;
- gnocchi board.

MAKE THE DOUGH Make your dough of choice, replacing the water with red wine in the Durum Wheat & Water Pasta Dough if you'd like. Let it rest, tightly covered, at room temperature for 30 minutes.

SET UP YOUR WORKSPACE Line a sheet pan with semolina or a dry dishcloth. Gather your tools.

ROLL THE DOUGH INTO A ROPE Cut off a slice of dough, about the width of one or two fingers. Keep the rest covered.

Roll the dough into a thin rope, a scant ¼ inch (6 mm) thick (or a little thinner than a pencil): Start in the center and use your fingers or the palms of your hands to roll the dough, first back and forth, until the surface is smooth, and then outward in opposite directions, eventually making your way toward the ends. If the dough slides and it's difficult to get a grip, wet your hands a little and try again. The rope does not need to be perfectly even.

CUT THE ROPE INTO PIECES Cut the rope into pieces that are the width of your gnocchi board, about 3 inches (7.5 cm).

MAKE THE SPIZZULUS Position the gnocchi board horizontally on your work surface and place a piece of dough north to south (perpendicular to the grooves) in the center. Use the spine of a table knife, tilted upward at a 45-degree angle, or the blade of a bench scraper to drag the dough across the board, with firm pressure, until it curls over into a tube. It will look like an elongated cavatello with the seam sealed shut.

With the seam facing downward, join the ends to form a teardrop-shaped loop and pinch them together firmly to seal.

Arrange the finished spizzulus in a single layer on the prepared sheet pan. Repeat with the remaining pieces, and then the remaining dough. You can leave the pasta uncovered at room temperature until you're done, up to 5 hours.

COOK OR STORE THE PASTA Cook the spizzulus according to the instructions on page 205 until tender but with some bite, 3 to 5 minutes, depending on their thickness and drying time. For storage options, see page 206.

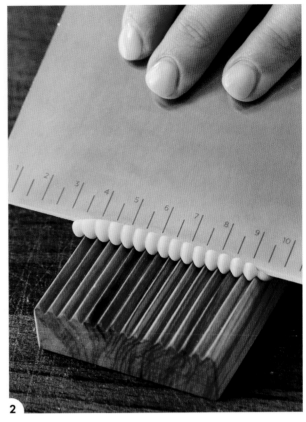

Durum Wheat & Water Spizzulus

MAKE THEM WITH
Whole Wheat & Water Dough (38)
Durum Wheat & Water Dough (37)

PAIR THEM WITH
Anchovy & Onion Sauce with Breadcrumbs (331) ·
Citrus & Pistachio Pesto (275) · No-Cook Tomato
& Basil Sauce (259) · Tomato & Almond Pesto (274)

busiate

What they are

Ancient pasta spirals from Sicily, and a remnant of the region's Arab influence. Their signature ringlet shape was first created by coiling long ropes of dough around a reed called a busa, from the Arabic "bus"; today, a metal rod known as a ferretto, or ferro, is used to achieve the same effect. It took me years to find a ferretto, so instead I used a knitting needle from my local crafts store—it made no less beautiful busiate. (A wooden or metal barbecue skewer works wonders, too.)

How they're traditionally served

With a refreshing tomato and almond pesto (pesto alla trapanese), tomatoes and fresh tuna, and other seafood.

What you need

- A work surface, preferably wooden;
- metal bench scraper or sharp knife;
- rolling pin or wine bottle;
- ferretto, knitting needle, or other skewer.

MAKE THE DOUGH Make your dough of choice and let it rest, tightly covered, at room temperature for 30 minutes.

SET UP YOUR WORKSPACE Dust a sheet pan with semolina or line it with a dry dishcloth. Gather your tools.

ROLL THE DOUGH INTO A SLAB Cut off a quarter of the dough and keep the rest covered. Flatten the dough with the palm of your hand into a rough oval. With a rolling pin (or wine bottle), roll the dough into a scant ¼-inch (6-mm) thick slab, about the thickness of pita bread.

CUT THE DOUGH INTO STRIPS Slice the dough into strips a little thinner than ½ inch (1.25 cm) wide. They will all be different lengths.

ROLL THE STRIPS INTO STRANDS Position one of the strips horizontally on your work surface and cover the other pieces with a dishcloth. Starting in the center, use your fingers to roll the strip of dough into a thin strand that's about a scant ¼ inch (6 mm) thick, or a little thicker than pici.

MAKE THE BUSIATE If using a ferretto, cut the rope into 8-inch (20-cm) lengths; if using a knitting needle or other skewer, cut the rope into pieces that are a little shorter than what you have.

Position a piece of dough vertically on your work surface. Place your skewer at a 45-degree angle toward the left-hand side in an upside-down V.

Holding the bottom of the skewer loosely in place with your left hand, use your right hand to roll the other end—where the dough and skewer meet— toward you as if tracing an arc. (I like to think of it as drawing a rainbow). The pasta will naturally wrap around the skewer like a telephone cord.

Once the dough is completely twisted around the skewer, position it horizontally on your work surface. Gently roll the skewer, with the pasta still attached, back and forth once or twice to flatten the dough. Twist the skewer to loosen the pasta and slide it off.

Arrange the finished busiate in a single layer on the prepared sheet pan. Repeat with the remaining pieces, and then the remaining dough. If you have the time, let the pasta dry for an hour (or up to 5 hours) before cooking.

COOK OR STORE THE PASTA Cook the busiate according to the instructions on page 205 until tender but with some bite, 3 to 5 minutes, depending on their thickness and drying time. For storage options, see page 206.

Whole Wheat Busiate

MAKE THEM WITH

Durum Wheat & Water Dough (37)
Whole Wheat & Water Dough (38)

PAIR THEM WITH

Broccoli Sauce (281) · Spicy Garlic & Anchovy Sauce with
Broccoli (335) · Tomato Sauce with Olives & Fried Capers
(264) · White Bean Soup with Parmesan & Kale (350)

orecchiette

What they are

The pride of the Puglian table. In the port city of Bari, this pasta has graced women's hands for almost a thousand years; walk the narrow stone streets today and you'll meet mothers and daughters stretching dough into pasta at roadrunner speed. Big and little ears—orecchione and orecchiette, respectively—are scattered across mesh drying racks by every doorway, their hollow coves dancing with shadow and light under the beating sun. The women of Bari are so good at their craft that they've developed their own method entirely, called "arco basso," in which the pasta is fashioned in one continuous movement instead of two, like you'll see here. And if I *had* to pick a favorite pasta, both to make and to eat, this would be it.

How they're traditionally served

The smaller versions with meat sauces, the larger with vegetables, and especially with cima di rapa (broccoli rabe), which grows abundantly in Italy's south.

What you need

- A work surface, preferably wooden;
- metal bench scraper or sharp knife;
- table knife, butter knife, or try a few knives to find what works best for you.

MAKE THE DOUGH Make your dough of choice and let it rest, tightly covered, at room temperature for 20 minutes.

SET UP YOUR WORKSPACE Dust a sheet pan with semolina or line it with a dry dishcloth. Gather your tools.

ROLL THE DOUGH INTO A ROPE Cut off a slice of dough, about the width of one or two fingers. Keep the rest covered.

Roll the dough into a ½-inch (1.25-cm) thick rope. Start in the center and use your fingers or the palms of your hands to roll the dough, first back and forth, until the surface is smooth, and then outward in opposite directions, eventually making your way toward the ends. If the dough slides and it's difficult to get a grip, wet your hands a little and try again. The rope does not need to be perfectly even.

CUT THE ROPE INTO PIECES Cut the rope into roughly ½-inch (1.25-cm) pieces.

MAKE THE ORECCHIETTE Place a nugget of dough on your work surface. Then use the serrated edge of a table or butter knife to drag the dough toward or away from you, with firm pressure, tilting the blade downward into the dough at a 30- to 45-degree angle, until the dough curls over on itself like an ocean wave crashing on shore. If dragging the dough toward you, you can use your non-dominant index finger to apply more pressure on top of the tip of the knife as you drag for more control.

Don't be shy with the pressure; the more tension you feel between the dough and the knife, the rougher the surface will be, which will help catch sauce.

Peel the curled edges apart with your fingers and invert the dough over your thumb to expose the rough interior, stretching it a little into a small dome.

Arrange the finished orecchiette, rough side up, in a single layer on the prepared sheet pan. Repeat with the remaining pieces, and then the remaining dough. If you have the time, let the pasta dry for an hour (or up to 5 hours) before cooking.

COOK OR STORE THE PASTA Cook the orecchiette according to the instructions on page 205 until tender but with some bite, 3 to 5 minutes, depending on their thickness and drying time. For storage options, see page 206.

Whole Wheat Orecchiette

MAKE THEM WITH

Basil Dough (38) · Saffron Dough (41) ·
Colorful Flour & Water Doughs (54) · Durum Wheat
& Water Dough (37)

PAIR THEM WITH

Basil Pesto (270) · Kale & Arugula Pesto (277) ·
No-Cook Tomato & Basil Sauce (259) · Salsa Verde (357) ·
Tomato Sauce with Olives & Fried Capers (264)

foglie d'ulivo

What they are

Tender "olive leaves" with rugged bellies, an ode to the olive groves of Puglia, Sicily, and Calabria, though also found up north in Liguria. They're orecchiette's prettier cousins, made similarly but stretched flat so they can strike a pose on your plate. You'll find both plain and green versions; I infuse flour and water dough with basil or spinach in summer, and saffron, beets, or red peppers in autumn.

How they're traditionally served

In Puglia, with tomatoes, burrata, and chilies, or with mushrooms, seafood, and meat sauces; in Liguria, with fish, olives, and lemon.

What you need

- A work surface, preferably wooden;
- metal bench scraper or sharp knife;
- table knife.

MAKE THE DOUGH   Make your dough of choice and let it rest, tightly covered, at room temperature for 20 minutes.

SET UP YOUR WORKSPACE   Dust a sheet pan with semolina or line it with a dry dishcloth. Gather your tools.

ROLL THE DOUGH INTO A ROPE   Cut off a slice of dough, about the width of one or two fingers. Keep the rest covered.

Roll the dough into a thin rope, about ¼ inch (6 mm) thick, or the thickness of a pencil. Start in the center and use your fingers or the palms of your hands to roll the dough, first back and forth, until the surface is smooth, and then outward in opposite directions, eventually making your way toward the ends. If the dough slides and it's difficult to get a grip, wet your hands a little and try again. The rope does not need to be perfectly even.

CUT THE DOUGH INTO PIECES   Cut the rope into 1½-inch (4-cm) pieces. Roll each piece back and forth between your hands, putting more pressure on the ends so they become tapered and the result looks like a squat green bean.

MAKE THE FOGLIE D'ULIVO   Position a piece of dough vertically, at a slight angle, on your work surface. Hold a table knife, preferably with a serrated edge, with your dominant hand and press it into the dough at the opposite edge (I'm left-handed, so I hold the knife in my left hand to start at the right edge).

Dig the knife into the dough, so it's at a 30-degree angle to the work surface, then slowly begin to drag it outward in the opposite direction (so, in my case, I drag the dough from right to left). You want to feel the tension between the dough and the knife but still be gentle with the pressure so as not to tear the pasta.

Once the edge of the dough curls over the knife, use a couple of fingers from your non-dominant hand to peel it back and anchor the center part of the dough's edge to the work surface. Then continue stretching the dough outward with the knife until you reach the opposite edge—as you go, scoot the non-dominant fingers inward, toward the center, so they don't leave an imprint. The result should look like a leaf with a rough interior.

I'll admit: This one takes practice. Play around with the orientation of the dough, the angle of the knife, and the amount of pressure to see what works best for you.

Arrange the finished pasta in a single layer on the prepared sheet pan. Repeat with the remaining pieces, and then the remaining dough.

COOK OR STORE THE PASTA Cook the foglie d'ulivo according to the instructions on page 205 until tender but with some bite, 2 to 4 minutes, depending on their thickness and drying time. For storage options, see page 206.

how to roll pasta sheets
(with a pasta machine)

Before we jump into hand-cut, short-cut, and stuffed pastas, there's one thing we need to do first: Roll the dough into sheets. Every pasta maker does this a little differently. Here's my method; you'll no doubt develop your own:

Cut off a quarter of the dough and keep the rest covered. Keep extra 00 or all-purpose flour nearby.

Set your pasta machine to its widest setting. For a Marcato Atlas 150, that's setting 0; for most KitchenAid attachments, that's setting 1.

Flatten the dough with your palm into a rough oval—smush it between your fingers if you need to, or use a rolling pin to roll it into an oval that's about ¼ inch (6 mm) thick. Position one of the dough's tapered ends in the center of your pasta machine and roll it through once. (If you're using the KitchenAid attachment, don't run the motor too fast; I usually prefer speed 2.) You should now have a longer oval-ish shape.

Rotate the dough 90 degrees, so the tapered ends run horizontally. Fold the ends toward the center like an envelope so that the width of the dough is similar to the width of the machine's rollers (about 6 inches/15 cm; hold it up to the machine to check). The ends might overlap in the center, or there might be a wide gap between them—it doesn't matter.

Flatten the dough again and, with the folded ends on either side, roll it through the widest setting once more.

Continue rolling the pasta through the machine in the same orientation, once on each progressive setting, until you reach the thickness of the pasta you're making (see chart on page 116). Feed the dough straight down into the roller instead of letting it hang off the back of the machine so it doesn't pull or tear.

If the dough is sticky or the surface starts to tear—this happens often with a KitchenAid, especially after setting 5—dust both sides with 00 or all-purpose flour, spreading it around evenly and removing any excess.

Shape the pasta as desired.

THICKNESS

Following are thickness guidelines for two of the most widely used pasta machines—the Marcato Atlas 150 hand-crank machine and the KitchenAid stand mixer attachment—but of course there are many more. So take my setting suggestions as just that: suggestions.

A pasta's thickness is, in part, informed by tradition, but it's also subject to personal taste. Some prefer ultra-delicate stuffed pastas so they'll roll their sheets thinner than I do, while others prefer a more equal dough-to-filling ratio. Instead of relying on numbers, there are other cues that can help: When it comes to feathery tagliatelle and most stuffed pastas, for example, you want to be able to see your hand through the sheet when held up to the light, and it should feel delicate but not fragile. With time you'll find the thicknesses that work best for you. And remember that pasta expands as it cooks, so it'll always be a little thicker when you take a bite.

PASTA ROLLING & THICKNESS GUIDE

Machines vary and stretch over time, so adjust these settings as needed and preferred. The Marcato Atlas 150 hand-crank machine and KitchenAid stand mixer attachment settings are similar up to a point, but the Marcato will produce thinner sheets from about setting 7 onward. Note that this guide is based on the Standard Egg Pasta Dough recipe on page 45, so if a dough feels too thick or too thin, go with your gut.

Shape	Style	Setting for Marcato Atlas 150	Setting for KitchenAid
Lagane	Hand-formed	4	4
Strozzapreti	Hand-formed	5	5
Fettuccine	Hand-cut	6	6
Lasagne	Hand-cut	6	6
Pappardelle	Hand-cut	6	6
Tagliatelle	Hand-cut	7	7, twice through
Tagliolini	Hand-cut	4 or 5	4 or 5
Corzetti stampati	Short-cut	5	5
Farfalle	Short-cut	6, twice through	7
Garganelli	Short-cut	5, twice through	5, twice through
Sorpresine	Short-cut	7	7, twice through
Agnolotti & agnolotti del plin	Stuffed	7	7, twice through
Cappelletti	Stuffed	6, twice through	7
Caramelle	Stuffed	7	7, twice through
"Classic" ravioli	Stuffed	6, twice through	7
Double-stuffed ravioli (ravioli doppi)	Stuffed	7	7, twice through
Egg yolk ravioli (uovo in raviolo)	Stuffed	7	7, twice through
Scarpinocc	Stuffed	6	6
Tortelloni	Stuffed	6, twice through	7

rolling pasta by hand

There is a very particular way to roll pasta by hand in Italy. It's a dance between the pasta and its maker, with the sound of dough slapping against wood like waves lapping at the shore; quick, methodical turns; and an enormous rolling pin called a mattarello. This—the art of rolling sfoglie—is how I first learned to make pasta in Modena. The process changes the pasta's texture entirely: Instead of smooth ribbons of tagliatelle, you create a pebbly surface that coaxes sauce to adhere to it. Rolling sfoglie is challenging and takes practice, but I encourage you to give it a try anyway. You can find in-depth tutorials on YouTube; better yet, there are many pasta makers in Italy who are eager to share their knowledge.

Tradition aside, you can, of course, roll your dough with a regular rolling pin and a little elbow grease. Some tips to keep in mind:

- Let the dough rest for at least 1 hour at room temperature. A more relaxed dough will make for a much easier rolling experience.

- Don't stress and do your best! Roll the dough as thin as you can, but don't drive yourself crazy. Remember that it's just pasta, it's supposed to look handmade, and it'll taste good anyway.

- If you find yourself itching to make pasta more regularly, consider investing in a pasta machine or borrow one from a friend.

Rolling Gluten-Free Pasta Dough

I probably sound like a broken record, but: Gluten-free pasta dough tears easily and doesn't like to stretch. So use the Gluten-Free Egg Pasta Dough on page 57 and follow the sheeting instructions above, but note the following:

- The dough will crack, particularly around the edges, as it goes through the machine. You can patch up the especially egregious tears but don't worry about it too much.

- Roll the dough as thin as you can before it breaks—for me, that's setting 4 on the Marcato and KitchenAid machines.

- Stick with simple shapes: Wider hand-cut pastas like fettuccine and pappardelle work well, as do some short-cut pastas like farfalle and sorpresine.

- Starch-heavy gluten-free blends will leave behind a sticky film on the surface of the rollers (this goes for naturally gluten-free flours like chestnut and chickpea, too). Make sure to clean it off, gently, with a dry cloth. If necessary, use a lightly damp cloth and dry thoroughly.

playing
with
patterns
& colors

Now that we've covered the basics, think of your pasta sheet as a blank canvas, ready for a splash of color and all the creativity your heart desires.

herb-laminated pasta sheets

Herb-laminated pasta—pasta embedded with whole herbs—is like edible stained glass. Held up to the light, its pretty patterns dance and glow, and it's my favorite way to usher in the warmer seasons. Luckily, like most things in pasta, it's far simpler to make than it looks.

Herb lamination is a modern technique, so creativity is more than welcome. **Tender leaves** like sage, parsley, mint, basil, stripped thyme, and dill are all great options; skip firm needles like rosemary and avoid tougher stems, which can puncture the pasta during lamination. Edible flower petals, if you can find them, make a stunning addition, too. Know that whatever you choose, **the flavor will be subtle**, so you can still use dill even if you're not a big fan (the fronds are especially beautiful here). **Stick with small and medium-sized leaves** to prevent tears as the dough stretches—large leaves also contain more moisture, which can burst and make the pasta sticky.

Herb-laminated pasta can be used to make any of your favorite sheeted shapes, from farfalle to ravioli.

What you need
- A work surface, preferably wooden;
- pasta machine;
- metal bench scraper or sharp knife.

MAKE THE DOUGH Make a batch of Standard Egg Pasta Dough or Almost All-Yolk Pasta Dough (page 45) and let it rest, tightly wrapped, at room temperature for 30 minutes.

SET UP YOUR WORKSPACE Gather your herbs and remember: Use only small and medium-sized tender leaves, no stems. Set up your pasta machine.

SHEET THE DOUGH Roll a quarter of your pasta dough into a sheet following the directions on page 114, stopping at the setting suggested for the type of pasta you're making on page 116.

CUT THE SHEET Lay the pasta horizontally on your work surface; if using a countertop, dust it with a little 00 or all-purpose flour first. Trim away any uneven ends (ball them up and cover them or save them for soup). Fold the sheet in half crosswise, like a book, make a crease at the midpoint, then unfold it again. Cut the pasta in half along the crease.

ADD THE HERBS If the dough feels dry, cover one of the pasta sheets with a damp dishcloth and set aside. Scatter the herbs across the other sheet in whatever pattern you like and press them into the dough to adhere.

If the dough feels very dry, spritz it with a little water. Lay the unused half of the pasta on top, sandwiching the herbs between them. Smooth out the air pockets and press down firmly to seal.

ROLL THE SHEET (AGAIN) Trim a thin strip of dough from the longer sides of the pasta so the sheet is slightly narrower than the width of your pasta machine. Dust both sides of the dough very lightly with 00 or all-purpose flour.

Set your pasta machine back two settings wider than it was before. Roll the sheet through once, then set the machine back to your original setting and roll the dough through again.

VOILÀ—HERB-LAMINATED PASTA! Shape as desired.

Herb-Laminated Pasta Sheets

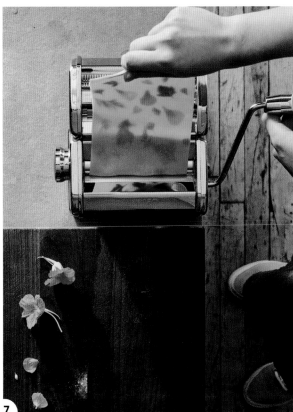

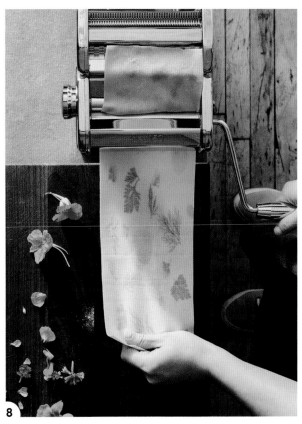

patterned pasta sheets

Stripes, polka dots, diamonds; pink, orange, green—for anyone who thinks a plate of pasta isn't much to look at, let this technique prove otherwise. I'm partial to clean lines made with one or two colors, but here's a chance to really let your creativity run wild. There are several methods for creating patterned pasta sheets, but here are the ones I use the most.

What you need
- A work surface, preferably wooden;
- pasta machine;
- metal bench scraper or sharp knife;
- pasta machine cutter attachments (optional);
- cookie cutters (optional);
- rolling pin or wine bottle.

MAKE THE DOUGHS   Make 1 batch of Standard Egg Pasta Dough or Almost All-Yolk Pasta Dough (page 45) and either a half or full batch of the Colorful Egg Pasta Dough of your choice (page 54). (You'll only need a small amount of colorful dough to create the patterns, but if you prefer to make a full batch, use the leftovers for any egg-based shapes as desired.) Let them rest, tightly covered, at room temperature for 30 minutes.

SET UP YOUR WORKSPACE   Gather your tools and set up your pasta machine.

SHEET THE DOUGH   Roll half (of a half-batch) or a quarter (of a full batch) of the colorful pasta dough into a sheet following the directions on page 114, stopping at setting 6 for both the Marcato and KitchenAid machines. Trim the uneven ends and cut the pasta sheet in half crosswise, or to fit your workspace. Set it out of the way and cover with a dishcloth (if you're using a countertop, dust the surface with some 00 or all-purpose flour first).

Roll a quarter of the egg pasta dough into a sheet following the directions on page 114, stopping at setting 6 for both the Marcato and KitchenAid machines. Trim the ends and cut it to the size of the colorful sheet.

CUT THE COLORFUL SHEET   If the colorful sheet feels sticky, dust both sides with a little 00 or all-purpose flour.

For striped pasta: If your pasta machine has a fettuccine and/or tagliolini cutter attachment, feed the colorful sheet through slowly, catching the strands as they pass through the other side. If you prefer to cut the strands by hand, follow the instructions on page 113. Cut it into strips that are ¼ inch (6 mm) wide or thinner.

For polka dots and other designs: Use a small cookie cutter to cut out circles or a knife to cut diamonds or other shapes from the colorful sheet. You can also use thin tagliolini to make a crisscross or other abstract pattern.

CREATE AND SET THE PATTERN   Arrange the colorful strips lengthwise on top of the egg pasta sheet—it's totally fine if they hang over the edges—or arrange the other shapes in whatever pattern you wish. Use your fingers to press the colorful dough firmly into the egg dough to set the pattern and remove any trapped air.

With a rolling pin or wine bottle, gently roll over the entire sheet once or twice to seal the two layers together. Trim away any overhanging strips so you have a neat rectangle.

For striped pasta: If the dough feels sticky, dust both sides of the sheet with a little 00 or all-purpose flour, shaking off any excess. Set the machine back two settings wider (setting 4) and slowly feed the pasta sheet through, then set the machine back to your original setting (6) and roll it through again. If the combined sheet still feels thick, roll it through once more one setting thinner (7).

For polka dots and other designs: Open the machine wider (setting 3) and roll the pasta through once to set the pattern.

Shape the pasta as desired—patterned pasta sheets dry out quickly, so make sure to keep any pieces you're not immediately using covered with a damp dishcloth or plastic wrap.

VARIATIONS

Two-Toned Pasta Sheets: Make two colorful or other pasta doughs of choice. After resting, roll a quarter of each dough into a thin sheet, stopping on setting 6 for both the Marcato and KitchenAid machines. Then lay one sheet on top of the other and press them together to seal, removing any air pockets. Trim the edges so you have a neat rectangle. Set your pasta machine back two settings wider than you last left it—so, setting 4—and roll the combined sheets through. Then skip to the final setting of the pasta you're making (based on the chart on page 116) and roll through once more.

Note: Two-toned pasta looks best with thicker sheets, so I'd recommend fettuccine, pappardelle, garganelli, or corzetti. If you want to use them for sorpresine or farfalle, stop at setting 6 on both machines.

Two-Toned Polka Dots: Follow the instructions for two-toned pasta above but use a small cookie cutter or sharp knife to cut circles—or any shape—out of one of the pasta sheets before overlaying it on top of the other. Set the machine back and roll the pasta through setting 4, then setting 5, to fuse the sheets together.

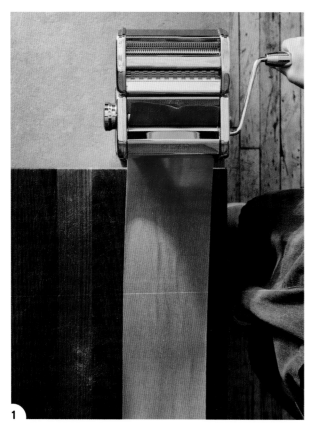

Patterned Pasta Sheets

hand-cut pastas

Hand-cut pastas—ribbons long and short, thick and thin—are at home in every part of Italy. Up north, in Lombardy, near Switzerland, you'll find pizzoccheri, stout strips of buckwheat pasta tossed with potatoes, cabbage, and plenty of cheese. Down south, there's lagane, the wide, toothsome semolina noodles we already talked about (page 86) and lasagne's great-great grandmother. Fine strands of **tagliolini**—known by a dozen other names—are omnipresent and served every which way, from seafood to truffles, broths to bakes.

Of course, it's the ribbons of central Italy, sensuous and golden, that most often come to mind. Let's start with **tagliatelle**, the pride of Bologna, deeply etched into the city's DNA. So serious are the Bolognesi about this pasta that a single strand dipped in gold—literally the gold standard, at an exacting 8 millimeters wide when cooked—is displayed at the Chamber of Commerce. Legend has it that this pasta, like so many other things, was inspired by a beautiful woman. At the turn of the 16th century, one of Bologna's powerful noblemen, Giovanni II Bentivoglio, requested his cook Zefirano prepare a feast to honor the Pope's daughter, Lucrezia Borgia, who was soon to be married. Upon catching a glimpse of the bride, Zefirano was so taken by her luminous blonde locks that he rushed to the kitchen and tagliatelle were born! Today, a tangle of yellow and green tagliatelle called paglia e fieno, "straw and hay," is also a popular dish, usually served with meat sauce or with cream, vegetables, and prosciutto.

Next, let's stop in Tuscany, where you'll find **pappardelle**, from the word "pappare," which in local dialect has the most wonderful meaning: to eat with gusto, joy, and pleasure. These undulating ribbons are perhaps my favorite of the bunch, since I'm a sucker for any wide noodle. They're primarily served with hearty game or mushroom sauces—wild boar ragù is a must—and enjoyed in the colder months, around hunting season.

Finally, to Lazio we go to meet America's beloved "little ribbons," **fettuccine** (thanks, Alfredo). Examine a plate of fettuccine beside another of tagliatelle and you might think they're the same dish. They mostly are, though fettuccine is usually a hair narrower and always thicker than tagliatelle. If we're getting technical here—which I suppose we are.

Whatever size or thickness you choose, these are proof that yes, you *can* make fresh pasta on a weeknight. Here's the method I use to cut them by hand, a simple technique that's easily customizable. You can also cut tagliolini and fettuccine with the relevant pasta machine attachments, if you have them, as directed on page 131.

Pappardelle, 131

Fettuccine, 131

Tagliatelle, 131

Tagliolini, 131

MAKE THEM WITH

Standard Egg Dough (45)
Almost All-Yolk Dough (45)
Whole Wheat Egg Dough (45)
Parsley-Speckled Dough (46)
Black Pepper Dough (46)
Chestnut Dough (49)
Citrus-Scented Dough (50)
Colorful Egg Dough (54)

PAIR THEM WITH

TAGLIOLINI
Fiery Calabrian Chili Sauce (267)
Pantry Tuna & Tomato Sauce (332)
*White Fish Ragù with Lemon &
Capers (327)*

TAGLIATELLE
Braised Onion Ragù (289)
Casual Bolognese (312)
*Slow-Roasted Salmon and Crème
Fraîche Sauce (328)*

FETTUCCINE
Butter & Parmesan Sauce (294)
Citrus & Pistachio Pesto (275)

PAPPARDELLE
Port-Braised Lamb Ragù (321)
Wild Mushroom Sauce (285)

tagliolini, tagliatelle, fettuccine & pappardelle

How they're traditionally served

For tagliolini, with light sauces, particularly seafood, vegetable, and cream sauces, but also with meat, as well as in soups, baked, and fried. For tagliatelle, with Bolognese meat sauce (page 312), of course, or prosciutto, though other variations, made elsewhere and with other flours, are served with walnut sauce, vegetable sauces, and cream sauces, as well as baked. For pappardelle, with gamey meat sauces made from duck, boar, rabbit, and the like, or mushroom and onion ragùs (pages 285 and 289, for something similar). For fettuccine, with meat and vegetables and, of course, butter and Parmigiano-Reggiano (page 294).

What you need

- A work surface, preferably wooden;
- pasta machine;
- sharp knife.

MAKE THE DOUGH Make your pasta dough of choice and let it rest, tightly covered, at room temperature for 30 minutes. To make "straw and hay" tagliatelle (paglia e fieno), make a half batch of Standard Egg Pasta Dough and a half batch of Green Colorful Egg Pasta Dough.

SET UP YOUR WORKSPACE Dust a sheet pan with semolina or line it with a dry dishcloth. Gather your tools and set up your pasta machine.

SHEET THE DOUGH Roll a quarter of your pasta dough into a sheet following the directions on page 114.

For tagliolini, roll the dough semi-thin, stopping at setting 4 or 5 for both the Marcato and KitchenAid machines.

For tagliatelle, roll the dough to setting 7 (Marcato) or twice through setting 7 (KitchenAid).

For fettuccine and pappardelle, roll the dough to setting 6 (both machines).

Lay the sheet on your work surface; if using a countertop, dust the bottom with 00 or all-purpose flour. For thicker tagliolini, you can leave the sheet as is or cut it in half; for the thinner ribbons, cut the sheet in half crosswise so you have two even pieces.

DRY THE SHEET (A LITTLE) Let the sheet dry for about 10 minutes per side, or until the surface feels leathery and doesn't stick to your hands, work surface, or itself when folded over and pressed (but is still pliable). In the meantime, roll out another sheet if you have the space.

continues

Making a Pasta Nest

To make a pasta nest

Gather the ends of about 15 strands in the palm of your non-dominant hand. Using the other hand, loosely wrap the strands around your non-dominant hand as many times as you can. Position your hand with the pasta on your work surface or sheet pan and let go—the ribbons should release into a small nest. For shorter strands like tagliolini, simply fold them in half wallet-style into a U shape.

Using pasta machine cutter attachments

Roll your pasta sheet as described above; reduce the drying time to 5 minutes per side (a very dry sheet has trouble catching in the machine). Dust both sides with 00 or all-purpose flour—be generous with the flour when making tagliolini.

Line up one edge of the sheet with one edge of the machine's cutting slot and feed it through—for the KitchenAid, this process is intuitive; for the Marcato, hold the sheet with your non-dominant hand while cranking the machine with your dominant hand, then, about halfway through, catch the strands on the other side with your non-dominant hand as you continue to crank. If the sheet doesn't catch, try cutting the corners off one of the ends at an angle so you have little notches that can help feed the sheet through the machine.

Gently shake out the strands to separate them, then lay them across the prepared sheet pan. Dust the pasta with semolina flour and spread the strands out a little if using right away or form them into nests if storing for future use.

CUT THE PASTA Dust both sides of the sheet with 00 or all-purpose flour, spreading it around and removing any excess. If making *tagliolini*, generously sprinkle the top with semolina, too.

Position the pasta sheet horizontally along your work surface. Fold the ends toward the center like an envelope so they meet in the middle. Then continue to fold up each side, carpet-style, once or twice more until they, too, meet in the middle and you have a little packet that looks like flat scrolls.

Rotate the dough 90 degrees, so the center line runs horizontally. Use a knife to trim the ends so you have straight edges, then cut strips across the dough.

For tagliolini, these strips should be about ⅛ inch (2 to 3 mm) wide;

for fettuccine, ¼ inch (6 mm) wide;

for tagliatelle, ¼ inch or a touch (6 to 7 mm) wider;

for pappardelle, 1 inch (2.5 cm) wide.

Slide the blade of the knife under the pasta so its spine is directly under the center line and lift—the strands should unfurl like Rapunzel's hair.

Gently shake out the strands to separate them, then lay them across the prepared sheet pan. Dust the pasta with semolina flour and spread the strands out a little if using right away, or form them into nests if storing for future use. Repeat with the remaining dough.

COOK OR STORE THE PASTA Cook the pasta according to the instructions on page 205 until tender but still with some bite, 2 to 3 minutes, depending on the shape, thickness, and drying time. For storage options, see page 206.

Cutting Tagliatelle by Hand

5

6

7

8

short-cut pastas

Little butterflies, tubes, and surprises first created on a whim, or as a joke, or fashioned from scraps. I love the sculptural nature of these shapes, their peaks and valleys an invitation for any sauce. It's amazing what can become of a small square of pasta—so give these a try and then, like generations before us, fold, pinch, and twist any which way you like. Maybe you'll invent something new.

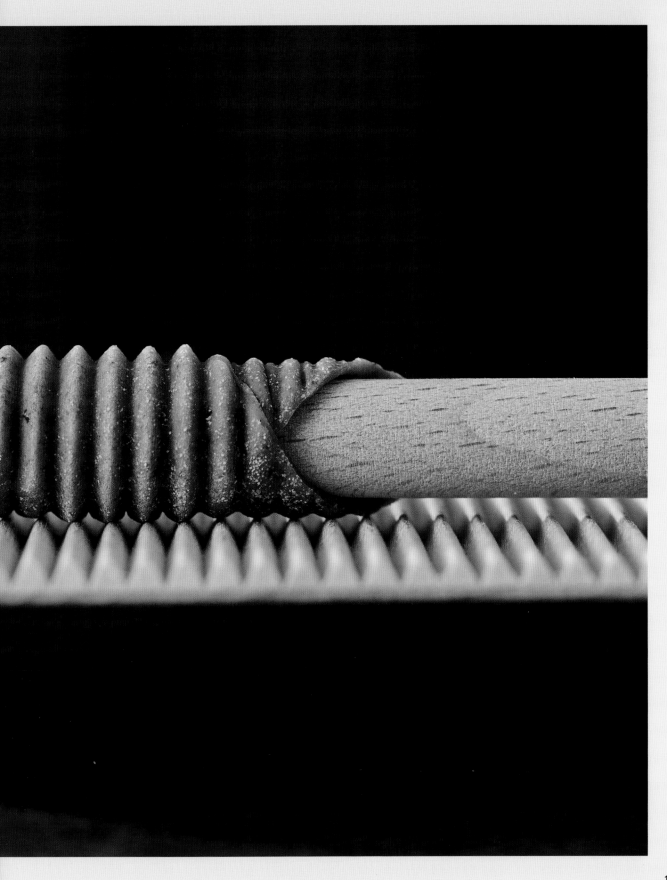

MAKE THEM WITH
*Standard Egg Dough (45) • Almost All-Yolk
Dough (45) • Whole Wheat Egg Dough (45) •
Parsley-Speckled Dough (46) • Black Pepper Dough (46) •
Colorful Egg Dough (54)*

PAIR THEM WITH
*All-Purpose Tomato Sauce (256) • Grandma Ruthe's
Chicken Soup (346) • Italian Meat Broth (345) •
Pantry Tuna & Tomato Sauce (332) • Tomato Broth (338)*

sorpresine

What they are

"Little surprises" and a cheeky joke made by women of centuries past. Remember the story about strozzapreti, and how farmers would, begrudgingly, pay their local priests in pasta (page 88)? Well, it's said that those priests had a penchant for inviting themselves over to the farmers' homes for Sunday lunch. The priests were known to love cappelletti (page 168), a meat- or cheese-filled pasta usually served in broth, and, on Sundays, they came to expect it. But the farmers' wives, with limited financial means, had other plans: They made sorpresine instead, which looked *just* like cappelletti on the outside but—surprise!—not a bit of filling to be found. This story always makes me laugh as I picture a dumbfounded priest, spoon mid-air, chewing slowly and unwilling to admit his defeat. You'll also see these called tortellini bugiardi ("lying tortellini") and igannapreti ("priest foolers").

How they're traditionally served

In broths and other soups, and with tomato sauces.

What you need

- A work surface, preferably wooden;
- pasta machine;
- bicycle pastry cutter or sharp knife.

MAKE THE DOUGH Make your dough of choice and let it rest, tightly covered, at room temperature for 30 minutes.

SET UP YOUR WORKSPACE Dust a sheet pan with semolina or line it with a dry dishcloth. Gather your tools and set up your pasta machine.

SHEET THE DOUGH Roll a quarter of your pasta dough into a sheet following the directions on page 114, stopping at setting 7 for a Marcato or twice through setting 7 for a KitchenAid machine.

CUT THE SHEET INTO SQUARES Cut the sheet into 1¼-inch to 1½-inch (3- to 4-cm) squares, either with a bicycle pastry cutter or by hand.

To cut the squares by hand: Position the pasta sheet horizontally on your work surface. Trim a thin strip of dough, about ¼ inch (6 mm) from the top and bottom (longer) edges so the sheet is a little narrower. Fold the pasta into thirds like a letter, first folding the bottom third upward about halfway and making a crease, then folding the top edge downward to meet the bottom and making another crease. Unfold the pasta sheet and cut along the creases—you should have three rows. Cut the rows into squares (just eyeball it).

Save any scraps for soups or a snack, or ball them up and cover them so they can be reused at the end.

MAKE THE SORPRESINE Cover any squares you're not using with a damp dishcloth or plastic wrap. Hold a square in one hand like a diamond. Bring the bottom point up to meet the top, forming an open triangle, almost like a hammock. Pinch the points together firmly to seal. Flip the triangle over so the sealed point is facing downward. Then bring the remaining two points together at the top and pinch to seal.

Arrange the finished sorpresine in a single layer on the prepared sheet pan. Repeat with the remaining squares, and then the remaining dough.

COOK OR STORE THE PASTA Cook the sorpresine in boiling water or broth according to the instructions on page 205 until tender, 3 to 5 minutes, depending on thickness and drying time. For storage options, see page 206.

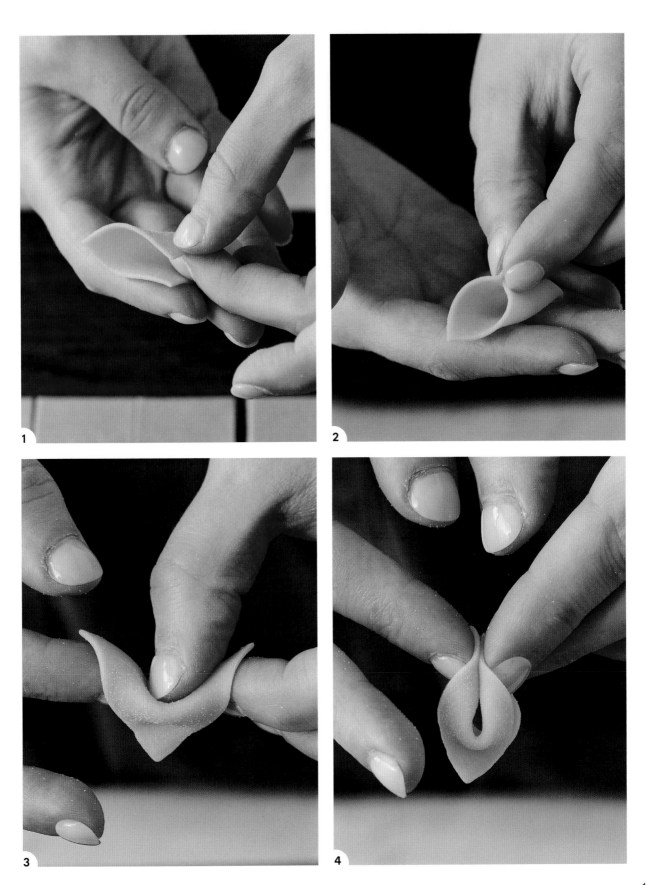

Standard Egg Sorpresine

MAKE THEM WITH
Standard Egg Dough (45) • Almost All-Yolk Dough (45) •
Whole Wheat Egg Dough (45) • Parsley-Speckled
Dough (46) • Black Pepper Dough (46) •
Chestnut Dough (49) • Citrus-Scented Dough (50) • Colorful
Egg Dough (54) / Patterned Pasta Sheets (124)

PAIR THEM WITH
Butter & Parmesan Sauce (294) • Four-Cheese Sauce (306) •
Pecorino, Pepper & Lemon Sauce (298) •
Slow-Roasted Salmon and Crème Fraîche Sauce with Peas
(328) • Sweet & Sour Eggplant Sauce with Burrata (286) •
Tomato-Cream Sauce (260)

farfalle

What they are

The name means "butterflies," although I grew up calling them bow ties. They're an old favorite in Lombardy and Emilia-Romagna, where they're known as strichetti ("pinches"), and became especially popular in the 1970s. At the beginning, farfalle were the offcuts of filled pastas made delicate and pretty; today, you'll find them in all sorts of sizes and colors, from tiny farfalline (perfect for soups) to oversized farfallone.

How they're traditionally served

With peas and prosciutto, cream and meat sauces, and with seafood, particularly salmon (they're also a popular choice for pasta salads). In Lombardy, you'll find them sweetened with amaretti biscuits, butter, and sage.

What you need

- A work surface, preferably wooden;
- pasta machine;
- bicycle pastry cutter or sharp knife;
- fluted pasta cutter (optional).

MAKE THE DOUGH Make your dough of choice and let it rest, tightly covered, at room temperature for 30 minutes.

SET UP YOUR WORKSPACE Dust a sheet pan with semolina or line it with a dry dishcloth. Gather your tools and set up your pasta machine.

SHEET THE DOUGH Roll a quarter of your pasta dough into a sheet following the directions on page 114, stopping at twice through setting 6 for a Marcato or setting 7 for a KitchenAid machine.

CUT THE SHEET INTO RECTANGLES Either with a bicycle pastry cutter or by hand, cut the sheet lengthwise into 1½-inch (4-cm) strips.

To cut the strips by hand: Position the pasta sheet horizontally on your work surface. Trim a thin strip of dough, about ¼ inch (6 mm) from the top and bottom (longer) edges so the sheet is a little narrower. Fold the pasta into thirds like a letter, first folding the bottom third upward about halfway and making a crease, then folding the top edge downward to meet the bottom and making another crease. Unfold the pasta sheet and cut along the creases—you should have three rows.

Using a fluted pasta cutter if you have one, a bicycle pastry cutter, or a sharp knife, cut the sheet crosswise—north to south—at 2-inch (5-cm) intervals (just eyeball it). You should have rectangles that are wider than they are tall and look like an old-fashioned arcade or circus ticket.

Save any scraps for soups or a snack, or ball them up and cover them so they can be reused at the end.

continues

Almost All-Yolk Farfalle

MAKE THE FARFALLE   Cover the rectangles you're not using with a damp dishcloth or plastic wrap.

There are many ways to make farfalle. Here's what works best for me:

Hold a rectangle between your thumbs (in front) and index fingers (at the back), with the shorter, fluted edges at top and bottom. Start folding the rectangle inward like a book and then, just as your thumbs start to knock against each other, use them to peel the center part of the side edges back, away from you, so it starts to look like a butterfly (or bow tie). Pinch the center firmly to seal, then fan out the wings a little bit more.

Arrange the finished farfalle in a single layer on the prepared sheet pan. Repeat with the remaining rectangles, and then the remaining dough.

COOK OR STORE THE PASTA   Cook the farfalle according to the instructions on page 205 until tender, 3 to 5 minutes, depending on thickness and drying time. For storage options, see page 206.

MAKE THEM WITH
*Standard Egg Dough (45) • Almost All-Yolk Dough (45) •
Whole Wheat Egg Dough (45) • Parsley-Speckled Dough
(46) • Black Pepper Dough (46) • Colorful Egg Dough (54)*

PAIR THEM WITH
*Braised Onion Ragù (289) • Casual Bolognese (312) •
Fried Zucchini Sauce (282) • Slow-Roasted Salmon and
Crème Fraîche Sauce with Peas (328) • Smoky Pumpkin
Sauce (305) • The Meatiest Meatless Ragù (317)*

garganelli

What they are

Quill-shaped hollow tubes wrapped in deep ridges from Emilia-Romagna. They're the invention, some say, of a housewife whose cat ate her tortellini filling just as her dinner guests walked through the door. Quick on her feet, she spotted a loom comb nearby and rolled her already-cut pasta squares across it with a stick. Even now, traditional garganelli are made with a comb called a pettina and a wooden dowel called a bastoncino. You can also use a gnocchi board—some come with garganelli-making dowels—but the handle of a wooden spoon works too, or improvise with a sushi mat and a Sharpie marker.

How they're traditionally served

With meat sauces; seasonal vegetables like peas, mushrooms, pumpkin, and zucchini; often with ham and pancetta.

What you need

- A work surface, preferably wooden;
- pasta machine;
- bicycle pastry cutter or sharp knife;
- pettina, garganelli board, or gnocchi board;
- wooden dowel or the handle of a wooden spoon.

Note

Garganelli have an affinity for collapsing, so don't worry if they start to deflate over time. Rolling the dough into a semi-thin sheet and letting the squares dry for a few minutes before shaping will help them keep their shape. You can also dry the garganelli for up to 5 hours before cooking.

MAKE THE DOUGH Make your dough of choice and let it rest, tightly covered, at room temperature for 30 minutes.

SET UP YOUR WORKSPACE Dust a sheet pan with semolina or line it with a dry dishcloth. Gather your tools and set up your pasta machine.

SHEET THE DOUGH Roll a quarter of your pasta dough into a sheet following the directions on page 114, stopping at twice through setting 5 for both the Marcato and KitchenAid machines.

CUT THE SHEET INTO SQUARES Cut the sheet into 1¼- to 1½-inch (3- to 4-cm) squares, either with a bicycle pastry cutter or by hand.

To cut the squares by hand: Position the pasta sheet horizontally on your work surface. Trim a thin strip of dough, about ¼ inch (6 mm) from the top and bottom (longer) edges so the sheet is a little narrower. Fold the pasta into thirds like a letter, first folding the bottom third upward about halfway and making a crease, then folding the top edge downward to meet the bottom and making another crease. Unfold the pasta sheet and cut along the creases— you should have three rows.

Save any scraps for soups or a snack (page 79), or ball them up and cover them so they can be reused at the end.

Let a few of the squares dry for about 5 minutes before forming the garganelli, or a little longer if it's a humid day. Cover any squares you're not using with a damp dishcloth or plastic wrap.

continues

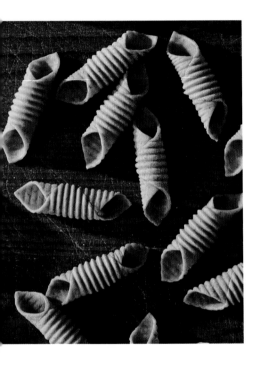

MAKE THE GARGANELLI Place your garganelli board on your work surface. Transfer a square to the center of the board in a diamond orientation. Position the wooden dowel at the bottom third of the diamond. Curl the bottom point of the pasta over the dowel, making sure the dough is flush. Holding either side of the dowel, continue rolling the dough away from you, with firm pressure, until it completely wraps around the dowel and the two points seal.

Gently twist the pasta off the dowel—if the dough sticks, leave it to dry for a few moments and try again. You should have a hollow tube imprinted with deep ridges.

Arrange the finished garganelli in a single layer on the prepared sheet pan. Repeat with the remaining squares, and then the remaining dough.

COOK OR STORE THE PASTA Cook the garganelli according to the instructions on page 205 until tender, 3 to 5 minutes, depending on thickness and drying time. For storage options, see page 206.

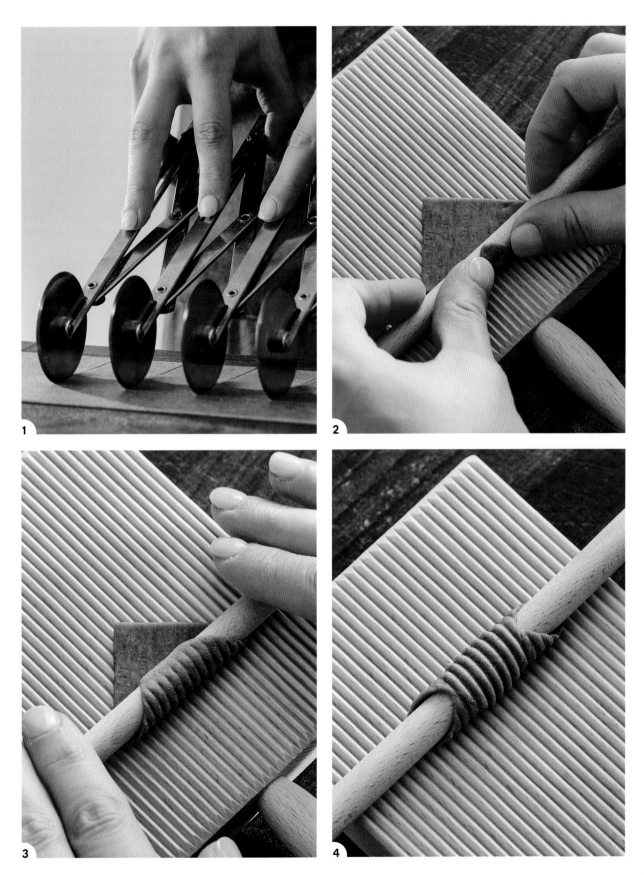

Spinach & Egg Garganelli

MAKE THEM WITH
White Wine Dough (56)
Standard Egg Dough (45)

PAIR THEM WITH
All-Purpose Tomato Sauce (256) · Basil Pesto (270) ·
Casual Bolognese (312) · Ligurian Walnut Sauce (279)

corzetti stampati

What they are

Also known as croxetti, these embossed pasta medallions hail from Genoa, in Liguria, and date back to the 13th century. It's likely they were first created with metal coins, which over time developed into elaborate, customizable wooden stamps reserved for the rich. You'll still find a few corzetti stamp artisans working today, including Filippo Romagnoli, whose family has been in the business for generations and who's crafted my entire collection. But if you're not quite ready to invest in a traditional stamp, try a cookie stamp, or cut out rounds of dough and press them with whatever sturdy textured surface you have.

How they're traditionally served

With Ligurian favorites like marjoram pesto and walnut sauce (salsa di noci).

What you need

- A work surface, preferably wooden;
- pasta machine;
- corzetti stamp.

MAKE THE DOUGH Make your dough of choice and let it rest, tightly covered, at room temperature for 30 minutes.

SET UP YOUR WORKSPACE Dust a sheet pan with semolina or line it with a dry dishcloth. Gather your tools and set up your pasta machine.

SHEET THE DOUGH Roll a quarter of your pasta dough into a sheet following the directions on page 114, stopping at setting 5 for both the Marcato and KitchenAid machines.

CUT THE SHEET INTO ROUNDS Dust both sides of the pasta sheet with a bit of 00 or all-purpose flour. Use the hollow cutter side of your corzetti stamp to cut as many rounds from the dough as you can.

Save any scraps for soups or a snack, or ball them up and cover them so they can be reused at the end.

MAKE THE CORZETTI Flip the corzetti stamp over so the patterned side is facing up and place a round of dough in the center. Align the other patterned piece of the corzetti stamp on top. Press down firmly, sandwiching the dough between the wood. Remove the round to reveal a beautifully printed medallion. If the pasta sticks to the stamp, dust the rounds or the stamp with a little more flour moving forward.

Arrange the finished corzetti in a single layer on the prepared sheet pan (if you'd like, stack the pieces by placing a sheet of parchment between each layer or dusting them with semolina). Repeat with the remaining rounds, and then the remaining dough.

COOK OR STORE THE PASTA Cook the corzetti according to the instructions on page 205 until tender, 3 to 5 minutes, depending on thickness and drying time. For storage options, see page 206.

———————— • ————————

corzetti ravioli

A hand-crafted corzetti stamp is too beautiful to stay hidden in a cupboard for long. Right now, my collection consists of seven stamps (they're a bit of an obsession), so I'm always looking for new ways to use them. Enter corzetti ravioli. I'm certain I'm not the first one to think of this, but when I first made them years ago, I hadn't seen them elsewhere. When we served them at the supper club, we filled them with a fudgy, caramelized cheese from Norway called Ski Queen (try it; it's available at many grocery stores) and dressed them with corzetti's typical condiment of marjoram and pine nuts. Flavor-wise, they were a hit, but their pretty printed faces were the real showstopper.

What you need

- A work surface, preferably wooden;
- pasta machine;
- cookie cutters;
- corzetti or cookie stamp;
- small bowl or spray bottle of water.

MAKE THE DOUGH AND FILLING   Make your egg pasta dough (pages 45–57) and filling (pages 214–243) of choice. Let the dough rest, tightly covered, at room temperature for 30 minutes, and let the filling chill as needed.

SET UP YOUR WORKSPACE   Line a sheet pan with semolina or a dishcloth. Gather your tools and set up your pasta machine.

SHEET THE DOUGH   Roll a quarter of your pasta dough into a sheet following the directions on page 114, stopping at setting 6 for both the Marcato and KitchenAid machines.

CUT AND STAMP THE DOUGH   Dust both sides of the pasta sheet with a little 00 or all-purpose flour. Then use a 3-inch (7.5-cm) cookie cutter to cut out as many rounds as you can. Any scraps can be reused later if they're still pliable or cut into pieces and saved for soup.

Press the corzetti stamp very firmly into the center of each cut round so the pattern is clearly visible.

MAKE THE RAVIOLI   Flip the rounds over so the blank sides face up. Spoon or pipe dollops of filling, 1 to 2 teaspoons each, in the center of a few of the rounds, leaving a generous border of dough around them. Cover the rest of the pieces with a damp dishcloth or plastic wrap. If the dough feels dry, add a small amount of water with your finger to the edge of half of the round.

Fold each round into a half-moon, gently pressing out the air around the filling as you do so but being careful to keep the outer pattern intact. Once the filling is encased, press the edges firmly between your fingers once more to seal and thin out the dough.

Arrange the finished pieces in a single layer on the prepared sheet pan. Repeat with the remaining dough and filling.

COOK OR STORE THE PASTA   Cook the ravioli according to the instructions on page 205 until tender, 3 to 4 minutes. For storage options, see page 206.

White Wine Corzetti Stampati

stuffed pastas

Stuffed parcels of dough are some of gastronomy's oldest veterans, present in every culture. In Italy, they were first recorded around the 13th century, and even those writings referenced earlier versions. Variations have since evolved in every region, all similar in concept yet different in the details, which as usual depended on the ingredients available in a particular place, at a particular time. By the 19th century, more formal recipes emerged and classic dishes like spinach and ricotta ravioli became popular. Now they're known by many names—agnolotti, anolini, cappellacci, cappelletti, tortelli, tortellini—but at their core they're still just pasta hugging something delicious.

Making stuffed pasta (pasta ripiena) is much simpler than it seems. In fact, you could bypass all the other shapes and start your pasta-making journey here. Once you've made great pasta dough, all that's left to do is make something tasty to tuck inside (pages 214–243) and put the two together. Here are my top tips for successful stuffed pastas:

- **REMEMBER THE LAYERS:** Folding, pinching, and creasing creates more layers of dough that need to be cooked, so keep the pasta sheets thin to ensure delicate, not doughy, results.

- **A LITTLE LESS FILLING GOES A LONG WAY:** We all want well-filled ravioli, but it can be easy to get carried away. Although there are exceptions, piling on the filling will increase your chances of exploding pasta down the line, and it can be devastating to see all that hard work undone. Always make sure there's a border of dough between the filling and the pasta's edge—at least ¼ inch (6 mm)—so you have plenty of space for sealing. I suggest doing a few tests: Fill one piece conservatively, see how it goes, and adjust as needed. It's easier to add than to take away.

- **GOODBYE, AIR POCKETS:** Too much air trapped inside the filling pocket causes the pasta to inflate rapidly as it cooks. This means the pasta might burst if it's not properly sealed or deflate just as quickly into a shriveled version of your creation. Know that there will always be some air left inside (so don't drive yourself crazy), but making even a small effort to remove it will do wonders.

- **SEAL ONCE, THEN SEAL AGAIN:** Well-sealed pasta will not only reach your plate intact, but it'll also cook more evenly. Seal once, gently, to encase the filling and remove some of the air. Seal a second time, firmly, to thin out the edges. Any touch points between layers of dough will take longer to cook than the single-layered filling pocket, so pressing these edges flat will encourage all parts of the pasta to cook at a similar rate.

MAKE THEM WITH

Standard Egg Dough (45)
Almost All-Yolk Dough (45)
Whole Wheat Egg Dough (45)
White Wine Dough (50)
Parsley-Speckled Dough (46)
Sour Cream & Rye Dough (49)
Colorful Egg Dough (54)

PAIR THEM WITH

Eggplant & Burrata Filling (233)
+ Basil Pesto (270)

Honeymoon Cheese & Herb
Filling (221) + All-Purpose Tomato
Sauce (256)

Roasted Salmon & Mascarpone Filling
(240) + Lemon-Chive Butter (297)

Sausage & Spinach Filling (245) +
Grandma Ruthe's Chicken Soup (346)

Spinach & Ricotta Filling (218)
+ Butter & Sage Sauce (293)

Winter Squash & Brown Butter
Filling (234) + Golden Saffron Sauce
(301)

"classic" ravioli

What they are

Ravioli are the pici of stuffed pasta: If you're unsure of where to start, it's here. The word itself, "ravioli," immediately conjures a particular image—rounds or squares with plump bellies and flowery edges. But the term actually describes a whole cast of pasta characters: rounds and squares, yes, but also rectangles, half-moons, triangles, and little buttons, to name a few. "Tortelli"—not to be confused with tortellini—is another word you might come across, and one that also encompasses many shapes. The differences between ravioli and tortelli are, like everything with pasta, murky, but in general tortelli tend to be more intricate than ravioli (caramelle, page 182, are a version of tortelli).

What you need

- A work surface, preferably wooden;
- pasta machine;
- fluted pasta cutter, pasta wheel, sharp knife, or cookie cutters; small bowl or spray bottle of water.

Squares & Rounds

MAKE THE DOUGH AND FILLING Make your dough and filling of choice. Let the dough rest, tightly covered, at room temperature for 30 minutes, and let the filling chill as needed.

SET UP YOUR WORKSPACE Dust a sheet pan with semolina or line it with a dishcloth. Gather your tools and set up your pasta machine.

SHEET AND CUT THE DOUGH Roll a quarter of your pasta dough into a sheet following the directions on page 114, stopping at twice through setting 6 for a Marcato or setting 7 for a KitchenAid machine.

Lay the pasta sheet horizontally on your work surface—if you're using a countertop, dust it with some 00 or all-purpose flour first—and trim any uneven edges. Save the scraps for soups or a snack, or ball them up and cover them so they can be reused at the end.

Fold the pasta sheet in half crosswise, like a book, and make a crease to mark the midpoint. Unfold it and cut along the crease so you have two even pieces. Set one aside and cover it with a damp dishcloth or plastic wrap.

FILL THE RAVIOLI
For square ravioli: Position the uncovered pasta sheet horizontally along your work surface. Fold the dough in half lengthwise and make a crease at the midpoint, then unfold it—you should be left with a faint line along the equator designating two rows. Using the crease as a guide, spoon or pipe generous filling dollops, 1 to 2 tablespoons each, across each row at regular intervals, leaving about 1 inch (2.5 cm) of space between each one and the edges of the sheet.

For round ravioli: Gently press a round cookie cutter—I usually use a 2-inch (5-cm) or 2½-inch (6-cm) size—across the uncovered pasta sheet, just enough to see the circles' outlines but not enough to cut through. Fit as many outlines as possible while leaving a finger's worth of space between them and the edges of the sheet. Spoon or pipe a dollop of filling in the center of each outline. Add enough to fill the round while leaving ¼ inch (6 mm) of space between the dollop and the outline.

SEAL THE RAVIOLI   If the dough feels dry, dip a finger in a small amount of water and trace around the dollops of filling, or lightly mist the dough with a spray bottle.

Uncover the other pasta sheet and carefully lay it on top of the filling (if there's flour on it, make sure that side is facing up), aligning the two sheets at one edge and draping it over. It's okay if the top layer doesn't look like it'll quite cover everything—you can stretch the dough if needed.

Trace and press your index fingers around each filling pocket to remove the air, lifting the top layer of pasta as needed and pushing the air out toward the nearest edge. Once the mounds of filling are sealed, lift the pasta up to make sure it's not sticking to your work surface.

To make the ravioli look more uniform, gently press the rim of a small glass or the blunt side of a smaller cookie cutter around each filling pocket. They'll puff up as the filling concentrates; it's incredibly satisfying but totally optional.

CUT THE RAVIOLI

For square ravioli: Use a fluted pasta cutter, pasta wheel, or sharp knife to cut lengthwise between the two rows, then crosswise between the filling pockets to create individual squares. Pinch around the edges to seal and thin out the dough. If you don't have a fluted pasta cutter, press the tines of a fork along the edges for a crimped effect if you'd like.

For round ravioli: Cut out the ravioli with the cookie cutter, twisting it as you do so, then pinch around the edges of each piece to seal and thin out the dough.

If the scraps are filling-free and feel pliable and hydrated, ball them up and cover them again. If they're dry or covered in filling, wipe away the filling and cut them into pieces to save for a snack or soups.

Arrange the finished ravioli in a single layer on the prepared sheet pan. Repeat with the remaining dough and filling.

COOK OR STORE THE PASTA   Cook the ravioli according to the instructions on page 205 until tender, 2½ to 3 minutes. For storage options, see page 206.

How they're traditionally served

With anything and everything, depending on the region. The rules and expectations that surround some stuffed pastas (looking at you, tortellini) don't apply to ravioli—order a plate in the south and you'll probably taste fresh cheeses like mozzarella and ricotta, herbs like marjoram and mint, and plenty of fresh tomatoes. Farther north the experience will be wholly different, with pasta full of warming ingredients like rye flour, potatoes, squash, butter, sage, nutmeg, and chestnuts.

Good news

The most familiar ravioli are also the simplest and most efficient to make. Think of these techniques as making a pasta-filling sandwich (squares and rounds) or taco (triangles and half-moons). For round shapes, I prefer the versatility of cookie cutters, but if you have ravioli stamps or molds, by all means use them.

continues

Triangles & Half-Moons (Triangoli & Mezzelune)

MAKE THE DOUGH AND FILLING Make your dough and filling of choice. Let the dough rest, tightly covered, at room temperature for 30 minutes, and let the filling chill as needed.

SET UP YOUR WORKSPACE Dust a sheet pan with semolina or line it with a dishcloth. Gather your tools and set up your pasta machine.

SHEET THE DOUGH Roll a quarter of your pasta dough into a sheet following the directions on page 114, stopping at twice through setting 6 for a Marcato or setting 7 for a KitchenAid machine.

Lay the pasta sheet horizontally on your work surface—if you're using a countertop, dust it with some 00 or all-purpose flour first—and trim any uneven edges. Save the scraps for soups or a snack, or ball them up and cover them so they can be reused at the end.

CUT THE SHEET INTO SQUARES OR ROUNDS
For triangoli: Cut the dough into 2½-inch (6-cm) squares using a bicycle pastry cutter or by hand. For the latter, fold the dough in half lengthwise and make a crease at the midpoint, then unfold it—you should be left with a faint line along the equator designating two rows. Use a fluted pasta cutter, pasta wheel, or sharp knife to cut along the crease. Then cut crosswise to create individual squares (just eyeball it).

For mezzelune: Use a 2½- or 3-inch (6- or 7.5-cm) cookie cutter to cut out as many rounds from the pasta sheet as you can. Any scraps can be reused later if they're still pliable, or cut into pieces and saved for soup.

FILL THE RAVIOLI Spoon or pipe dollops of filling, 1 to 2 teaspoons each, in the center of a few squares or rounds, leaving a generous border of dough around them. Cover the rest of the pieces with a damp dishcloth or plastic wrap. If the dough feels dry, add a small amount of water with your finger to two adjoining edges (triangoli) or along half of the round (mezzelune).

SEAL THE RAVIOLI
For triangoli: Fold each square into a triangle, first joining two opposite points, then sealing the sides, gently pressing out the air around the filling as you do so. Once the filling is encased, press the edges firmly between your fingers once more to seal and thin out the dough. If you'd like, press the tines of a fork along the edges for a crimped effect.

For mezzelune: Fold each round into a half-moon, gently pressing out the air around the filling as you do so. Once the filling is encased, press the edges firmly between your fingers once more to seal and thin out the dough.

Arrange the finished pieces in a single layer on the prepared sheet pan. Repeat with the remaining dough and filling.

COOK OR STORE THE PASTA Cook the ravioli until tender according to the instructions on page 205, 2½ to 3 minutes. For storage options, see page 206.

Spinach & Ricotta Ravioli

5

6

7

8

MAKE THEM WITH

Standard Egg Dough (45)
Almost All-Yolk Dough (45)

PAIR THEM WITH

Asparagus & Spring Pea Filling
with Mint (229) + Lemon-Chive
Butter (297)

Black Pepper & Pecorino Filling (219)
+ Brown Butter (291)

Mushroom, Garlic & Thyme
Filling (231) + Parmesan-Garlic
Butter (297)

Spinach & Ricotta Filling (218)
+ Butter & Sage Sauce (293)

Whipped Ricotta Filling (214)
+ Simple Butter Sauce (290)

egg yolk ravioli

uovo in raviolo

In 1974, chefs Nino Bergese and Valentino Marcattilii of the Michelin-starred Ristorante San Domenico in Imola (near Bologna) changed ravioli forever. Encased within delicate sheets of egg pasta and a towering nest of spinach and ricotta was an egg yolk. With one satisfying cut, the humble yolk became unctuous liquid gold, pooling alongside the cheesy filling to create its own decadent sauce. The dish was, of course, finished with a shower of freshly shaved truffles.

These ravioli are more common today, but they're no less spectacular. Try them for Valentine's Day, a birthday, or another special occasion—or, in my case, I first enjoyed them at the hands of my wonderful husband, who spent hours rolling dough and separating eggs just to make an average Sunday exceptional. Serve them in a simple butter sauce to keep the focus on the yolk.

Tips and tricks

- The key to fully cooked pasta with a still-runny egg yolk is **very thin pasta sheets**, so if you don't have a pasta machine, I suggest skipping ahead. **A piping bag** is another helpful tool here since it'll make it much easier to create the filling "nest" that holds the yolk in place (a large zip-top bag with a corner snipped off will work in a pinch).

- **Use a thick, creamy filling** that can stand tall; a very soft, runny filling won't encase the yolk properly. I especially recommend the black pepper and Pecorino filling, the mushroom filling, or, of course, the spinach and ricotta filling, pictured opposite, to honor tradition.

- To separate the eggs, I prefer to crack them into a bowl, then gently scoop up each yolk with my hands, passing it back and forth between them to remove all of the white. You can do them all at once or one at a time, but make sure to place each yolk in its own small bowl or cup.

Notes

- These ravioli are decadent, so two per person is usually plenty. Use the leftover dough and filling as you please: Make "classic" ravioli or cut the dough into any pasta shape and cook it, then thin out your filling with some pasta water to make a creamy sauce.

- It's best to cook these as soon as you're done making them, but they'll keep on a semolina-dusted sheet pan, uncovered, in the refrigerator, for up to 2 hours.

- The leftover egg whites can be stored in an airtight container in the refrigerator for 2 to 3 days. Use them in frittatas or omelets, or shake them into cocktails.

What you need

- A work surface, preferably wooden;
- pasta machine;
- fluted pasta cutter, pasta wheel, sharp knife, or large cookie cutter;
- small bowl or spray bottle of water.

continues

MAKE THE DOUGH AND FILLING Make your pasta dough and filling of choice. Let the dough rest, tightly covered, at room temperature for 30 minutes. Transfer the filling to a piping bag and chill thoroughly.

SET UP YOUR WORKSPACE AND SEPARATE THE EGGS Dust a sheet pan with semolina or line it with a dishcloth. Gather your tools and set up your pasta machine. Separate two or more eggs and place each yolk into its own small bowl or cup.

SHEET AND CUT THE DOUGH Roll a quarter of your pasta dough into a sheet following the directions on page 114, stopping at setting 7 for a Marcato or twice through setting 7 for a KitchenAid.

Lay the pasta sheet horizontally on your work surface—if you're using a countertop, dust it with some 00 or all-purpose flour first—and trim any uneven edges. Save the scraps for soups or a snack, or ball them up and cover them so they can be reused at the end.

Fold the dough in half crosswise, like a book, and make a crease to mark the midpoint. Unfold it again and cut along the crease so you have two even pieces. Then fold each of those smaller pieces in half crosswise, like a book, and cut them down the middle, too, so you have four squares, roughly 6 inches (15 cm) in size. Set two pieces aside and cover them with a damp dishcloth or plastic wrap.

PIPE THE FILLING With the piping bag tip snipped at about ½ inch (1.25 cm), pipe an open circle of filling in the center of the remaining two squares—it should be large enough to fit an egg yolk snugly, about 2 inches (5 cm) in diameter (you can use the blunt side of a cookie cutter or rim of a glass to mark an outline if you'd like). Then pipe another layer of filling directly on top of the first, so you have a little nest.

ADD THE EGG YOLKS   Quickly and carefully slide an egg yolk from its small cup or bowl into each nest. If needed, carefully pipe a little more filling around the yolk to keep it in place.

SEAL AND TRIM THE PASTA   If the dough feels dry, dip a finger in a small amount of water and trace around the filling, or lightly mist the dough with a spray bottle.

Gently lay the other two squares of pasta on top of the filling and yolks. Push out any air pockets around the filling, lifting the top sheet of pasta to remove the air as needed, then press around the filling firmly to seal.

Using a fluted pasta cutter, pasta wheel, sharp knife, or large cookie cutter, trim the excess pasta dough into a square or round—if the scraps are hydrated, ball them up and cover them to reuse later; if they're dry, cut them into pieces and save them for a snack or soup.

Firmly pinch the edges of each raviolo to seal once more and thin them out (if you'd like, use the tines of a fork to press the edges closed for a crimped effect).

Arrange the ravioli in a single layer on the prepared sheet pan. Repeat with the remaining dough and filling until you have as many ravioli as you like.

COOK THE RAVIOLI   To cook, bring a large, deep pan of water to a gentle (not rolling) boil, then salt it generously. Working with no more than four ravioli at a time, cook until the edges are tender, about 4 minutes. Use the back of a spoon to push the edges under the water as needed; when they're done, remove them from the water using a spider sieve or slotted spoon.

MAKE THEM WITH

Standard Egg Dough (45)
Almost All-Yolk Dough (45)

FILL THEM WITH

Four-Cheese Filling (215)
+ Any-Greens Filling (226)

Black Pepper & Pecorino Filling (219)
+ Asparagus
& Spring Pea Filling with Mint (229)

Mushroom, Garlic & Thyme
Filling (231) + Roasted Garlic &
Rosemary Filling (222)

Smoky Caramelized Onion
Filling (239) + Mashed Potato & Chive
Filling (232)

double-stuffed ravioli
ravioli doppi

Double the filling, double the fun! I've seen several techniques that pack in twice the flavor, but this one's become my favorite.

Tips and tricks

- Because you're wrapping each filling in two layers of pasta, a thin, tender dough that cooks quickly is key. It'll also highlight the contrast between the two fillings beautifully. The Almost All-Yolk Dough is a great option.

- This technique calls for a wooden dowel (the same one you'd find with a garganelli board) to seal the edges of the pasta, along with a fluted pasta cutter. If you don't have a dowel, try a pencil. A durable brass cutter will serve you best here since it cuts and seals the pasta at the same time.

What you need

- A work surface, preferably wooden;
- pasta machine;
- dowel from a garganelli/gnocchi board, pencil, or handle of a wooden spoon;
- fluted pasta cutter, preferably brass.

MAKE THE DOUGH AND FILLINGS Make your dough and half batches of your two fillings of choice. Let the dough rest, tightly covered, at room temperature for 30 minutes. Transfer the fillings to individual piping bags if you have them and chill thoroughly.

SET UP YOUR WORKSPACE Dust a sheet pan with semolina or line it with a dishcloth. Gather your tools and set up your pasta machine.

SHEET AND CUT THE DOUGH Roll a quarter of your pasta dough into a sheet following the directions on page 114, stopping at setting 7 for a Marcato or twice through setting 7 for a KitchenAid machine.

Lay the pasta sheet horizontally on your work surface—if you're using a countertop, dust it with some 00 or all-purpose flour—and trim any uneven edges. Save the scraps for soups or a snack, or ball them up and cover them so they can be reused at the end.

Cut the dough into 6-inch (15-cm) squares. Position one square on your work surface and cover the rest with a damp dishcloth or plastic wrap.

Fold a square of dough in half crosswise, like a book, and make a crease to mark the midpoint. Unfold it again and cut along the crease so you have two even rectangles that are 6 inches (15 cm) tall and 3 inches (7.5 cm) wide.

PIPE THE FILLINGS Pipe a stout tube of filling just above one short edge of each rectangle, leaving a small rim of dough, about ¼ inch (6 mm), on each side. Repeat the process with the second filling on the other short edge.

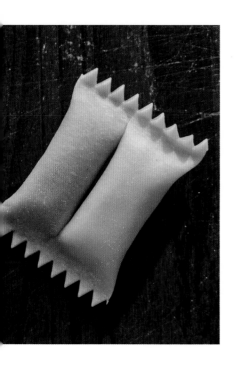

SEAL AND TRIM THE RAVIOLI   Lift the bottom two corners of each rectangle and roll them over the filling to encase it—the edge of the dough should just graze the upper edge of the filling. Then roll it over again so you have a tight tube. Repeat the process: Bring the top two corners of dough over the second filling to encase it, then roll it up again so the two fillings meet in the middle.

Use the dowel from a garganelli or gnocchi board, or whatever you have, and rest it on top of one of the rectangle's unsealed outer edges so that one side is flush with the filling. Press down firmly and gently roll the dowel back and forth to seal. Repeat on the other side, and with the other raviolo.

Trim the outer edges of each piece with a fluted pasta cutter, close to the filling but leaving a little bit of overhang. The cutter should do all the work for you, but, if needed, pinch the edges closed to ensure they're fully sealed.

Arrange the finished ravioli in a single layer on the prepared sheet pan. Repeat with the remaining dough and filling.

COOK OR STORE THE PASTA   Cook the ravioli according to the instructions on page 205 until tender, 3 to 4 minutes. For storage options, see page 206.

Black Pepper & Pecorino and Asparagus & Spring Pea Double-Stuffed Ravioli

MAKE THEM WITH

Sour Cream & Rye Dough (49)
White Wine Dough (50)
Standard Egg Dough (45)
Black Pepper Dough (46)
Whole Wheat Egg Dough (45)

PAIR THEM WITH

Alpine Cheese Fondue Filling (225)
+ Simple Butter Sauce (290) +
Balsamic Reduction (356)

Braised Beef & Caramelized Cabbage
Filling (243) + Braising Liquid (236)

Mashed Potato & Chive Filling (232)
+ Caramelized Onion Cheese Sauce
(308)

Roasted Salmon & Mascarpone Filling
(240) + Lemon-Chive Butter (297)

scarpinocc

What they are

The name comes from "scarpa," the Italian word for shoe—it's pronounced *scar-pee-noch*, by the way—and once you see it, it's hard to get the image a yodeler's clog out of your head (though a small boat and a banana also come to mind). That's no coincidence either: This pasta hails from Parre, a small town in Lombardy that neighbors Switzerland, with plenty of snow and German-inspired food to go around. They're traditionally filled with Grana Padano cheese (which is produced nearby), breadcrumbs, and spices, and the dough itself is made extra-tender with milk and butter—an homage to the region's plentiful sheep and dairy.

How they're traditionally served

With butter, which pools generously in the pasta's dimpled bellies, and local cheeses.

What you need

- A work surface, preferably wooden;
- pasta machine;
- cookie cutters;
- small bowl or spray bottle of water.

MAKE THE DOUGH AND FILLING Make your pasta dough and filling of choice. Let the dough rest, tightly covered, at room temperature for 30 minutes and let the filling chill as needed.

SET UP YOUR WORKSPACE Line a sheet pan with semolina or a dishcloth. Gather your tools and set up your pasta machine.

SHEET AND CUT THE DOUGH Roll a quarter of your pasta dough following the directions on page 114, stopping at setting 6 for both the Marcato and KitchenAid machines.

Lay the pasta sheet horizontally on your work surface (if you're using a countertop, dust it with some 00 or all-purpose flour first). Use a 2½-inch (6-cm) round cookie cutter to cut out as many rounds from the pasta sheet as you can. Any scraps can be reused later if they're still pliable or cut into pieces and saved for soup.

FILL THE PASTA Spoon or pipe about 1 teaspoon filling in the center of a few rounds, leaving a generous border of dough around them. Cover the rest of the dough with a damp dishcloth or plastic wrap.

If the dough feels dry, add a small amount of water to half of the edges of the rounds.

MAKE THE SCARPINOCC Fold each round into a half-moon, gently pressing out the air around the filling as you do so. Once the filling is encased, press the edges firmly once more to seal and thin out the dough.

Position a half-moon so its curve is facing downward. Tuck the seam to one side, creating a little fold, and prop the pasta upright on your work surface.

Use your index finger to make a dimple in the center of the filling—like poking the Pillsbury Doughboy—so it balloons outward and the pasta stands up on its own.

Arrange the finished scarpinocc in a single layer on the prepared sheet pan. Repeat with the remaining dough and filling.

COOK OR STORE THE PASTA Cook the scarpinocc according to the instructions on page 205 until tender, 3 to 4 minutes. For storage options, see page 206.

Sour Cream & Rye Mashed Potato & Chive Scarpinocc

MAKE THEM WITH

Standard Egg Dough (45)
Almost All-Yolk Dough (45)
Sour Cream & Rye Dough (49)
White Wine Dough (50)
Black Pepper Dough (46)
Colorful Egg Dough (54)

PAIR THEM WITH

Roasted Garlic & Rosemary
Filling (222) + Parmesan Broth (342)

Sausage & Spinach Filling (245)
+ Grandma Ruthe's Chicken
Soup (346)

Smoky Caramelized Onion Filling
(239) + Parmesan Broth (342)

Spinach & Ricotta Filling (218)
+ Tomato Broth (338)

Summer Corn & Basil Filling (230)
+ Corn Broth (341)

cappelletti

What they are

"Little hats" from Emilia-Romagna, easily mistaken for tortellini but more forgiving than their all-star cousins. They're often filled with cheese, but also meat or greens, then served in broth or sometimes in sauce, and can be fashioned from varying-sized rounds or squares. Like many small stuffed pastas, they were savored on special occasions like Christmas lunch and, until the modern age, reserved for the rich.

The love of this pasta runs deep: Cappelletti were once in such high demand that contests were held to see how many pieces could be downed in one sitting. Oretta Zanini De Vita's *Encyclopedia of Pasta* quotes one observer: "The greed for this dish is so general that *everyone*, especially the priests, places bets on who can eat the largest number, with some reaching four hundred or five hundred, and each year this custom leads to the death of some individual, who succumbs to grave indigestion." Not the worst way to go if you ask me!

How they're traditionally served

Usually filled with meat or cheese and served in broth.

What you need

- A work surface, preferably wooden;
- pasta machine;
- bicycle pastry cutter, sharp knife, or cookie cutters;
- small bowl or spray bottle of water.

MAKE THE DOUGH AND FILLING   Make your pasta dough and filling of choice. Let the dough rest, tightly covered, at room temperature for 30 minutes and let the filling chill as needed.

SET UP YOUR WORKSPACE   Dust a sheet pan with semolina or line it with a dishcloth. Gather your tools and set up your pasta machine.

SHEET AND CUT THE DOUGH   Roll a quarter of your pasta dough following the directions on page 114, stopping at twice through setting 6 for a Marcato or setting 7 for a KitchenAid machine.

Lay the pasta sheet horizontally on your work surface (if you're using a countertop, dust it with some 00 or all-purpose flour first).

Cut the dough into 2-inch (5-cm) squares with a bicycle pastry cutter (or eyeball them with a knife) or use a 2½-inch/6-cm (for broth) or 3-inch/7.5-cm (for sauce) round cookie cutter to cut out as many rounds from the pasta sheet as you can. Any scraps can be balled up, covered, and reused later if they're still pliable or saved for soup.

FILL THE CAPPELLETTI   Spoon or pipe dollops of filling, ½ to 1 teaspoon each (depending on the size), in the center of a few pieces, leaving a generous border of dough around them. Cover the rest of the dough with a dishcloth or plastic wrap.

If the dough feels dry, mist it with a spray bottle or add a small amount of water with your finger to half of the edges of each square or round.

FOLD THE CAPPELLETTI   Fold each square into a triangle, or each circle into a half-moon, gently pressing out the air around the filling as you do so. Once the filling is encased, press the edges firmly between your fingers once more to seal and thin out the dough.

There are many ways to shape cappelletti, but here's mine: Position the triangle or half-moon so the top point or curved edge is facing downward. Use your index finger to make an indentation in the center of the filling pocket—it'll look like it's smiling at you.

Bring the two ends toward you in a circular motion, then overlap them slightly and pinch firmly to seal. The squares might remind you of pointed pirate hats, and the rounds of sun hats with their brims turned up. When I make larger round cappelletti, sometimes I like to gently press on the filling pocket to flatten it.

Arrange the finished cappelletti in a single layer on the prepared sheet pan. Repeat with the remaining dough and filling.

COOK OR STORE THE PASTA   Cook the cappelletti in boiling water or broth according to the instructions on page 205 until tender, 2½ to 3 minutes. For storage options, see page 206.

Any-Greens Cappalletti

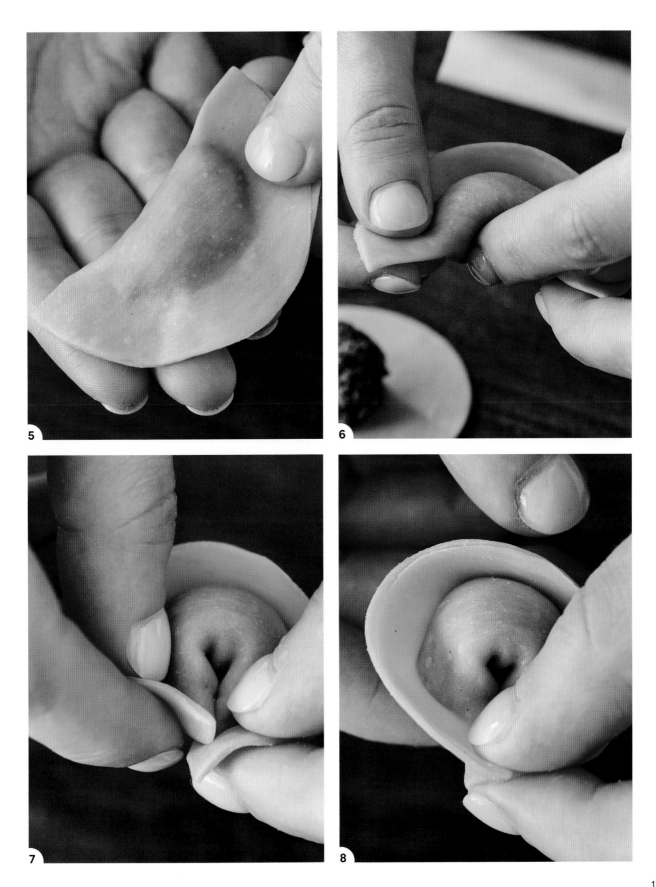

MAKE THEM WITH

Standard Egg Dough (45)
Almost All-Yolk Dough (45)
Colorful Egg Dough (54)

Four-Cheese Filling (215) + All-Purpose Tomato Sauce (256)

Roasted Garlic & Rosemary Filling (222) + Braised Onion Ragù (289)

Mushroom, Garlic & Thyme Filling (231) + Brown Butter (291)

PAIR THEM WITH

Whipped Ricotta Filling (214) + Butter & Sage Sauce (293) + Balsamic Reduction (356)

Winter Squash & Brown Butter Filling (234) + Butter & Sage Sauce (293) or Sage & Hazelnut Pesto (278)

tortelloni (& tortellini)

What they are

Tortellini's origin story begins at an inn between Bologna and Modena, with the Roman gods Venus and Jupiter. Exhausted after battle, the two deities retire at the inn for the night. Venus arises the next morning to find herself alone and calls for the innkeeper. When he arrives, so awestruck is he by her naked beauty—particularly the shape of her belly button—that he returns to his kitchen and creates the first tortellino!

Like tagliatelle and Bolognese meat sauce, tortellini are particular, filled with particular ingredients and served in a particular way. They're also so small that seven pieces can snuggle comfortably into the curve of a spoon. Today, the shape is made larger into tortelloni (and larger still into tortellacci), which are easier to make and far more flexible in their preparation. So, to keep things simple, these instructions are for tortelloni, but if you want to make tortellini, cut the dough into 1¼-inch (3-cm) squares, use pea-sized amounts of filling, and rope in your family and friends to help.

How they're traditionally served

For tortelloni, with a variety of fillings and sauces; for tortellini, always filled with meat and usually served in broth, though sometimes with cream.

What you need

- A work surface, preferably wooden;
- pasta machine;
- bicycle pastry cutter or sharp knife;
- small bowl or spray bottle of water.

MAKE THE DOUGH AND FILLING Make your dough and filling of choice. Let the dough rest, tightly covered, at room temperature for 30 minutes and let the filling chill as needed.

SET UP YOUR WORKSPACE Dust a sheet pan with semolina or line it with a dishcloth. Gather your tools and set up your pasta machine.

SHEET AND CUT THE DOUGH Roll a quarter of your pasta dough following the directions on page 114, stopping at twice through setting 6 for a Marcato or setting 7 for a KitchenAid machine.

Lay the pasta sheet horizontally on your work surface (if you're using a countertop, dust it with some 00 or all-purpose flour first).

Cut the dough into 2½-inch (6-cm) squares with a bicycle pastry cutter or by hand. For the latter, fold the dough in half lengthwise and make a crease at the midpoint, then unfold it—you should be left with a faint line along the equator. Use a pasta wheel or sharp knife to cut along the crease. Then cut crosswise to create individual squares (just eyeball it).

FILL THE PASTA Spoon or pipe 1 to 2 teaspoons filling in the center of a few pieces, leaving a generous border of dough around it. Cover the rest of the dough with a damp dishcloth or plastic wrap.

If the dough feels dry, mist it with a spray bottle or add a small amount of water with your finger to two adjoining edges of each square.

FOLD THE TORTELLONI Fold each square into a triangle, pressing out the air around the filling as you do so. Once the filling is encased, press the edges firmly between your fingers once more to seal and thin out the dough.

Position one of the bottom corners of the triangle between your index finger and thumb so they echo its angle. Fold the sides inward like a book, meeting at the center, and pinch firmly so it looks like a little "tail" with a wrinkle at the base of the filling pocket. Repeat on the other side.

Use your thumb to create a gentle curve along the filling pocket, pushing the filling so it concentrates toward the triangle's point. Then bring the two "tails" together, overlapping them a bit, and press firmly to flatten and seal.

Arrange the finished tortelloni in a single layer on the prepared sheet pan. Repeat with the remaining dough and filling.

COOK OR STORE THE PASTA Cook the tortelloni in boiling water according to the instructions on page 205 until tender, 2½ to 3 minutes. For storage options, see page 206.

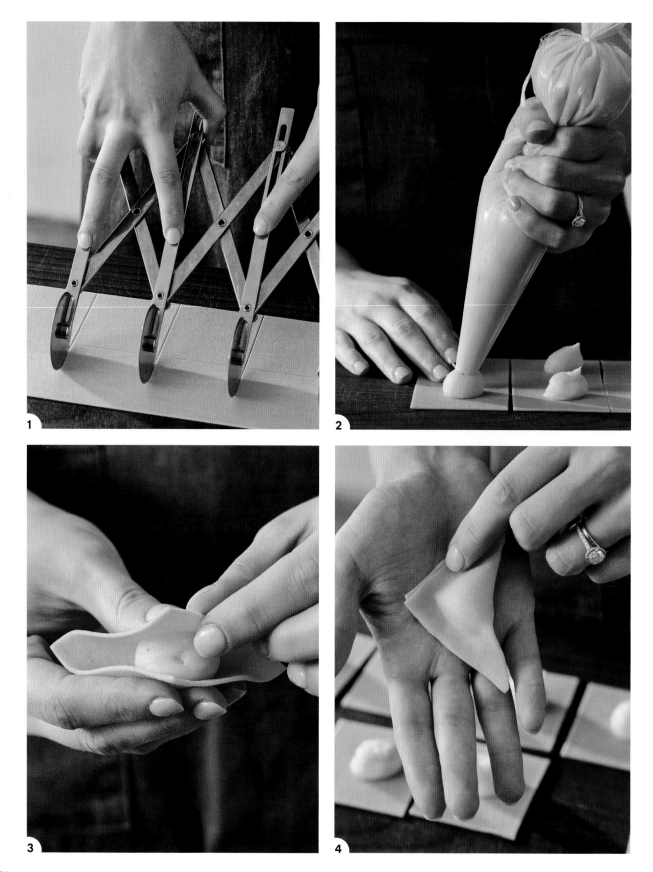

Alpine Cheese Fondue Tortelloni

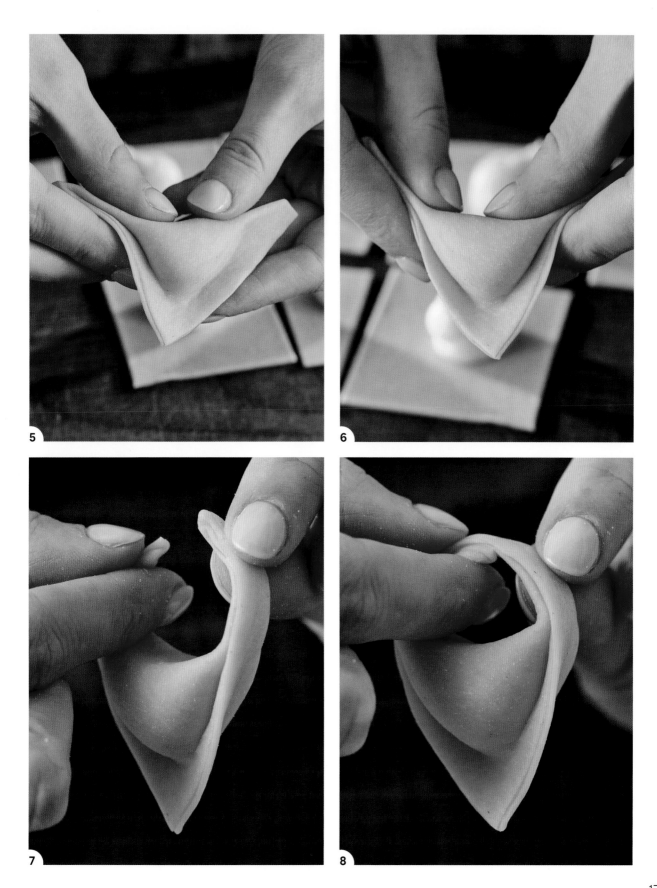

MAKE THEM WITH
Standard Egg Dough (45)
Almost All-Yolk Dough (45)

PAIR THEM WITH (AGNOLOTTI)
Asparagus & Spring Pea Filling with Mint (229) + Lemon-Chive Butter (297)

Summer Corn & Basil Filling (230) + Brown Butter (291)

Whipped Ricotta Filling (214) + Sage & Hazelnut Pesto (278)

PAIR THEM WITH (AGNOLOTTI DEL PLIN)
Alpine Cheese Fondue Filling (225) + Butter & Sage Sauce (293)

Braised Beef & Caramelized Cabbage Filling (243) + Braising Liquid (236)

Braised Shallot & Grana Padano Filling (236) + Braising Liquid (236)

agnolotti & agnolotti del plin

What they are

Piedmontese pasta parcels that take many forms, some of which are rectangular and the most famous being agnolotti del plin (meaning "pinched"). Tiny, plump, and usually filled with meat, plin crinkle at the edges and smile up at you. They're a remnant of elaborate feasts and Sunday suppers, when cooks made good use of leftovers by tucking them into pasta (though in some areas they're also filled with cheese and finished with truffles).

As for me, I first fell in love with agnolotti fresh out of culinary school, during my time making desserts at Lilia. If you've been to the restaurant, or know someone who has, then you've no doubt heard about the agnolotti: puffy tubes of pasta filled with tangy sheep's milk cheese, sauced with sweet saffron and honey, and studded with dried tomatoes—simple ingredients enlightened by time and technique. It's a dish I won't forget, and the one that put agnolotti firmly on my list of favorite pastas.

Note: Tubular agnolotti are well-suited for any pasta maker, but I'll admit plin can be finicky so I'd suggest giving them a try after a few practice rounds with other shapes.

How they're traditionally served

For agnolotti, with various fillings, including greens, cheese, and breadcrumbs (agnolotti di magro) and veal or other meats (agnolotti di grasso), and with various sauces, including broths and butter. Plin are usually filled with meat and served in broth or with leftover braising liquid, but also filled with cheese and served with truffles.

What you need

- A work surface, preferably wooden;
- pasta machine;
- fluted pasta cutter or pasta wheel, preferably brass;
- small bowl or spray bottle of water.

MAKE THE DOUGH AND FILLING   Make your dough and filling of choice. Let the dough rest, tightly covered, at room temperature for 30 minutes. Transfer your filling to a piping bag and let it chill as needed.

SET UP YOUR WORKSPACE   Dust a sheet pan with semolina or line it with a dishcloth. Gather your tools and set up your pasta machine.

SHEET AND TRIM THE DOUGH   Roll a quarter of your pasta dough into a sheet following the directions on page 114, stopping at setting 7 for a Marcato or twice through setting 7 for a KitchenAid machine.

Lay the pasta sheet horizontally on your work surface (if you're using a countertop, dust it with some 00 or all-purpose flour first).

Trim away the uneven ends and cut the sheet into sections to fit your work surface, covering any dough you're not immediately using with a damp dishcloth. Any scraps can be balled up, covered, and reused later if they're still pliable, or saved for soup.

continues

To make agnolotti

FILL THE PASTA Pipe a long cylinder of filling, as thick as your thumb, along the pasta sheet, starting about ½ inch (1.25 cm) above the bottom edge and leaving 1-inch (2.5-cm) gaps at either end. If it looks scant, pipe another layer of filling on top.

SEAL THE PASTA If the dough feels dry, mist it with a spray bottle or trace a small amount of water with your finger around the top edge of the filling.

Starting at one of the bottom corners, lift and roll the dough up and over the filling, away from you, so it's completely encased. Use the side of an index finger to seal the seam where the layers of dough meet, pushing the filling back toward you so it's as taut as possible. Roll the encased filling over once more so the seam disappears and you're left with a tight tube.

FORM AND CUT THE AGNOLOTTI
Now for my favorite part: With your index fingers held 2 inches (5 cm) apart, firmly and confidently (!) press them down along the length of the tube to create individual pillows.

Using a fluted pasta cutter or pasta wheel, trim the excess dough, close to the filling but leaving a small amount of overhang. You can make more agnolotti out of the trimming.

Gently lift the pasta to make sure it's not sticking to your work surface, then use the cutter to slice between the filling pockets and form the individual agnolotti.

1

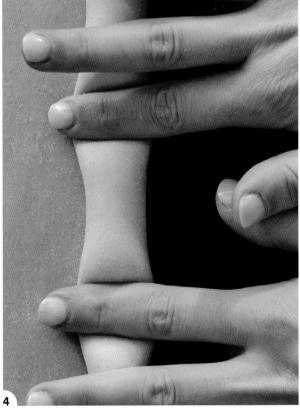

4

continues

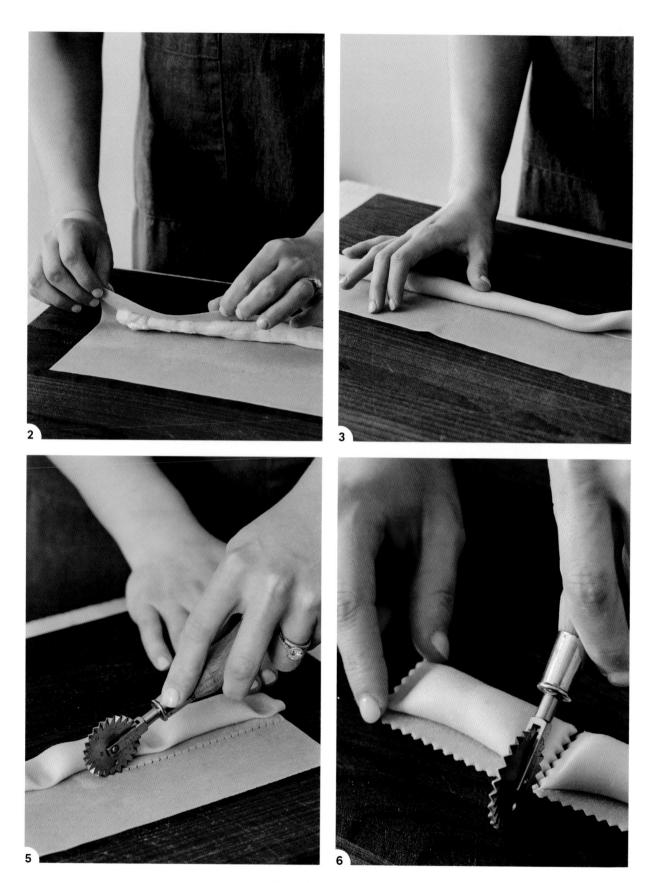

Whipped Ricotta Agnolotti

To make agnolotti del plin

FILL THE PASTA Pipe ½-teaspoon dollops of filling along the pasta sheet, starting about ¼ inch (6 mm) above the bottom edge and leaving ¾-inch (2-cm) gaps between them.

SEAL THE PASTA If the dough feels dry, mist it with a spray bottle or trace a small amount of water with your finger around the top edge of the filling.

Starting at one of the bottom corners, lift and fold the dough up and over the filling, away from you, so it's completely encased. Use the side of a finger to seal the seam where the layers of dough meet, pushing the filling back toward you so it's as taut as possible.

PINCH AND CUT THE AGNOLOTTI Now for the big moment: With your thumbs and index fingers, firmly and confidently (!) pinch the gaps between the filling dollops upward so they stand tall.

Using a fluted pasta cutter or pasta wheel, trim the excess dough, close to the filling but leaving a small amount of overhang. You can make more plin out of the trimming.

Gently lift the pasta to make sure it's not sticking to your work surface.

Finally, use the fluted cutter to forcefully cut forward between each filling pocket—smack in the middle of the pinches—to form the individual plin and signature wrinkles on each side.

Arrange the finished pasta in a single layer on the prepared sheet pan. Repeat with the remaining dough and filling.

COOK OR STORE THE PASTA Cook the agnolotti according to the instructions on page 205 until tender, 2½ to 3 minutes. For storage options, see page 206.

Braised Beef & Caramelized Cabbage Agnolotti del Plin

MAKE THEM WITH

Standard Egg Dough (45)
Almost All-Yolk Dough (45)
*Colorful Egg Dough (54) / Patterned
Pasta Sheets (124)*

PAIR THEM WITH

*Asparagus & Spring Pea Filling
with Mint (229) + Wild Mushroom
Sauce (285)*

*Eggplant & Burrata Filling (233)
+ Basil Pesto (270)*

*Four-Cheese Filling (215)
+ Golden Saffron Sauce (301)*

*Summer Corn & Basil Filling (230)
+ Lemon-Chive Butter (297)*

*Winter Squash & Brown Butter
Filling (234) + Butter & Sage Sauce
(293) or Sage & Hazelnut Pesto (278)*

caramelle

What they are

Playful pasta "candies" that I'd take over classic caramels any day. Their origins are hazy—they're probably from Emilia-Romagna and you might spot them in Parma and Modena around Easter—but now they've been happily adopted stateside. Some have round bellies like peppermints, while others stretch long like Jolly Ranchers. All are the perfect canvas for colors and stripes.

How they're traditionally served

With a variety of fillings and sauces, and now often with colorful patterns.

What you need

- A work surface, preferably wooden;
- pasta machine;
- bicycle pastry cutter or sharp knife;
- fluted pasta cutter (optional);
- small bowl or spray bottle of water.

MAKE THE DOUGH AND FILLING   Make your dough and filling of choice. Let the dough rest, tightly covered, at room temperature for 30 minutes. Transfer your filling to a piping bag and let it chill as needed.

SET UP YOUR WORKSPACE   Dust a sheet pan with semolina or line it with a dishcloth. Gather your tools and set up your pasta machine.

SHEET AND CUT THE DOUGH   Roll a quarter of your pasta dough into a sheet following the directions on page 114, stopping at setting 7 for a Marcato or twice through setting 7 for a KitchenAid machine.

Lay the pasta sheet horizontally on your work surface (if you're using a countertop, dust it with some 00 or all-purpose flour first).

Cut the sheet lengthwise into 2½-inch (6-cm) strips with a bicycle pastry cutter or by hand. For the latter, fold the dough in half lengthwise and make a crease at the midpoint, then unfold it—you should be left with a faint line along the equator. Use a pasta wheel or sharp knife to cut along the crease. With a fluted pasta cutter if you have one, a bicycle pastry cutter, or a sharp knife, cut the sheet crosswise—north to south—at 3- to 3½-inch (7.5- to 9-cm) intervals (just eyeball it). You should have rectangles that are wider than they are tall, similar to an old-fashioned arcade or circus ticket.

Any scraps can be balled up, covered, and reused later if they're still pliable or saved for soup.

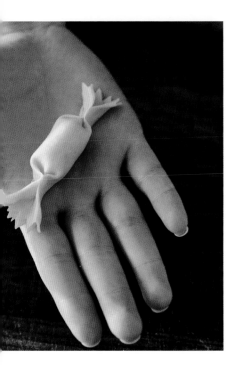

MAKE THE CARAMELLE   Cover the rectangles you're not immediately using with a damp dishcloth or plastic wrap.

Position a rectangle so the fluted (short) ends are east and west on your work surface. Pipe a stout cylinder of filling just above the bottom edge of the dough, leaving ½ inch (1.25 cm) of unfilled space on each side.

If the dough feels dry, add a small amount of water with your finger around the filling or mist it with a spray bottle.

Lift the bottom two corners of the rectangle and roll them up and over the filling, tucking the edge of the dough around to encase it. Then roll it over again so you have a tight tube.

Use your index fingers to locate where the filling begins on each side. Then firmly and confidently (!) press downward to seal—the filling pocket should puff up in the center, *à la* agnolotti. It's totally fine if some of the filling leaks out on either side as long as the pasta is sealed well.

At either side of the filling, pinch the top and bottom edges of the pasta together, then fan out the ends to complete the candy-wrapper look.

Arrange the finished caramelle in a single layer on the prepared sheet pan. Repeat with the remaining dough and filling.

COOK OR STORE THE PASTA   Cook the caramelle according to the instructions on page 205 until tender, 2½ to 4 minutes. For storage options, see page 206.

Four-Cheese Caramelle

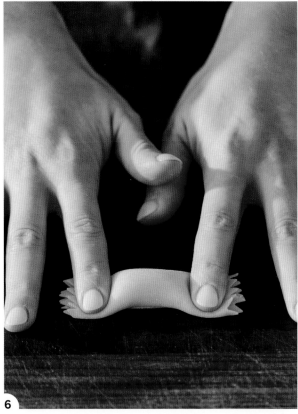

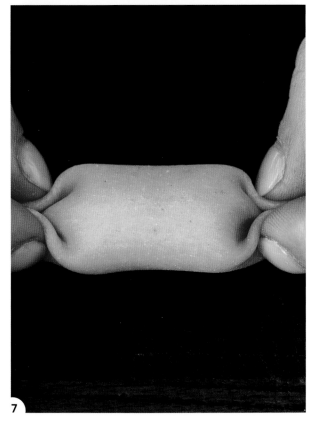

gnocchi

Always irregular, gnocchi come in many forms, depending on where you are. In Lazio, you'll find gnocchi alla romana, buttery discs of cooked semolina baked until golden and covered in Parmesan. In Sorrento, gnocchi alla sorrentina (page 202)—potato gnocchi prepared ziti-style with tomato sauce, fresh mozzarella, and basil—is a Sunday staple. Head to the Amalfi Coast for ricotta dumplings called 'ndunderi, or to the border of Austria, in Trentino Alto-Adige, for matzah ball–like canederli served in broth. Familiar shapes like cavatelli from Puglia and malloreddus from Sardinia are gnocchi, too.

There are two methods I use to shape gnocchi, one geared toward sturdier doughs like potato and ricotta, and another for softer and more delicate doughs made with vegetables like sweet potatoes and squash. The pillows themselves can be kept smooth or rolled across the back of a fork or a wooden board to create sauce-grabbing ridges—it's totally up to you.

MAKE THEM WITH

*Meyer Lemon & Herb Ricotta
Gnocchi Dough (64)*
Ossola-Style Gnocchi Dough (66)
Potato Gnocchi Dough (67)
Ricotta Gnocchi Dough (60)

PAIR THEM WITH

**MEYER LEMON & HERB RICOTTA
GNOCCHI**
Basil Pesto (270) ·
Lemon-Chive Butter (297) ·
Parmesan-Garlic Butter (297)

OSSOLA-STYLE GNOCCHI
Butter & Sage Sauce (293) ·
Four-Cheese Sauce (306) ·
Ligurian Walnut Sauce (279) ·
Wild Mushroom Sauce (285)

POTATO GNOCCHI
Casual Bolognese (312) ·
*Pecorino, Pepper & Lemon Sauce
(298)* · *Tomato-Cream Sauce (260)*

RICOTTA GNOCCHI
All-Purpose Tomato Sauce (256) ·
The Meatiest Meatless Ragù (317) ·
Broccoli Sauce (281) · *Kale &
Arugula Pesto (277)*

standard gnocchi method

What you need

- A work surface, preferably wooden;
- metal bench scraper or sharp knife;
- gnocchi board or fork (optional).

MAKE THE DOUGH   Make your gnocchi dough of choice.

SET UP YOUR WORKSPACE   Line a sheet pan with parchment paper and dust it with all-purpose flour. Keep a small bowl of flour nearby.

CUT THE DOUGH   Dust your work surface and the dough with flour. Using a bench scraper or sharp knife, cut the dough into wedges or thick slices about the width of two fingers—they don't need to be even.

ROLL THE DOUGH INTO ROPES   Sprinkle a piece of dough with flour and roll it back and forth to create a smooth exterior. Then gently roll the dough outward into a thick rope, about ¾ inch (2 cm) in diameter. If the dough gets sticky, dust it with more flour.

MAKE THE GNOCCHI   Cut the rope into bite-sized pillows. Leave the gnocchi as they are, or roll them across the back of a fork or gnocchi board until they curl over. The motion is similar to cavatelli (page 96) but with a much gentler touch.

Arrange the pieces in a single layer on the prepared sheet pan—they can be close together but not touching. For maximum efficiency, roll all the dough into ropes first, then cut them into pieces in one go. The finished gnocchi can sit at room temperature or uncovered in the refrigerator for up to 2 hours if needed.

COOK OR STORE THE PASTA   Cook the gnocchi according to the directions on page 205 until they float, plus a few seconds longer. Enjoy as is or pan fry if desired (page 205). For storage options, see page 206.

Ricotta Gnocchi

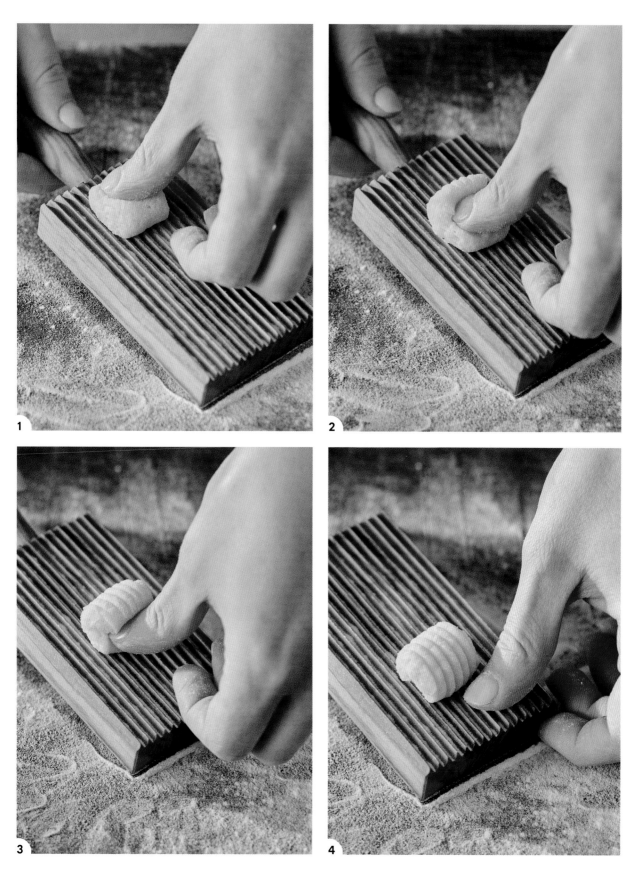

Rolling Potato Gnocchi on a Gnocchi Board

MAKE THEM WITH

*Meyer Lemon & Herb Ricotta
Gnocchi Dough (64)
Ossola-Style Gnocchi Dough (66)
Pumpkin & Ricotta
Gnocchi Dough (65)
Ricotta Gnocchi Dough (60)
Sweet Potato Gnocchi
Dough (70)*

PAIR THEM WITH

**MEYER LEMON & HERB RICOTTA
GNOCCHI**
*Basil Pesto (270) •
Lemon-Chive Butter (297) •
Parmesan-Garlic Butter (297)*

OSSOLA-STYLE GNOCCHI
*Butter & Sage Sauce (293) •
Four-Cheese Sauce (306) •
Ligurian Walnut Sauce (279) •
Wild Mushroom Sauce (285)*

PUMPKIN & RICOTTA GNOCCHI
*Brown Butter (291) • Butter & Sage
Sauce (293) • Ligurian Walnut Sauce
(279) • Sage & Hazelnut Pesto (278)*

RICOTTA GNOCCHI
*All-Purpose Tomato Sauce (256) • The
Meatiest Meatless Ragù (317) • Broccoli
Sauce (281) • Kale & Arugula Pesto (277)*

SWEET POTATO GNOCCHI
*Brown Butter (291) • Butter & Sage
Sauce (293) • Four-Cheese Sauce
(306) • Sage & Hazelnut Pesto (278)*

delicate gnocchi method

What you need

- A work surface, preferably wooden;
- metal bench scraper or sharp knife;
- rolling pin or wine bottle;
- gnocchi board or fork (optional).

MAKE THE DOUGH   Make your gnocchi dough of choice.

SET UP YOUR WORKSPACE   Line a sheet pan with parchment paper and dust it with all-purpose flour. Keep a small bowl of flour nearby.

ROLL AND CUT THE DOUGH   Dust your work surface and the dough with flour. Using a rolling pin or wine bottle, gently flatten and roll the dough into a rough square about ¾ inch (2 cm) thick. Slice the square into ¾-inch (2-cm) strips—dust your knife or bench scraper in some flour if it's sticking to the dough.

Dust each dough strip in a little more flour, then gently roll back and forth until it becomes a smooth log. Cut the log into bite-sized pillows.

MAKE THE GNOCCHI   Leave the gnocchi as they are, roll them into balls, or gently roll them across the back of a fork or gnocchi board.

Arrange the pieces in a single layer on the prepared sheet pan. For maximum efficiency, roll all the dough into ropes first, then cut them into pieces in one go.

COOK OR STORE THE PASTA   Cook the gnocchi according to the directions on page 205 until they float, plus a few seconds longer. Enjoy as-is or pan fry if desired (see page 205). For storage options, see page 206.

Sweet Potato Gnocchi

stuffed gnocchi
gnocchi ripieni

Stuffed gnocchi are "kind of a modern thing," according to a friend from Abruzzo who first introduced me to the concept. Sweet plum-filled gnocchi from Friuli in northeastern Italy (and neighboring Slovenia), known as gnocchi di susine, are as traditional as it gets, so there's plenty of room for experimentation. The key to making these with ease is a very cold, firm filling—the Mushroom, Garlic & Thyme Filling (page 231) and Roasted Salmon & Mascarpone Filling (page 240) are my favorites. Or keep it simple and wrap the dough around cold ½-inch cubes of melty, oozy cheese like fresh mozzarella, taleggio, or gorgonzola. You'll need 1½ to 2 cups (360 to 500 grams) filling for the Potato Gnocchi Dough recipe on page 67.

MAKE THE DOUGH AND FILLING   Make the Potato Gnocchi Dough (page 67) and your filling of choice—see my recommendations at left. Make sure the filling is cold but pliable.

SET UP YOUR WORKSPACE   Line a sheet pan with parchment paper and dust it with all-purpose flour. Keep a small bowl of flour nearby.

CUT THE DOUGH INTO PIECES   If you have a kitchen scale, cut a quarter of the dough into ½-ounce (15-gram) pieces. If you don't have a scale, cut off a portion of the dough about the thickness of two fingers. Dust it with flour and roll it into a thick rope, about 1 inch (2.5 cm) in diameter. Cut the rope into walnut-sized pieces.

FILL AND SEAL THE GNOCCHI   Roll one of the pieces of dough into a ball, then gently press it into a flat round.

Place ½ teaspoon filling or a cube of cheese in the center of the round. Carefully wrap the dough around the filling and pinch the seams together to seal. If the filling gets soft and difficult to manage as you go along, pop it in the freezer to firm up.

Turn the dumpling over so it's seam-side down and roll and adjust the shape into a neat disc—it should look a little like mochi.

Arrange the finished gnocchi in a single layer on the prepared sheet pan. Repeat with the remaining dough and filling.

COOK OR STORE THE PASTA   Cook the gnocchi according to the directions on page 205 until they float, plus a few seconds longer, then pan-fry if desired (page 206). For storage options, see page 206.

Roasted Salmon & Mascarpone Stuffed Gnocchi

lasagne

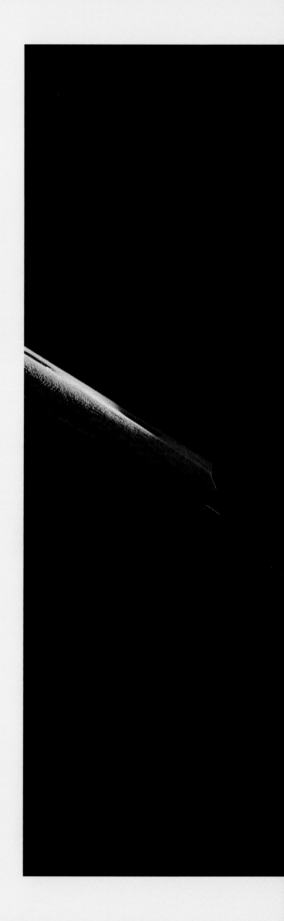

Few things cure the blues like a lasagna. Its remedy lies not only in the comfort of eating it (and sliding a fork through all those layers!), but also in the ritual of making it. In my house, that ritual is always a (delicious) mess that somehow requires every surface and utensil I own—but by now I've learned to embrace the chaos, knowing that the moment will come when the dishes are clean and everyone's smiling just as the bubbling top turns golden.

I love lasagne made with dried pasta as much as I do fresh, and it really comes down to preference and time. If you're looking for sturdy, al dente layers and need to speed things up, use what comes in the box; if your goal is silky and tender and you have an extra hour, opt for fresh. If you do choose the fresh route, I find blanching the pasta sheets yields better texture than layering them in raw. Without blanching, the lasagna takes longer to cook and the pasta can get gummy.

Like all pasta dishes, lasagne are a combination of components—layers of dough and various fillings and sauces—so there's ample room for flavor exploration. I've included recipes and guidelines for my four favorite lasagne here, but let the "mix and match" mantra of this book guide you, too. A standard 9 x 13-inch lasagna will serve 8 and, using a standard batch of dough in this book, you should get enough pasta sheets for about five layers. (If you prefer store-bought noodles, a 1-pound box will yield about four layers.)

Lasagne Storage

Any lasagna can be assembled in advance. Refrigerate the unbaked lasagna for up to 24 hours, or freeze it in a disposable dish, tightly wrapped in plastic and then foil, for 2 to 3 months. Defrost a frozen lasagna in the refrigerator overnight, and let a cold lasagna stand at room temperature for an hour before baking. And, just in case, increase the lasagna's covered baking time by 20 minutes.

Cheesy Spinach Lasagne

my favorite lasagne & how to make them

	Bolognese-Style Meat Lasagne (Lasagne alla Bolognese)	Portofino-Style Pesto Lasagne (Lasagne alla Portofino)	Cheesy Spinach Lasagne	Autumn Squash Lasagne
What You Need	1 batch Standard Egg Pasta Dough (page 45) or Green Colorful Egg Pasta Dough (page 54) 2 batches Casual Bolognese (page 312) or, for a vegetarian-friendly version, Meatiest Meatless Ragù (page 317) 1 batch Besciamella (page 203) 3½ ounces (100 grams) finely grated Parmigiano-Reggiano	1 batch Standard Egg Pasta Dough (page 45) 1½ batches Basil Pesto (page 270) 1 batch Besciamella (page 203) 16 to 20 thin slices provolone (optional) 2 ounces (55 grams) finely grated Parmigiano-Reggiano	1 batch Standard Egg Pasta Dough (page 45) 1½ batches Any-Greens Filling (page 226) 16 ounces (450 grams) full-fat ricotta 1 large egg, lightly beaten 1 batch Besciamella, Cheesy Spinach Lasagne variation (page 203) 2 ounces (55 grams) grated Fontina and/or low-moisture mozzarella, for topping 1 ounce (30 grams) finely grated Parmigiano-Reggiano, for topping	1 batch Standard Egg Pasta Dough (page 45) 1½ batches Winter Squash & Brown Butter Filling (page 234) 8 ounces (225 grams) full-fat ricotta 1 large egg, lightly beaten 1 batch oven-caramelized red or yellow onions from the Smoky Caramelized Onion Filling (page 239) 1 batch Besciamella, Autumn Squash Lasagne Variation (page 203) 2 ounces (55 grams) grated Fontina, Gruyère, and/or Asiago, for topping 1 ounce (30 grams) finely grated Parmigiano-Reggiano, for topping 16 fried sage leaves, for topping post-bake
Extra Notes			Omit the mozzarella from the Any-Greens Filling, if you'd like. Add the ricotta to the food processor with the Any-Greens Filling and pulse until combined but not pureed, then fold in the egg.	Omit the brown butter from the Winter Squash Filling, if you'd like. Add the ricotta to the food processor with the Winter Squash Filling and pulse until well-combined, then fold in the egg. I prefer using red onions for color.

MAKE THE COMPONENTS   Make your dough, filling(s), and/or sauce(s) of choice; if using besciamella, hold off for now. Grate your cheese.

ROLL AND BLANCH THE PASTA   Bring a large pot of water to a boil and salt it generously. Fill a large bowl with ice water. Line a sheet pan with a clean, tightly woven (not terry cloth) dishcloth and keep a few more on hand.

Roll a quarter of your pasta dough following the directions on page 114, stopping at setting 6 for both a Marcato and KitchenAid machine. Cut the sheet into about 6-inch (15-cm) squares—the size doesn't really matter; you'll be cutting them again to fill your dish. Ball up any scraps and cover them—they can be rerolled at the end if needed.

Depending on your counter space, roll and cut as much of the remaining dough as you can.

Drop four to five pasta squares into the boiling water and gently stir. Cook for 30 seconds, then use a spider sieve and/or tongs to carefully transfer to the ice water. Arrange the pasta in a single layer on the dishcloth and pat dry. Repeat with the remaining squares, layering them between clean dishcloths.

If using dried pasta sheets, prepare them according to the package directions.

MAKE THE BESCIAMELLA AND PREHEAT THE OVEN   Make the besciamella or, for the Cheesy Spinach Lasagne and Autumn Squash Lasagne, make the suggested variations. Heat the oven to 375°F/190°C.

ASSEMBLE THE LASAGNE   Grease your baking dish with butter or oil.

FOR BOLOGNESE-STYLE MEAT LASAGNE

Ladle some besciamella into the dish, spreading it out in a thin layer with the bottom of the ladle or a spoon. Layer some pasta on top to fill the dish, cutting and overlapping the pieces as needed (for crispy edges, let some of the pasta go up the sides of the dish). Spoon over a layer of meat sauce and spread it across the pasta using the back of the spoon or spatula—don't worry if there are gaps. Then add another layer of besciamella, spreading it over the sauce, and sprinkle with Parmigiano-Reggiano. Repeat (pasta, sauce, besciamella, Parmigiano), ending with pasta, then the remaining sauce, followed by the remaining besciamella, and top with plenty of Parmigiano-Reggiano.

FOR PORTOFINO-STYLE PESTO LASAGNE

Ladle some besciamella into the dish, spreading it out in a thin layer with the bottom of the ladle or a spoon. Layer some pasta on top to fill the dish, cutting and overlapping the pieces as needed (for crispy edges, let some of the pasta go up the sides of the dish). Ladle another layer of besciamella on top, then spoon over some of the pesto and spread it across the pasta using the back of the spoon or spatula—don't worry if there are gaps. Layer a few slices of provolone on top, if using. Repeat (pasta, besciamella, pesto, provolone) ending with pasta, then pesto, followed by besciamella, and finishing with the Parmigiano-Reggiano.

FOR CHEESY SPINACH LASAGNE

Ladle some besciamella into the dish, spreading it out in a thin layer with the bottom of the ladle or a spoon. Layer some pasta on top to fill the dish, cutting and overlapping the pieces as needed (for crispy edges, let some of the pasta go up the sides of the dish). Spoon over a layer of greens filling and spread it across the pasta using the back of the spoon or a spatula—don't worry if there are gaps. Then add another layer of besciamella. Repeat (pasta, greens, besciamella), ending with pasta, then greens, then besciamella, and finish with plenty of grated Fontina, low-moisture mozzarella, and Parmigiano-Reggiano.

FOR AUTUMN SQUASH LASAGNE

Ladle some besciamella into the dish, spreading it out in a thin layer with the bottom of the ladle or a spoon. Layer some pasta on top to fill the dish, cutting and overlapping the pieces as needed (for crispy edges, let some of the pasta go up the sides of the dish). Spoon over a layer of squash filling and spread it across the pasta using the back of the spoon or a spatula—don't worry if there are gaps. Then scatter some caramelized onions on top, followed by another layer of besciamella. Repeat (pasta, squash, onions, besciamella), ending with pasta, then squash, then besciamella, then onions, and finish with plenty of grated Fontina, Asiago, and/or Gruyère, and Parmigiano-Reggiano.

BAKE THE LASAGNA   Cover the baking dish with foil and bake on the middle rack for 30 minutes. Uncover and bake until bubbling and golden around the edges, 15 to 20 minutes more. Broil the top for a few minutes for extra color. Remove from the oven and let stand for 15 to 30 minutes before serving. If making the Autumn Squash Lasagne, scatter the fried sage on top.

besciamella

4 tablespoons (55 grams) **unsalted butter**

A scant ⅓ cup (55 grams) **all-purpose flour**

3½ cups (800 ml) **whole milk**, plus more as needed

Kosher salt

Whole nutmeg

All the components for making a great lasagna (or cannelloni, or stuffed shells, or baked ziti, for that matter) are already in this book—all except one. I grew up on lasagne layered with ricotta, but in Italy you'll find besciamella (béchamel)—milk thickened with butter and flour—instead. It's a smooth, snowy "mother sauce" that's luxurious yet mild, the perfect companion for more robust flavors.

In a medium saucepan, melt the butter over medium heat. Add the flour and cook, using a whisk to mix constantly, until it smells nutty and the mixture starts to loosen and bubble, 2 to 3 minutes.

While continuing to whisk, gradually add the milk, either in a slow, steady stream or a splash at a time.

Increase the heat to medium-high and, still whisking, cook until it thickens to the consistency of a creamy soup and coats the back of a spoon, about 5 to 7 minutes more (it'll continue to thicken as it cools). Turn off the heat. Season to taste with salt and freshly grated nutmeg.

To hold for more than 10 or 15 minutes, cover the surface of the sauce with a layer of plastic wrap to prevent a skin from forming. Whisk again before use—once cool, if it seems too thick, loosen it with a splash of milk.

The besciamella can be stored in an airtight container in the refrigerator for up to 3 days or the freezer for up to 1 month. Reheat over low heat and loosen with more milk or warm water as needed.

VARIATIONS

Besciamella for Cheesy Spinach Lasagne: After the sauce thickens, turn off the heat and whisk in 6 ounces (170 grams) grated Fontina and 4 ounces (115 grams) grated low-moisture mozzarella, one handful at a time, until smooth, letting each addition melt before adding the next. Season to taste with salt, pepper, and nutmeg. Reserve more grated cheese for topping.

Besciamella for Autumn Squash Lasagne: After the sauce thickens, turn off the heat and whisk in 10 ounces (285 grams) grated Fontina, Gruyère, Asiago, or a mix, one handful at a time, until smooth, letting each addition melt before adding the next. Season to taste with salt and nutmeg. Reserve more grated cheese for topping.

Vegan Besciamella: Swap out the butter for oil or a dairy-free butter alternative and the milk for an unflavored plant-based option like oat milk.

sorrento-style baked gnocchi
gnocchi alla sorrentina

1 batch **Potato Gnocchi** (dough, page 67; shape, page 188)

1 batch **All-Purpose Tomato Sauce** (page 256)

1 pound (450 grams) **fresh mozzarella**, cut into cubes

Fresh basil

1 ounce (30 grams) finely grated **Pecorino Romano** (optional)

Okay, not a lasagne, but similar in spirit and too good to pass up.

Boil the gnocchi in a large pot of well-salted water until they float. Use a spider sieve or slotted spoon to transfer the gnocchi to the tomato sauce and gently stir to coat. Scoop half of the gnocchi into a 9 x 13-inch baking dish and scatter half of the mozzarella and a few torn basil leaves on top. Then layer on the remaining gnocchi and mozzarella, and sprinkle with Pecorino. Bake at 400°F/205°C until the cheese melts, 10 to 15 minutes. Broil briefly until the top is golden. Serve with more basil.

LASAGNE

203

cooking & storing fresh pasta

Pasta is a simple food and cooking it should be simple, too. But in true Italian fashion, there are rules about cooking pasta that change a little here, a little there, depending on who you ask. And for most of us, those rules give rise to three questions: *How much salt should I put in the pot? How many minutes should I boil my pasta? What really is "al dente"?* Good questions, with somewhat subjective answers.

cooking dried pasta: finding al dente

Let's start with the goal: pasta that's pleasant to eat. For dried pasta, the holy grail is usually "al dente," which literally means "to the tooth." Simply put, al dente pasta bites back. It has texture and resistance; it banishes the thought of mushy noodles. Luckily, **al dente isn't a bullseye**—it's not one moment that, if not seized upon in its exactness, will leave you with lesser-quality food. **It's a whole target**, a sliding scale. There's always the element of personal taste, and my version of al dente might be more toothsome than yours.

To discover which ring of the al dente target suits you requires practice and observation. When you fish a noodle from the boiling water and bite into it—because **you should always taste your pasta as it cooks**—you'll notice a line between outer tenderness and inner rawness. When pasta is al dente, a whisper of that inner rawness, a speck of chalky white in the center, should linger. The timeframe will depend on the brand and the shape, but the cook time stated on a packet of high-quality dried pasta is more or less correct (still, start tasting about 3 minutes shy of what it tells you). If you're finishing the cooking process in the sauce—which I

recommend in nearly every circumstance—remove the pasta from the water just shy of your preferred doneness.

cooking fresh pasta

First things first: **Fresh pasta doesn't take long to cook.** Where a box of the dried stuff might suggest 10 or 12 minutes, freshly made shapes are far more eager to reach your plate, softening at 2, 3, or 5 minutes (which is *not* the moment they float, by the way—except for gnocchi). **Fresh pasta favors tenderness over true "al dente,"** but that doesn't mean it shouldn't have a bit of chew, so taste-test until the texture is right for you. Here are a few other factors to consider:

FORM: Flat ribbons, hollow spirals, and delicate ravioli will take less time to cook than stubbier shapes like capunti and strozzapreti. Pici rolled thin will take less time to cook than pici rolled thick.

FRESHNESS: As pasta dries, its cook time increases. Leave a tray of orecchiette to bask in the sun for a few hours and it'll take a couple of extra minutes to cook than if it was just made. Refrigerated and frozen pastas will take about a minute longer than if they were fresh; partially dried then frozen pastas will take longer still.

SAUCE: As with boxed pasta, fresh pasta that continues to cook in its sauce should be removed from the water a few moments prior to doneness. Exceptions include raw sauces and pasta salads, as well as gnocchi and stuffed pastas which, best enjoyed delicate and tender, should be cooked through before saucing.

Cooking Gnocchi

Unlike other pastas, gnocchi are direct in their doneness and are nearly ready when they float (just give them another 30 seconds in the water).

After boiling, I love to pan-fry them, particularly potato varieties (crunchy on the outside + fluffy on the inside = superior potatoes). Here's how: While the gnocchi boil, heat a large nonstick pan over medium-high and coat with a shallow layer of oil or clarified butter. Transfer the gnocchi with a spider sieve to a sheet pan or platter, then carefully slide some of them—just enough to sit comfortably in a single layer—into the hot pan (watch out for splatter). Cook until golden and crisp, 3 to 5 minutes, then flip and cook until golden on the other side. Repeat with the remaining gnocchi. Toss with sauce or eat them like popcorn.

let's talk about salt

Whether you add a pinch of salt to your pasta dough (and I don't, as you now know), adding salt to the pasta's cooking water is the best way to season the pasta itself. You might have been told that pasta water should taste "like the sea," but this has always confounded me, probably because I grew up alongside the Atlantic. I prefer **"season your pasta water like a soup,"** a phrase I first heard from chef Evan Funke of Felix Trattoria. I encourage you to taste your cooking water to see what I mean, but if you're not one to sip boiling water, then when checking your pasta for doneness, it should taste pleasant (not bland, not sea-like), as if someone sprinkled just a hint of salt on top.

But how much salt? I'll give you a formula, but first, understand that not all salts are the same.

I always use kosher salt in the kitchen, and within that category I use Diamond Crystal, which I love for its flaky texture and mild salinity. Morton's kosher salt is more common but it's also much saltier. A grain of Morton's is coarse and compressed, and holds its shape instead of fully dissolving; a granule of Diamond Crystal looks like a crystal (surprise!), so it's lighter, easily crushed, and more forgiving. In Italy, pasta water is seasoned with sale grosso ("coarse salt"), which can

Well-Cooked Pasta in Seven Steps

1. Fill a large pot (I use an 8-quart) about two-thirds with water. (This is about 5 quarts—good for a full batch of fresh pasta or box of dried.) Bring the water to a boil. Set your pot, pan, or bowl of sauce next to the pot.

2. When the water is boiling, season it generously with kosher or other coarse salt, enough so it tastes pleasantly salty, like a soup. Let it dissolve for a few seconds. (See bottom of page 205 for my suggested amount of salt per quart.)

3. Add the pasta to the pot, shaking out any excess flour from fresh pasta to avoid gumminess, and stir for a few moments to prevent sticking.

4. Cook the pasta to your desired doneness, or just shy of your desired doneness if finishing the pasta in a sauce. Stir and taste the pasta as it cooks, not once, but several times.

   • For dried pastas, aim for what al dente means to you, and start tasting a few minutes before the instructions on the package.

   • For fresh pastas, aim for tender but not mushy. They cook quickly, generally between 2 and 5 minutes.

5. While the pasta cooks, warm your sauce.

6. Transfer the pasta to the sauce **with a spider sieve, slotted spoon, pasta basket, or tongs.** If these tools aren't an option, scoop out 1 cup (240 ml) of cooking water with a heatproof measuring cup or mug and drain the pasta in a colander over the sink—then immediately tip the pasta into the sauce (don't rinse, don't let it cool).

7. Marry pasta and sauce together—see page 252—and enjoy!

refer to kosher salt, but also sea salt, pickling salt, and rock salt—anything but table salt, the saltiest of all.

In general, **8 to 10 grams of coarse salt** (1 scant tablespoon of Diamond Crystal; about 2 teaspoons of Morton's) **for every 1 liter (quart) of water** should do the trick. I cook a full batch of fresh pasta or a 1-pound

Cooking Stuffed Pastas

A rigorous boil is preferred for most pastas, but I opt for a gentler approach when it comes to stuffed shapes. After adding the pasta, let the water return to a boil, then turn down the heat to a lively simmer—this will make bursting less likely, and also prevent cheese-filled pastas from curdling.

box of dried pasta in 5 quarts of water, give or take, so there's plenty of room to tumble and expand (no need to measure; fill an 8-quart stockpot two-thirds of the way). Ultimately, you're using about a palmful of salt, but don't let that scare you; the pasta only absorbs a fraction of it. Use whatever coarse salt you prefer; over time, adding the right amount will become muscle memory.

One more thing: **Salt the water *after* it comes to a boil and just before adding your pasta.** If you add salt at the start, it will concentrate as water evaporates, leaving you with a saltier result than intended.

storing fresh pasta

It would be reasonable to assume that because boxes of dried pasta line an entire aisle at the market that fresh pasta can—and should—be stored the same way. But **fresh pasta tastes best when it's, well, fresh.** Yes, there are exceptions—orecchiette, busiate, and garganelli hold their shape better after a few hours of drying—but in general homemade pastas left to dry for an extended period become brittle, tough, and discolored. So, what to do? I always end up in the same place: the freezer.

Freezing fresh pasta locks in its color and texture. Cook a batch of freshly cut pappardelle alongside one frozen the night before and you'll be hard-pressed to tell the difference. The freezer is my solution to scraps, leftovers, and meal prep so I always have fresh pasta on hand. It also provides a scarce commodity: peace of mind.

Say you want to host a dinner party showcasing your new pasta-making skills (fantastic!). Make and freeze the pasta in advance so all that's left to do when your guests arrive is boil and cover it in sauce.

- **Hand-formed** (cavatelli, capunti, orecchiette, busiate, etc.) and **short-cut pastas** (sorpresine, farfalle, garganelli, corzetti) can be left at room temperature, uncovered, on a semolina- or parchment-lined sheet pan for up to 5 hours. Turn occasionally for even drying.

- **Hand-cut and other long strands** (pici, tagliolini, fettuccine, tagliatelle, pappardelle) are best cooked or frozen as soon as possible to prevent them from clumping together and becoming brittle. I also recommend this for strozzapreti.

- **Stuffed pastas** can be refrigerated, uncovered, on a semolina- or parchment-lined sheet pan for up to 3 to 4 hours. Check the bottoms to make sure they're not getting sticky. Refrigerated pastas will take about 1 minute longer to cook.

- **Larger stuffed pastas** like ravioli, scarpinocc, agnolotti (but not plin), tortelloni, and caramelle can be blanched, air-dried, and refrigerated for up to 3 days (see opposite). Do not blanch egg yolk ravioli; cook these as soon as possible or refrigerate for no more than 2 or 3 hours.

- **Gnocchi** can be left at room temperature or, if it's hot or humid, refrigerated uncovered for up to 2 hours. They can also be blanched, air-dried, and refrigerated for up to 5 days.

Cooking Pastas in Broths & Soups

For stuffed pastas and shapes served in broths or soups, you can cook the pasta in broth, or parboil it in water for a minute first (if your pasta is coated in a lot of excess flour, or for denser pastas, I recommend parboiling). Season your broth or soup to your liking, add the pasta, and cook at a lively simmer, stirring often, until tender. For stuffed pastas, turn off the heat, cover, and let stand for a couple more minutes so the pasta absorbs the flavor of the broth.

LONG-TERM STORAGE

- **Hand-formed, short-cut, and small filled pastas** (cappelletti, agnolotti del plin, tortellini) can be frozen for up to 3 months. To do this, arrange the pasta in a single layer on a semolina- or parchment-lined sheet pan. Freeze uncovered until the pieces are solid, 20 to 25 minutes (set a timer if you, like me, are forgetful), then shake off any excess semolina, transfer the pasta to a freezer-safe bag, and return to the freezer.

- **Hand-cut and other long strands** should be dusted with semolina before coiling (pici), stacking (lagane and pappardelle), or bundling into nests (tagliolini, tagliatelle, fettuccine, also pappardelle). Then freeze as above.

- **Large stuffed pastas** benefit from blanching and air-drying before freezing, though you can do without if short on time. Blanching creates a protective coating that prevents the pasta from cracking when exposed to frigid air.

- Always blanch **gnocchi** before freezing—without it, frozen gnocchi risk disintegrating when cooked.

Cook frozen pasta, blanched or not, directly from the freezer—no need to thaw—and add about a minute to its cook time (for gnocchi, boil them again until they float). Let frozen hand-cut pastas sit in the boiling water for a few seconds, then stir gently to separate the strands.

Blanching & Air-Drying

This is a storage technique taught to me by Tina Prestia, a friend and pasta maker in Bologna. Use it for ravioli (except egg yolk ravioli), scarpinocc, agnolotti (not plin), tortelloni, caramelle, and gnocchi. It can also be used for some hand-formed pastas like orecchiette and strozzapreti.

Bring a large pot of water to a boil and salt it well. Keep a wire rack or a sheet pan lined with a dry dishcloth nearby. Drop your pasta into the water and stir for a moment. Cook until the pasta floats, then use a spider sieve (or drain in a colander) to transfer it to the rack or sheet pan. Arrange the pasta in a single layer and allow to air-dry, turning the pieces occasionally, until they're no longer tacky to the touch.

If using within 3 days, transfer to an airtight container and refrigerate. For long-term storage, transfer to a freezer bag; it'll keep for up to 3 months. (If you're making gnocchi, arrange them on a parchment-lined sheet pan and freeze, uncovered, until solid, about 1 hour, before transferring to a freezer bag.)

FRESH PASTA COOK TIMES, MORE OR LESS	
Style	**Approximate Cook Time** *For partially dried or frozen pasta, add 1 to 2 minutes*
Hand-formed pastas	3 to 5 minutes
Hand-cut pastas	2 to 3 minutes
Short-cut pastas	3 to 5 minutes
Stuffed pastas	2 to 4 minutes
Gnocchi	Until they float, plus 30 seconds or so

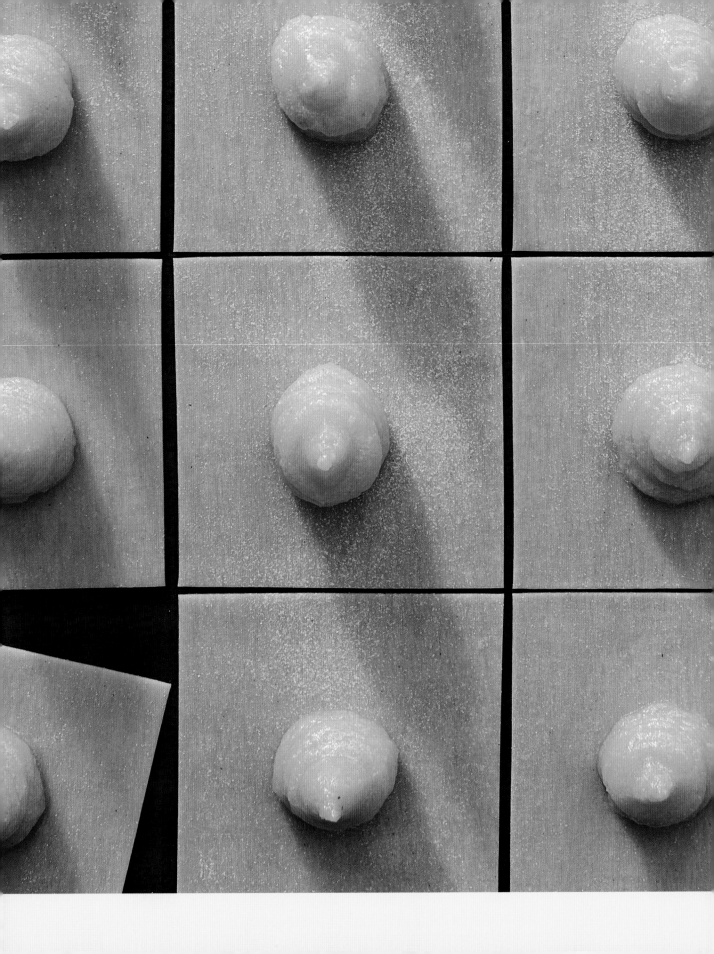

PART THREE

fillings

All kinds of pasta will satisfy and delight, but there's something particularly glorious about digging into a plate of ravioli, as if experiencing some great culinary magic trick—a hidden world of flavor suddenly unleashed.

Some of my clearest food memories revolve around stuffed pastas. At age six, there were tiny cheese ravioli gliding in a mushroom cream sauce, eaten feverishly by a marina in Sint-Maarten where I visited my grandparents every winter. At ten, there were spinach-stuffed triangles from Costco that were so good I'd eat them raw in the basement so no one would see. Then, in my twenties, there was the thrill of cutting into my first egg yolk–filled raviolo, carefully made by my husband, and the pleasure of savoring smoked ricotta tortelli with spritzes and friends shivering outside Via Carota in New York.

There's only one little hiccup: I always want more! Go to most restaurants and you'll be served four or six pieces, easily downed in a few moments and then— well, let's just say I could devour five more plates. (Having produced pasta for restaurants, I completely understand why: Pasta, especially stuffed pasta, takes time to make and people to make it.) But what if you could make the same pasta, just as delicious, at home in your sweats and enjoy as much as you pleased?

The filling recipes in this section can be used to make any of the stuffed pastas in this book, or whatever other stuffed shapes that catch your eye. Some are inspired by traditional fillings that are paired with particular shapes and sauces (or broths), which is noted where relevant. All are designed to match this book's dough quantities and, in turn, fill plenty of pasta, with occasional leftovers. Those leftovers can be frozen for a rainy day or thinned out with pasta cooking water and transformed into a quick sauce: The Black Pepper & Pecorino Filling (page 219) and the Smoky Caramelized Onion Filling (page 239) are especially good candidates for this.

Like the sauces that follow, the recipes here are organized according to their main ingredients, starting with cheese and ending with meat. You might notice that the meat filling recipes do not include pork or dairy products, two things that appear regularly in Italian stuffed pastas, particularly in Emilia-Romagna. This, again, is because I follow kosher dietary laws—no pork, no mixing of milk and meat—and while I think the recipes are delicious as they are, feel free to tailor them to your preferences.

I'll conclude by saying that, as with dough, **anything can be fashioned into a pasta filling**, not just the familiar cheeses, meats, and vegetables. So let this be a beginning; let your creativity run wild.

before we start

on flavor

One of the many wonderful things about stuffed pastas is that you'll know how they're going to taste from the start. Please tinker, adjust, and adjust again—add another spoonful of Parmesan, or a squeeze of lemon—until a filling is exactly how *you* like it.

My biggest piece of advice when it comes to flavor is to **season generously**. An extra pinch of salt, to the point where you think it might be too much, is exactly where you want to be. Remember that this little dollop of deliciousness is going to be wrapped in dough, so that extra salt will go a long way.

on texture

Most pasta fillings should have, more or less, the consistency of cake frosting. The goal (particularly for cheese and vegetable fillings) is something thick and creamy, firm yet malleable, like you can move a dollop around if you need to—or, better yet, stretch a piece of dough around it (meat-based fillings are more paste-like). Basically, fillings shouldn't be runny; runny fillings are difficult to handle, make the pasta harder to seal, and, in turn, can end up floating in the boiling water instead of in the pasta on your plate.

In practice, this means **avoid excess moisture**. Many of the recipes here call for ricotta, so opt for well-drained, full-fat varieties like the ones fresh from the deli counter or high-quality brands like Calabro (or make your own, page 61). Squeeze the water mightily out of cooked greens; cool meats and vegetables thoroughly.

On the flip side, fillings shouldn't be very dry. If you find yourself with a crumbly mixture, add an egg, a spoonful of ricotta, or a dash of heavy cream to bind it. Braise tough cuts of meat slowly and with plenty of liquid to keep them juicy; cook fish until just set to keep it tender.

HOW TO FIX A RUNNY FILLING
If you do find yourself with a too-wet filling, you can:

- **THICKEN IT:** A hard grating cheese like Parmigiano-Reggiano, Grana Padano, or Pecorino Romano can act as a thickener and absorb some of the extra water. Dry breadcrumbs are also commonly used, but add them sparingly to avoid a mealy texture.

- **DRAIN IT:** Let the filling sit in a fine-mesh sieve or colander lined with cheesecloth over a bowl in the refrigerator for a few hours or overnight.

- **CHILL IT:** Some fillings are softer and more difficult to work with when they're warm or even at room temperature, so try popping them in the fridge or freezer to firm up. This is especially helpful when making small pastas and stuffed gnocchi.

- **BIND IT:** Adding an egg won't thicken a filling, but it *will* bind it, which means that when the pasta cooks, the filling is more likely to hold together instead of leak.

- **USE IT, SPARINGLY:** If nothing else seems to work, use it anyway, but stick with larger shapes, which are more forgiving, and start with a small spoonful, adding more as you feel comfortable.

equipment

There are two pieces of equipment you'll see mentioned time and again: a **food processor** and a **piping bag**. Neither are necessary, but both are helpful. A food processor will whip grainy ricotta into silk and roasted squash into velvet. It'll also make filling preparation quicker and easier, effortlessly chopping greens, meats, and vegetables with just a few pulses. But if you don't have one, a few everyday kitchen tools and a mixing bowl will usually get the job done.

When making large batches of stuffed pasta or venturing into smaller and more intricate shapes, a piping bag will provide precision, and with precision comes speed. I never encourage rushing through pasta making; I will say, though, that working at a steady pace can be helpful so that the dough is less likely to dry out before you can seal it. (Piping also makes for more uniform pasta, which I'll admit pleases the perfectionist in me.) Of course, you won't find many (any?) Italian nonne using a piping bag. A bowl and a couple of spoons are all you really need.

storage

All fillings can be made a day ahead, and some—especially meat-based—are better the next day since time brings flavors together. Keep them refrigerated in an airtight container or sealed piping bag (if the tip is cut, cover the opening with some kitchen tape) for up to 3 days, though always taste before reusing. Fillings with little or no cheese freeze well for up to 3 months; use cheese fillings as soon as possible.

pairing fillings & sauces

Ninety percent of the time, the star of a filled pasta dish is, you guessed it, the filling. Which means one hundred percent of the time you can't go wrong with covering it in some variation of melted butter and grated cheese, a combination both delicious and delicate enough not to overshadow what's inside.

Unsurprisingly, most traditional filling–sauce combinations are a product of place, seasonality, and resourcefulness. Tortellini, filled with pork, mortadella, prosciutto, and Parmigiano-Reggiano, then served in meat broth, represent the best of Bologna in a single bite. Pansotti, pot-bellied ravioli from Liguria, filled with local greens and dressed in the area's famous walnut sauce (page 279), tell a similar story. Cappellacci (or tortelli) di zucca, tortelloni lookalikes from Lombardy, celebrate the region's exceptional pumpkin varieties and a favorite local condiment, butter and sage. And Piedmontese agnolotti del plin were born from leftover roasts, the uneaten meat and vegetables becoming a flavorful filling and the braising liquid its sauce.

Today there is far more flexibility, and most ingredients are available anywhere, anytime. But one rule, according to pasta experts Oretta Zanini De Vita and Maureen B. Fant, remains: "What goes inside doesn't go outside." I take this to mean that **filling and sauce should complement, not compete, with each other**. Light cheeses, greens, and potatoes are a blank canvas for bold ragùs, tomato sauces, and pestos; rich, meaty mushrooms shine on their own so a simple butter sauce will do. Squash can go either way—it's traditional in Bologna to serve it with butter and sage, and also as a slightly sweet counterpoint to a savory ragù. To be clear, I've seen pasta filled with meat and served with meat sauce in Tuscany, and fish ravioli served with seafood in Liguria. So although I've provided pairing recommendations with each recipe, trust your gut. And when in doubt, butter.

One more thought here: Fillings taste very much the same whether encased in squares, triangles, half-moons, or little hats. But I do find that, sometimes, pairing a certain filling with a certain shape (or size) can make for a marginally better eating experience. I'm primarily referring to fillings like the Alpine Cheese Fondue Filling on page 225 and the Braised Beef & Caramelized Cabbage Filling on page 243. Both are traditionally paired with agnolotti del plin, and for good reason: The strong flavors work well in a smaller format, a little "ooh!" moment fully enjoyed in one bite. Similarly, I find subtler fillings like the Whipped Ricotta Filling on page 214 and Any-Greens Filling on page 226 shine brighter in larger quantities, so I'll usually opt for something like ravioli.

MAKES ABOUT 2 CUPS
(500 GRAMS)
Active time: 10 minutes
Total time: 10 minutes

USE IT WITH
Agnolotti (117)
Caramelle (182)
"Classic" Ravioli (152)
Tortelloni (172)

PAIR IT WITH
All-Purpose Tomato Sauce (256)
Basil Pesto (270)
Butter & Sage Sauce (293)
Golden Saffron Sauce (301)

whipped ricotta filling

16 ounces (450 grams) **full-fat ricotta**, drained if needed (or make your own, page 61)

2 ounces (55 grams) finely grated **Parmigiano-Reggiano**, plus more to taste

Kosher salt and freshly ground black pepper

The push of a button is all you need to transform often-grainy ricotta into a fluffy, frosting-like cloud of cheese. Use it as is, or as a foundation for other flavors: A little lemon zest, a dusting of fresh nutmeg, or some finely chopped herbs are always a good idea. If you don't have a food processor, a hand mixer or a whisk and some elbow grease will work, too. Spread the leftovers on toast with honey and thyme, or toss them in a mixing bowl with hot pasta, a squeeze of lemon, and some fresh basil for a light lunch.

Add the cheeses and a generous pinch of salt and pepper to the bowl of a food processor. Pulse until very smooth, 30 to 60 seconds, scraping down the side of the bowl as needed.

Adjust seasoning to taste—don't be shy with the salt; it'll bring out the ricotta's mild sweetness. Transfer the filling to a bowl or piping bag and refrigerate until ready to use.

A NOTE ABOUT RICOTTA: If your ricotta is very loose, drain off any liquid, then spread the cheese on a paper towel–lined plate to absorb some of the excess moisture. (Alternatively, you can drain it in a sieve over a bowl for a few hours or overnight in the refrigerator.) If it's dry and crumbly, add a splash of heavy cream or a spoonful of mascarpone to loosen it up. Apply these methods as needed to any filling recipe that calls for a significant amount of ricotta.

Any-Greens
Filling (226)

Summer Corn & Basil
Filling (230)

Mushroom, Garlic & Thyme
Filling (231)

*Winter Squash & Brown
Butter Filling (234)*

Whipped Ricotta Filling (214)

*Spinach & Ricotta
Filling (218)*

MAKES ABOUT 2 CUPS
(515 GRAMS)

Active time: 15 minutes
Total time: 15 minutes

USE IT WITH
Caramelle (182)
Double-Stuffed Ravioli (162)
Tortelloni (172)

PAIR IT WITH
All-Purpose Tomato Sauce (256)
Butter & Sage Sauce (293)
Sage & Hazelnut Pesto (278)

four-cheese filling

10 ounces (300 grams) **full-fat ricotta**, drained if needed (or make your own, page 61)

4 ounces (115 grams) **fresh mozzarella**, cut into ½-inch cubes

2 ounces (55 grams) grated **Fontina**

1½ ounces (45 grams) finely grated **Parmigiano-Reggiano**

Kosher salt and freshly ground black pepper

When I have four cheeses to choose from, these are the ones I reach for most.

Add the cheeses and a generous pinch of salt and pepper to the bowl of a food processor. Pulse until smooth, 30 to 60 seconds, scraping down the side of the bowl as needed. Adjust seasoning to taste. Transfer the filling to a bowl or piping bag and refrigerate until ready to use.

MAKES ABOUT 2 CUPS
(500 GRAMS)

Active time: 20 minutes
Total time: 30 minutes

USE IT WITH
Cappelletti (168)
"Classic" Ravioli (152)
Egg Yolk Ravioli (159)

PAIR IT WITH
All-Purpose Tomato Sauce (256)
Butter & Sage Sauce (293)
Tomato-Cream Sauce (260)

spinach & ricotta filling

9 ounces (255 grams) **fresh baby or mature spinach**

Kosher salt and freshly ground black pepper

12 ounces (340 grams) **full-fat ricotta**, drained if needed (or make your own, page 61)

1½ ounces (45 grams) finely grated **Parmigiano-Reggiano**

Whole nutmeg (optional)

Spinach and ricotta are a classic combination for good reason, and a heavy dose of Parmigiano-Reggiano and fresh nutmeg makes these simple flavors complex.

Sauté, blanch, or steam the spinach until vibrant and wilted. Season to taste with salt and pepper. Transfer to a clean, tightly woven dishcloth and let cool, then wring out as much moisture as possible. Either finely chop the spinach and mix in a bowl with the cheeses, or add everything to a food processor and pulse in short bursts until the spinach is chopped but not puréed. Season generously with salt, pepper, and, if you'd like, freshly grated nutmeg. Transfer the filling to a bowl or piping bag and refrigerate until ready to use.

MAKES ABOUT 2 CUPS
(470 GRAMS)
Active time: 15 minutes
Total time: 15 minutes

USE IT WITH
Caramelle (182)
Egg Yolk Ravioli (159)
Tortelloni (172)

PAIR IT WITH
Brown Butter (291)
Butter & Sage Sauce (293)
Sage & Hazelnut Pesto (278)
The Meatiest Meatless Ragù (317)

black pepper & pecorino filling

1½ teaspoons **whole black peppercorns or freshly ground black pepper,** plus more to taste

12 ounces (340 grams) **full-fat ricotta,** drained if needed (or make your own, page 61)

4½ ounces (125 grams) finely grated **Pecorino Romano**

Kosher salt

As with traditional cacio e pepe, toasting whole peppercorns makes the flavors of this simple combination come alive. Pair the filling with egg yolk ravioli (page 159) and toss with butter and rendered guanciale for a show-stopping take on carbonara.

In a small dry skillet over medium heat, add the peppercorns and cook, shaking the pan often, until fragrant, about 3 minutes. Transfer to a spice grinder or mortar and pestle and crush until semi-fine.

Combine the pepper, ricotta, and Pecorino in the bowl of a food processor or mixing bowl. Pulse or mix vigorously until smooth and creamy. Add more Pecorino and/or pepper if you'd like; season to taste with salt.

Transfer the filling to a bowl or piping bag and refrigerate until ready to use.

MAKES ABOUT 2 CUPS
(475 GRAMS)
Active time: 15 minutes
Total time: 15 minutes

USE IT WITH
"Classic" Ravioli (152)
Scarpinocc (166)

PAIR IT WITH
All-Purpose Tomato Sauce (256)
No-Cook Tomato & Basil Sauce (259)

honeymoon cheese & herb filling

8 ounces (225 grams) **fresh mozzarella**, cut into ½-inch cubes

5¼ ounces (150 grams) grated **caciotta or Monterey Jack cheese**

1½ ounces (45 grams) finely grated **Parmigiano-Reggiano**

Fresh marjoram leaves to taste

Kosher salt and freshly ground black pepper

1 large **egg** and 1 large **egg yolk**, lightly beaten together

The first meal my husband and I shared while honeymooning in Italy was a perfect plate of cheese ravioli in tomato sauce. Only a couple of hours earlier we'd touched down in Naples and drove to nearby Sorrento, where we unloaded our luggage under the speckled shadows of fragrant orange trees. Lunch was served overlooking the Bay of Naples, its glittering waves nodding toward the island of Capri, and at that moment, we couldn't have asked for anything more.

This recipe is pieced together from memory and taste. After falling down a deep internet rabbit hole, I discovered that the ravioli we enjoyed that afternoon were inspired by ravioli Capresi, pasta parcels from Capri filled with caciotta, a local semi-soft cheese, its closest American relative is Monterey Jack, which I suggest here—although not quite the table cheese of Capri, it's a little something unexpected that makes this filling melt in your mouth.

Ravioli Capresi are traditionally made with a soft wheat and water dough (page 37) and served in a light tomato sauce with plenty of good extra-virgin olive oil. Try the No-Cook Tomato & Basil Sauce (page 259) or the fresh tomato version of the All-Purpose Tomato Sauce (page 256) to bring the spirit of the island into your own home.

Add the cheeses and a few marjoram leaves to the bowl of a food processor and pulse until well combined. Season to taste with salt and pepper, adding more marjoram if you'd like. Transfer to a mixing bowl and fold in the egg, egg yolk, and another pinch of salt. (You can also finely chop the mozzarella and marjoram and mix everything together in a bowl.)

The texture of this filling is a little different than usual, almost doughlike— not to worry, the cheeses will melt together when cooked. Keep the filling in the bowl or transfer it to a piping bag; if chilling overnight, allow the filling to soften at room temperature for 30 minutes before use.

Note: Marjoram is an herb you'll come across often in Italian cooking. It's similar to oregano, aromatic with hints of citrus and pine, and, like oregano, a little can go a long way. If you can't find it, use fresh (not dried) oregano or, in a pinch, sage.

MAKES ABOUT 2 CUPS
(450 GRAMS)

Active time: 20 minutes
Total time: 1 hour 15 minutes

USE IT WITH

Agnolotti del Plin (177)
Cappelletti (168)
"Classic" Ravioli (152)
Scarpinocc (166)

PAIR IT WITH

Braised Onion Ragù (289)
Parmesan Broth (342)
Wild Mushroom Sauce (285)
Butter & Sage Sauce (293) +
Balsamic Reduction (356)

roasted garlic & rosemary filling

2 large **garlic heads**, the tops cut off crosswise to expose the cloves

Extra-virgin olive oil

Kosher salt and freshly ground black pepper

16 ounces (450 grams) **full-fat ricotta**, drained if needed (or make your own, page 61)

1½ teaspoons minced **fresh rosemary** (from about 1 large sprig), or to taste

Sticky-sweet roasted garlic welcomes rosemary's wintry notes in this filling that's just as satisfying to eat as it is simple to make. Enjoy it in the colder months—it pairs beautifully with broths and soups—and save any leftovers for your next snack-time dip.

Heat the oven to 400°F/205°C. Place the garlic cut sides up on individual pieces of aluminum foil. Drizzle with olive oil and season with salt and pepper, then wrap tightly in the foil. Place directly on the middle oven rack (or on a baking sheet on the rack). Roast until tender and caramelized, about 45 minutes.

When the garlic is cool enough to handle, squeeze the softened cloves into a small bowl and mash into a paste.

Combine the garlic, ricotta, rosemary, and a generous pinch of salt and pepper in the bowl of a food processor or mixing bowl. Pulse in short bursts or mix vigorously until creamy and well combined. Adjust seasoning to taste—don't be shy with the pepper.

Transfer the filling to a bowl or piping bag and refrigerate until ready to use.

Roasted Garlic & Rosemary Spinach Tortelloni with Butter, Sage, and Balsamic Reduction

223

USE IT WITH
Agnolotti del Plin (177)
Cappelletti (168)
Scarpinocc (166)
Tortelloni (172)

PAIR IT WITH
Butter & Sage Sauce (293)
Braised Onion Ragù (289)
Parmesan Broth (342)
Sage & Hazelnut Pesto (278)

alpine cheese fondue filling

1 cup (240 ml) **heavy cream**

7 ounces (200 grams) rind-free melty cheese like **Fontina or Taleggio**, cut into small cubes and at room temperature

4 tablespoons (55 grams) cold **unsalted butter**, cut into pieces

1 large **egg yolk**

Kosher salt and freshly ground black pepper

Fonduta—oozy, melty cheese sauce thickened with egg yolks—is a hallmark of Italian Alpine cooking. The cheeses can vary, from Fontina (most common) to Taleggio to Parmigiano-Reggiano, but the result always hits the spot. Like its more familiar Swiss cousin, fonduta is often served with bread, potatoes, and other vegetables for dipping. But head to Piedmont and you'll find this luscious mixture tucked into pasta. It usually fills the bellies of little pinched agnolotti del plin, and the dish is finished with shaved truffles.

Don't be alarmed by the strength of the cheeses here—their aromas are far more pungent than their flavors. And if you can't find Fontina or Taleggio, any Alpine variety like Gruyère or Emmental will work, too. It's especially important to chill this mixture before using so it's thick and workable (if you have the time, chill it overnight and let it soften at room temperature for 30 minutes prior to use). When cooking the pasta, keep it at a gentle simmer; once plated, let it cool for a moment to let the cheese settle before digging in.

In a small saucepan, warm the cream over medium heat, stirring often with a whisk or spatula to make sure it doesn't scorch. When the cream starts to bubble, turn down the heat and cook at a bare simmer, stirring often, until thickened and reduced by almost half, about 7 minutes.

Turn the heat down to its lowest setting and whisk in the cheese, a little at a time, until fully melted. The mixture should be thick and glossy, like cake frosting. Take the pot off the heat and let cool for 5 minutes.

Add the butter and egg yolk. Return the pot to low heat and whisk constantly until the butter melts and the mixture is very thick. Season to taste—you won't need much salt, but remember you want the filling to be a *little* saltier than you'd feel comfortable eating on its own.

Let the mixture cool for 10 minutes, then transfer the filling to a bowl or piping bag and refrigerate until chilled, at least 2 hours. If holding overnight, let the filling soften at room temperature for about 30 minutes before using.

MAKES ABOUT 2 CUPS
(475 GRAMS)
Active time: 35 minutes
Total time: 35 minutes, plus chilling

USE IT WITH
Agnolotti (177)
Cappelletti (168)
"Classic" Ravioli (152)
Double-Stuffed Ravioli (162)
Tortelloni (172)

PAIR IT WITH
All-Purpose Tomato Sauce (256)
Butter & Sage Sauce (293)
Ligurian Walnut Sauce (279)
The Meatiest Meatless Ragù (317)
Tomato-Cream Sauce (260)

any-greens filling

- 1.1 pounds (500 grams) **leafy greens** like kale, chard, spinach, mustard, and/or dandelion greens

- 2 tablespoons (30 ml) **extra-virgin olive oil** or unsalted butter

- 1 small **shallot**, minced

- 2 **garlic cloves**, minced

- **Kosher salt and freshly ground black pepper**

- 1½ ounces (45 grams) finely grated **Parmigiano-Reggiano**

- 1½ ounces (45 grams) **mascarpone**

- 5 ounces (150 grams; 1 large ball) **fresh mozzarella**, cut into ½-inch cubes

- **Whole nutmeg**

I reach for this flexible filling when I want to take advantage of winter's hearty greens. It's also my solution to the wilting spinach in the crisper, or the leftover beet, carrot, or radish greens I might have from last week's dinner prep. Use it to fill any pasta; spread it between layers of lasagne; or spoon it into oversized shells, cover with cheese and tomato sauce, and bake until golden and bubbling.

Wash and roughly chop the greens; if using chard, kale, or mustard greens, remove the ribs and reserve for another use. Line a sheet pan with a clean dishcloth and keep it nearby.

In a Dutch oven or large pot with a lid, warm the oil over medium heat. Add the shallot, garlic, and a pinch of salt and pepper. Cook, stirring occasionally, until softened and fragrant, 3 minutes.

Reduce the heat to medium-low. Add half of the greens and stir to combine with the aromatics. Add a splash of water, cover, and cook for 2 minutes. Uncover the pot and stir until wilted, then press them down and add the rest of the greens, along with a generous pinch of salt and pepper. Stir to combine as best you can. Pour in another splash of water and cover the pot. Cook, uncovering occasionally to stir, until completely wilted, about 5 minutes more.

Drain the greens in a colander, pressing out as much liquid as possible with a flexible spatula, and let cool. Transfer to the dishcloth and wring out as much of the remaining moisture as you can.

Combine the greens and cheeses in the bowl of a food processor. Pulse until finely chopped but not puréed. Season to taste with salt, pepper, and freshly grated nutmeg.

Transfer the filling to a bowl or piping bag and refrigerate until chilled, about 30 minutes, or until ready to use.

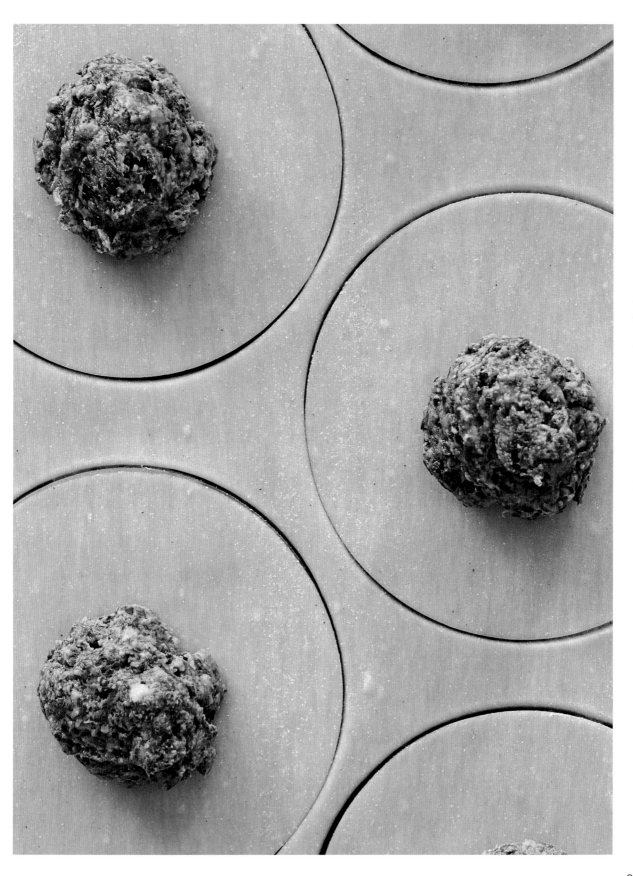

*Black Pepper & Pecorino and Asparagus & Spring Pea
Double-Stuffed Ravioli with a Simple Butter Sauce*

USE IT WITH
Agnolotti (177)
Double-Stuffed Ravioli (162)
Egg Yolk Ravioli (159)
Tortelloni (172)

PAIR IT WITH
Lemon-Chive Butter (297)
Simple Butter Sauce (290)
Slow-Roasted Salmon & Crème
fraîche Sauce with Peas (328)
Wild Mushroom Sauce (285)

asparagus & spring pea filling with mint

Kosher salt

1 pound (450 grams) **fresh asparagus**

1 cup (130 grams) **fresh or frozen peas**

4 ounces (115 grams) **mascarpone** (I prefer a very thick variety like BelGioioso or the one from Trader Joe's)

½ ounce (15 grams) finely grated **Parmigiano-Reggiano**

Grated zest of ½ **lemon**

¼ cup (a small bunch) **fresh mint leaves**, or to taste

Freshly ground black pepper

A garden of green—asparagus, fresh peas, fava beans, garlic scapes—at the grocery store is usually my cue that spring has arrived. This filling puts the season's most common vegetables to good use, and a quick blanch will keep their vibrant color intact. The result is sweet and vegetal, made creamy by just enough cheese to thicken and hold it together.

Bring a medium pot of water to a boil and season generously with salt. Remove the tough ends from the asparagus, then add them to the pot and cook for 1 minute. Add the peas and cook 2 minutes more, or until vibrant and tender. Immediately drain the vegetables in a colander and rinse with cold water to stop the cooking (alternatively, plunge into a bowl of ice water).

Snap the asparagus spears in half into a high-speed blender. Add the peas, mascarpone, Parmigiano-Reggiano, lemon zest, mint, and a generous pinch of salt and pepper. Purée until smooth, adding a *tiny* splash of water to get the motor running if needed. (Alternatively, spread the vegetables on a paper towel–lined sheet pan and thoroughly pat dry. Add everything to the bowl of a food processor and pulse until smooth—the result will be coarser in texture but still delicious.) Season to taste with salt and pepper.

Transfer the filling to a bowl or piping bag and chill thoroughly before use—it will thicken as it cools.

MAKE IT VEGAN
Swap out the mascarpone for dairy-free cream cheese, omit the Parmigiano-Reggiano.

MAKES ABOUT 2 CUPS
(475 GRAMS)
Active time: 30 minutes
Total time: 45 minutes, plus chilling

USE IT WITH
Agnolotti (177)
Agnolotti del Plin (177)
"Classic" Ravioli (152)
Cappelletti (168)
Tortelloni (172)
Caramelle (182)

PAIR IT WITH
Basil Pesto (270)
Brown Butter (291)
Corn Broth (341)
Parmesan Broth (342)
Simple Butter Sauce (290)

summer corn & basil filling

4 tablespoons (55 grams)
unsalted butter

12 ounces (340 grams) **fresh or
frozen and defrosted sweet
corn kernels**, from about 4
large ears

**Kosher salt and freshly ground
black pepper**

3 ounces (80 grams) **mascarpone**
(I prefer a very thick variety
like BelGioioso or the one from
Trader Joe's)

1½ ounces (42 grams) finely
grated **Parmigiano-Reggiano**

¼ cup (60 ml) **heavy cream**

½ cup (10 grams) **fresh basil**
leaves

Corn-stuffed pasta is always on my summer eating agenda, and few things scream Americana more than this sweet and starchy vegetable. Travel to Europe, though, and you'll be hard-pressed to find a freshly picked ear of corn, charred on the grill and slathered in butter—instead, you'll have to head to the canned foods aisle. It's perhaps less surprising, then, that many of my Italian pasta-making friends shudder at the thought of corn ravioli, and that the extent of sweet corn's appearance in Italian cooking is relegated to picnic dishes like pasta fredda and insalata di riso, both served cold. (Palermo is an exception, where boiled corn on the cob is a popular street food snack.)

Still, I like to think that corn pasta embodies the spirit of Italian cooking, rooted in a sense of place, the seasons, and making something delicious with what you have. So if you, like me, are a lover of corn—whether it's fresh ears at the height of summer or frozen kernels in the dead of winter—this filling's for you. And if you do opt for fresh corn, don't forget to save the cobs to make corn broth.

In a large sauté pan or skillet, melt the butter over medium heat, then continue to stir until the butter smells nutty and starts to brown, about 2 minutes. Add the corn and season generously with salt and pepper. Cook, stirring occasionally, until tender, 5 minutes. Remove from the heat and let cool completely.

Combine the cooled corn, mascarpone, Parmigiano-Reggiano, and cream in the bowl of a food processor. Run the machine until the mixture is smooth and creamy, about 1 minute, scraping down the side of the bowl as needed. Season to taste. Add the basil and pulse in short bursts until chopped and evenly distributed. (Alternatively, add everything except the basil to a high-speed blender, purée until smooth, and transfer to a bowl. Finely chop the basil and fold it into the corn mixture.)

Transfer the filling to a bowl or piping bag and refrigerate until chilled, at least 30 minutes. If chilling overnight, let the filling soften at room temperature for about 30 minutes before use.

MAKES ABOUT 2 CUPS
(500 GRAMS)
Active time: 30 minutes
Total time: 40 minutes, plus chilling

USE IT WITH
Cappelletti (168)
"Classic" Ravioli (152)
Stuffed Gnocchi (196)
Tortelloni (172)

PAIR IT WITH
Butter & Sage Sauce (293)
Four-Cheese Sauce (306)
Parmesan Broth (342)
Simple Butter Sauce (290)

mushroom, garlic & thyme filling

3 tablespoons (45 grams) **unsalted butter**

1 small **shallot**, finely chopped

1½ pounds (680 grams) **fresh mushrooms** like cremini, or a variety of wild mushrooms, cleaned and sliced

Kosher salt and freshly ground black pepper

6 **garlic cloves**, minced

¼ cup (60 ml) **dry vermouth, Madeira, sherry, or white wine** (optional)

2 teaspoons stripped **fresh thyme**

4 ounces (115 grams) **full-fat ricotta**

1¾ ounces (50 grams) finely grated **Parmigiano-Reggiano**

1 ounce (30 grams) **mascarpone**

This filling is reminiscent of French mushroom duxelles, usually wrapped between layers of pastry and prosciutto in beef Wellington, but equally delicious tossed with pasta, spread on toasted bread, or folded into potatoes. Use it for any stuffed shape; the paste-like texture works especially well with more intricate pastas like tortelloni, as well as stuffed gnocchi.

In a Dutch oven or large sauté pan, melt the butter over medium heat. Add the shallot and cook until softened, about 3 minutes. Increase the heat to medium-high. Stir in the mushrooms and cook, stirring occasionally, until they release their juices and begin to brown, 12 to 15 minutes. Season to taste with salt and pepper.

Stir in the garlic and cook until fragrant, 30 seconds. Pour in the alcohol, if using, and reduce it completely, scraping up any browned bits from the bottom of the pan. Add the thyme and stir to combine. Turn off the heat and let cool completely.

Combine the mushrooms, ricotta, Parmigiano-Reggiano, and mascarpone in the bowl of a food processor. Pulse in short bursts until the mushrooms are finely chopped but the mixture still has some texture. (Alternatively, finely chop the mushrooms and mix the ingredients together in a bowl.) Adjust the seasoning to taste.

Transfer the filling to a bowl or piping bag and refrigerate until chilled, about 30 minutes, or until ready to use.

MAKES ABOUT 2 CUPS
(500 GRAMS)
Active time: 30 minutes
*Total time: 1 hour 10 minutes, plus
chilling*

USE IT WITH
Agnolotti del Plin (177)
Cappelletti (168)
"Classic" Ravioli (152)
Scarpinocc (166)

PAIR IT WITH
All-Purpose Tomato Sauce (256)
Butter & Sage Sauce (293)
Braised Onion Ragù (289)
Parmesan Broth (342)
The Meatiest Meatless Ragù (317)
Wild Mushroom Sauce (285)

mashed potato & chive filling

1 pound (450 grams; about 2 large) **russet or Yukon Gold potatoes**, peeled and quartered

Kosher salt

¼ cup (60 ml) **heavy cream**

2 tablespoons (30 grams) **unsalted butter**

1 tablespoon (15 grams) **crème fraîche or sour cream**, plus more to taste

2 **garlic cloves**, minced

Freshly ground black pepper

1¼ ounces (35 grams) finely grated **Parmigiano-Reggiano**

1½ tablespoons minced **fresh chives**

MAKE IT VEGAN

*Swap the cream, butter,
and crème fraîche/sour cream
for dairy-free alternatives and
omit the cheese.*

Sometimes the only thing that'll make a bad day better are carbs wrapped in more carbs. Potato-stuffed pasta is a comfort across Italy: Start in the north and you're greeted by Ligurian potato, cheese, and mint-filled half-moons called turle. Head to Tuscany and you might dine on potato-packed tortelli di Mugello that are dressed in a rich wild boar, rabbit, or mushroom sauce. Stop all the way down south, in Sardinia, and you're in for one of the region's biggest treats, culurgiones: zipper-pleated potato, mint, and Pecorino-filled dumplings bathed in tomato sauce. This recipe pays homage to them all and is also rooted in my Eastern European and American heritages, with a hint of tang from crème fraîche and a mild garlicky finish from chives.

Add the potatoes to a pot and cover with an inch or two of cold water. Season generously with kosher salt and bring to a boil. Cook at a rapid simmer until tender and easily pierced with a knife, 10 to 15 minutes.

While the potatoes cook, combine the cream, butter, crème fraîche, garlic, and a generous amount of black pepper in a small saucepan. Warm over medium-low heat, stirring often; when the cream starts to bubble, remove from the heat. Let the mixture stand for 10 minutes, or until the potatoes are ready.

Drain the potatoes thoroughly. While they're still warm, pass them through a ricer into a heatproof bowl or mash with a potato masher or fork. Fold in the cream mixture and Parmigiano-Reggiano and mix until well combined. Season to taste with salt and lots of black pepper, and add a touch more crème fraîche if you'd like. Stir in the chives.

Transfer the filling to a piping bag or keep it in the bowl. Use warm or at room temperature, or refrigerate in an airtight container for up to 2 days and let soften at room temperature for 30 minutes before use.

USE IT WITH

Agnolotti (177)
Cappelletti (168)
Caramelle (182)
"Classic" Ravioli (152)

PAIR IT WITH

All-Purpose Tomato Sauce (256)
Basil Pesto (270)
Butter & Sage Sauce (293)
Golden Saffron Sauce (301)
Tomato & Almond Pesto (274)

eggplant & burrata filling

1½ pounds (680 grams) **globe, Italian, or Japanese eggplants**

3 tablespoons (45 ml) **extra-virgin olive oil**

Kosher salt and freshly ground black pepper

4 **garlic cloves**, unpeeled

4½ ounces (125 grams) **burrata**

½ packed cup (10 grams) **fresh basil** leaves

Smoky and sweet, eggplant is summertime's unsung hero. Here it's roasted until deeply caramelized and tender, then whipped with burrata and basil for a fresh, almost tangy finish. The combination is an ode to Sicily, where this vegetable gets its due—there, it's often paired with basil, too, as well as tomatoes and fresh cheeses.

Heat the oven to 450°F/230°C. Line a sheet pan with parchment paper.

Use a vegetable peeler to peel away a few strips of skin from the eggplants so you're left with a zebralike pattern, then cut them into 1-inch pieces.

Toss the eggplant with the oil and season generously with salt and pepper. Transfer to the sheet pan and nestle the unpeeled garlic among the pieces.

Roast the eggplant until tender and caramelized, 30 to 35 minutes, stirring halfway through.

Let the eggplant cool completely; peel the garlic. Transfer both to the bowl of a food processor. Add the burrata and basil and pulse until smooth. Adjust seasoning to taste.

Transfer the filling to a bowl or piping bag and chill thoroughly before use.

MAKES ABOUT 2 CUPS
(500 GRAMS)
Active time: 30 minutes
Total time: 1 hour 15 minutes, plus chilling

USE IT WITH
Agnolotti (177)
Caramelle (182)
"Classic" Ravioli (152)
Tortelloni (172)

PAIR IT WITH
Butter & Sage Sauce (293)
Brown Butter (291)
Four-Cheese Sauce (306)
Golden Saffron Sauce (301)
Sage & Hazelnut Pesto (278)
The Meatiest Meatless Ragù (317)

winter squash & brown butter filling

2 pounds (900 grams) **sweet winter squash** like honeynut, butternut, or kabocha

1 tablespoon (15 ml) **extra-virgin olive oil**

Kosher salt and freshly ground black pepper

4 tablespoons (55 grams) **unsalted butter**

2 ounces (55 grams) finely grated **Parmigiano-Reggiano**

Whole nutmeg

Pasta stuffed with squash—known as tortelli di zucca, or cappellacci di zucca—is a staple in northwest Italy, particularly in the area between the city of Mantova in Lombardy and Ferrara in Emilia-Romagna. The recipe varies from town to town, but the filling usually consists of firm-fleshed local pumpkin, Parmigiano-Reggiano, almondy amaretti biscuits, and mostarda di frutta (candied fruit preserved in a mustard-flavored syrup). This recipe is a little different, but the balance between savory and sweet is key: Pair it with butter, sage, and a drizzle of Balsamic Reduction (page 356), or try it with something meaty like Bolognese (page 312). If you happen to have amaretti on hand, crush 1 ounce (about four) of them in a food processor or by hand, then add most to the filling and reserve some crunchy crumbs for garnishing.

Heat the oven to 400°F/205°C.

PREPARE THE SQUASH   If using small honeynut squashes, trim the stems, cut them in half lengthwise, and scoop out the seeds. If using butternut, cut it in half crosswise (where the neck meets the base), then peel, deseed, and cut it into 1-inch cubes. If using kabocha, cut off the stem, then (carefully) halve it north to south and scoop out the seeds. Cut each half into four or five wedges.

Coat the squash with oil, season with salt and pepper, and arrange the pieces on a parchment-lined sheet pan. Roast, flipping halfway through, until very tender and easily pierced with a knife, about 35 minutes for butternut and 45 minutes for honeynut and kabocha. You're looking for the squash to be a little overcooked so it'll purée nicely.

234

BROWN THE BUTTER While the squash roasts, cook the butter in a small saucepan over medium heat, stirring constantly, until the milk solids separate, froth, and begin to turn golden, 5 to 7 minutes. Remove from the heat and continue to stir until the butter deepens to an amber color, 1 to 2 minutes. Transfer to a bowl and set aside.

When the squash is cool, discard any skin and transfer the flesh to the bowl of a food processor. Drizzle in the brown butter and pulse until very smooth and creamy, about 1 minute. (Alternatively, mash the squash with a potato masher or fork and mix the ingredients together in a bowl.) Add the Parmigiano-Reggiano and a generous grating of nutmeg and pulse again to combine. Season to taste.

Transfer the filling to a bowl or piping bag and refrigerate until chilled, about 30 minutes, or until ready to use.

MAKES ABOUT 2 CUPS
(500 GRAMS)
Active time: 25 minutes
Total time: 1 hour 10 minutes, plus chilling

USE IT WITH
Agnolotti del Plin (177)
Cappelletti (168)

PAIR IT WITH
Braising Liquid (recipe follows)
Butter & Sage Sauce (293)

braised shallot & grana padano filling

1 pound (450 grams; 8 to 10 medium) **shallots**

2 tablespoons (30 grams) **unsalted butter**

Kosher salt

¾ cup (180 ml) **dry vermouth**

1 cup (240 ml) **vegetable stock**, plus more as needed

1 large **Grana Padano** cheese rind

5 sprigs **fresh thyme**

2½ ounces (70 grams) finely grated **Grana Padano**

⅓ cup (80 grams) **full-fat ricotta**

A squeeze of **lemon juice**

Freshly ground black pepper

¼ cup (60 ml) **heavy cream**, for serving

4 tablespoons (55 grams) cold **unsalted butter**, for serving

Like so many of my favorite dishes, this one grew out of a craving. I was looking to create a vegetarian-friendly version of agnolotti del plin, which are typically filled with meat. I searched my kitchen and found (a lot of) shallots and a wedge of Grana Padano, a milder, sweeter alternative to Parmigiano-Reggiano that's stocked in most Italian households. I wondered if roasting the delicate alliums in a flavorful liquid, then showering them in a snowy mountain of cheese might be just as special as the traditional version. To me, the answer is yes, but you decide for yourself. It's a recipe I first shared years ago, and it's since become one of my most popular.

Heat the oven to 325°F/165°C.

Halve the shallots lengthwise and peel. Trim the hairy roots, but leave the base intact to keep the halves together. In a shallow Dutch oven or medium sauté pan, melt the 2 tablespoons butter over medium-high heat. Add the shallots, cut sides down, and sprinkle with salt. Cook until they begin to caramelize at the edges, 3 to 5 minutes. Turn down the heat if the butter starts to brown too quickly.

Pour in the vermouth, scraping up any browned bits from the bottom of the pan, and simmer until reduced by half, 3 minutes. If you're not using an ovenproof pan, transfer the shallots and remaining liquid to a baking dish that fits them snugly.

Add the stock, cheese rind, thyme, and a generous pinch of salt. Cover and braise in the oven until the shallots are very tender, about 45 minutes. Let cool completely. Strain and reserve the braising liquid—you should be left with about 1 cup (240 ml).

Pat the shallots dry, then roughly chop, removing any tough outer layers. Transfer to the bowl of a food processor and pulse until finely chopped. Add the Grana Padano and ricotta and pulse again until well combined. Adjust seasoning to taste with salt, pepper, and a squeeze of lemon juice.

Transfer the filling to a bowl or piping bag and refrigerate until chilled, at least 30 minutes, or until ready to use.

TO SERVE   Bring the braising liquid to a simmer over medium heat in a medium saucepan or large saucier. Add the cream and simmer until slightly thickened, then season to taste with salt. Cook the pasta in well-salted water and, when tender, transfer it directly to the sauce, along with the 4 tablespoons cold butter. Continue cooking, swirling the pan constantly, until the butter melts and the pasta is well coated. Divide the pasta among bowls and serve.

MAKES ABOUT 2½ CUPS
(560 GRAMS)
Active time: 15 minutes
Total time: 1 hour 45 minutes, plus chilling

USE IT WITH
Agnolotti del Plin (177)
Cappelletti (168)
"Classic" Ravioli (152)
Tortelloni (172)

PAIR IT WITH
Brown Butter (291)
Butter & Sage Sauce (293)
Parmesan Broth (342)

smoky caramelized onion filling

2 pounds (900 grams; about 4 medium) **yellow onions**, halved and thinly sliced

2 tablespoons (30 ml) **extra-virgin olive oil**

Kosher salt and freshly ground black pepper

2 sprigs **fresh thyme**

2 sprigs **fresh rosemary**

8 **fresh sage leaves**

4 tablespoons (55 grams) **unsalted butter**, cut into small pieces

1 tablespoon (15 ml) **aged sherry vinegar or balsamic vinegar**

½ cup (115 grams) **full-fat ricotta**

1½ to 2 ounces (50 grams) grated **smoked mozzarella or scamorza**

This one hits all the high notes: sweet, savory, smoky, and a little tangy, too. Roasting the onions in the oven turns an often-involved process into something almost entirely hands-off, while still yielding all the flavor complexity of stirring them over the stovetop. Use this filling for smaller shapes like cappelletti and serve them in broth.

Heat the oven to 375°F/190°C.

In a 9 x 13-inch baking dish, toss the onions with the oil and a generous amount of salt and pepper. Tuck the herbs under a layer of onions to prevent them from burning and scatter the butter cubes on top. Roast until very tender and amber in color, 60 to 90 minutes, stirring every 20 minutes.

Discard the herbs, as well as any scorched and tough onion pieces. Stir in the vinegar and season to taste. Let cool completely.

Combine the onions, ricotta, and mozzarella in the bowl of a food processor. Pulse until mostly smooth but still with some texture. Adjust the seasoning to taste.

Transfer the filling to a bowl or piping bag and refrigerate until chilled, about 30 minutes, or until ready to use.

Note: This recipe makes a lot of filling—loosen the leftovers into a sauce with pasta water or scoop it up as a snack with crunchy vegetables and crackers.

MAKES ABOUT 2 CUPS
(450 GRAMS)
Active time: 15 minutes
Total time: 35 minutes, plus cooling

USE IT WITH
"Classic" Ravioli (152)
Scarpinocc (166)
Stuffed Gnocchi (196)

PAIR IT WITH
Lemon-Chive Butter (297)
Butter & Sage Sauce (293)
Simple Butter Sauce (290)

roasted salmon & mascarpone filling

12 ounces (340 grams) **skinless boneless salmon fillet**, preferably sockeye

Kosher salt and freshly ground black pepper

1 **lemon**

1 tablespoon (15 ml) **extra-virgin olive oil**

8 ounces (225 grams) **mascarpone**

¼ cup (5 grams) **fresh dill** fronds

2 tablespoons minced **fresh chives**

Embrace the joy and lightness of spring with this mix of tender roasted salmon, sweet mascarpone, a zing of lemon, and plenty of herbs. Tuck it into ravioli or potato gnocchi, then drizzle with an herby compound butter and, if you'd like, finish the dish with a handful of sweet peas to bejewel every bite with the freshness of the season. I prefer to use wild-caught sockeye salmon here, which is flavorful without being fatty.

Heat the oven to 400°F/205°C.

Pat the salmon dry with paper towels and season generously all over with salt and pepper. Slice half of the lemon into thin rounds and arrange them on a parchment-lined sheet pan. Place the fish on top and coat with oil. Roast the salmon until just cooked through, usually 8 to 12 minutes, but potentially longer depending on its thickness. Flake the fish onto a plate and let cool completely.

Add the salmon and mascarpone to the bowl of a food processor and pulse until smooth and mousse-like, scraping down the sides of the bowl as needed. Add the dill and chives and pulse in short bursts until the dill is finely chopped. Season to taste with salt, pepper, and a squeeze of lemon juice.

Transfer the filling to a bowl or piping bag and refrigerate until chilled, about 1 hour. If chilling overnight, let the filling soften at room temperature for about 30 minutes before use.

smoked salmon filling

6 ounces (170 grams) **hot-smoked salmon or lox**, flaked or torn into pieces

5 ounces (140 grams) **mascarpone**

4 ounces (115 grams) **full-fat ricotta**

¼ cup (5 grams) **fresh dill** fronds

2 tablespoons minced **fresh chives**

Grated zest of 1 **lemon**, plus some juice

Combine all the ingredients in the bowl of a food processor and pulse until smooth. (Or finely chop the salmon and mix the ingredients together in a bowl.) Season to taste with salt, pepper, and a generous squeeze of lemon juice.

Roasted Salmon & Mascarpone Stuffed Gnocchi with Lemon-Chive Butter

MAKES ABOUT 2 CUPS
(500 GRAMS)
Active time: 30 minutes
Total time: 45 minutes, plus cooling

USE IT WITH
Agnolotti del Plin (177)
Cappelletti (168)
"Classic" Ravioli (152)
Tortelloni (172)

PAIR IT WITH
All-Purpose Tomato Sauce (256)
Grandma Ruthe's Chicken Soup (346)
Italian Meat Broth (345)

sausage & spinach filling

4 tablespoons (60 ml) **extra-virgin olive oil**, divided

8 ounces (225 grams) **fresh baby or mature spinach**

Kosher salt and freshly ground black pepper

½ medium **yellow onion**, finely chopped

4 **garlic cloves**, minced

1 teaspoon **sweet paprika**

¼ cup (60 ml) **dry white wine or water**

12 ounces (340 grams) **sweet or hot Italian-style ground sausage**, or a mix, any casings removed

MAKE IT VEGAN
Use a plant-based sausage alternative like Beyond Meat or Impossible.

This is one of the fillings I use to make kreplach, Jewish dumplings filled with beef, chicken, or potatoes and either fried or served in soup. Their long history converges with Ukrainian varenyky, Russian pelmeni, Polish pierogi, Italian tortellini, and Chinese wontons. Sometimes they're triangular, other times semi-circular, and always familiar. This recipe is flexible, too: Swap in a meat alternative like Beyond Meat or Impossible and no one will be the wiser, or combine the sautéed vegetables with cooked brisket instead, like the leftovers from a batch of Italian Meat Broth (page 345).

Pair the filling with dumpling-like doughs like the White Wine Dough on page 50. Then serve the pasta in broth or chicken soup topped with fresh dill, or pan-fry with caramelized onions for a deli-style meal that'll soothe the soul.

In a nonstick sauté pan, warm 2 tablespoons of the oil over medium heat. Add about a quarter of the spinach and stir for a few moments until mostly wilted, then repeat the process until all the spinach has cooked down. Turn off the heat and season to taste with salt and pepper. Transfer the spinach to a clean dishcloth and let cool. Then wring it dry over the sink, removing as much moisture as possible.

In the same pan that you used to cook the spinach, pour off any juices and warm the remaining 2 tablespoons oil over medium-high heat. Add the onion, season with salt and pepper, and cook, stirring occasionally, until softened, 3 to 5 minutes. Stir in the garlic and paprika and cook, stirring constantly, until fragrant, 30 seconds.

Pour in the wine and simmer, scraping up the browned bits from the bottom of the pan, until completely evaporated. Transfer the mixture to a bowl.

Add the sausage to the pan and season with salt and pepper. Cook, breaking the meat into small pieces with a wooden spoon or spatula, until cooked through and beginning to brown, about 10 minutes (if using a meat alternative, this will happen in about half the time).

Return the onion to the pan and cook, stirring often, for a couple of minutes more. Adjust seasoning to taste and let cool completely.

Add the meat mixture and spinach to the bowl of a food processor and pulse until well combined and paste-like. Transfer the filling to a bowl or piping bag and refrigerate until ready to use. If storing overnight, let the filling soften at room temperature for 30 minutes before using.

MAKES 1 SCANT QUART
(750 GRAMS)
Active time: 1 hour
Total time: 3 hours, plus chilling

USE IT WITH
Agnolotti del Plin (177)
Cappelletti (168)
"Classic" Ravioli (152)
Scarpinocc (166)

PAIR IT WITH
Braising Liquid (recipe follows)
Grandma Ruthe's Chicken Soup (346)
Italian Meat Broth (345)

braised beef & caramelized cabbage filling

1½ pounds (680 grams) **braising beef** like chuck, cut into 1½-inch pieces

Kosher salt and freshly ground black pepper

¼ cup (35 grams) **all-purpose flour**

2 tablespoons (30 ml) **extra-virgin olive oil**

1 **yellow onion**, halved and sliced into ¼-inch half-moons

2 tablespoons (30 grams) **unsalted butter or dairy-free butter alternative**

12 ounces (340 grams; about ½ small) **Savoy or green cabbage**, core removed, roughly chopped

½ cup (120 ml) **dry white wine**

1 sprig **fresh rosemary**

2 sprigs **fresh thyme**

2 **garlic cloves**, peeled and smashed

2 cups (500 ml) **low-sodium chicken stock, beef stock, or water**

Whole nutmeg

4 tablespoons (55 grams) cold **unsalted butter or dairy-free butter alternative**, for serving

Picture for a moment a Renaissance banquet hall, just gone dark after a night of merriment. I see long wooden tables, wisps of smoke emanating from ornate candelabras, empty goblets and alcohol stains, and oversized platters of half-eaten roasts. It's this image that comes to mind when I make this filling, which is inspired by the traditions of Piedmont, where lavish leftovers were pinched between delicate sheets of pasta to become the now famous agnolotti del plin.

This recipe can be made as is or, channeling the Italian no-waste mentality, with any leftover slow-cooked meat and vegetables you might have on hand (like from a batch of Italian Meat Broth, page 345). I've used cabbage here, as is often traditional, but spinach is also common. And if you don't observe kosher dietary laws like I do, feel free to add some grated Parmigiano-Reggiano.

SEAR THE BEEF   Pat the beef dry, season it generously with salt and pepper, and dust the cubes with flour. In a Dutch oven or wide, heavy-bottomed pot, warm the oil over medium-high heat. Add the beef and sear until golden, 2 to 3 minutes per side. Transfer the meat to a plate and turn down the heat to medium.

COOK THE VEGETABLES   Add the onion and a splash of water to deglaze the bottom of the pan and scrape up the browned bits. Cook the onion, stirring occasionally, until soft, about 5 minutes.

Increase the heat to medium-high. Add the 2 tablespoons butter and the cabbage and stir until the butter melts. Season with salt and pepper and cook, stirring often, until the cabbage caramelizes around the edges, about 10 minutes. Use more water to deglaze the pan as needed.

Pour in the wine and simmer until slightly reduced, about 2 minutes. Return the meat to the pot, then add the rosemary, thyme, garlic, and enough stock or water so that everything is mostly covered. Bring to a lively simmer, then reduce the heat to medium-low. Cover the pot and cook at a slow but steady simmer, turning the pieces halfway through, until the meat is tender, about 2 hours. When the meat is done, remove it from the pot and let cool completely. Cut away any fat and gristle.

continues

243

*Braised Beef & Caramelized
Cabbage Agnolotti del Plin
with Braising Liquid*

STRAIN THE BRAISING LIQUID   Discard the herb sprigs and carefully strain the leftover cooking liquid through a fine-mesh sieve into a heatproof container, pushing as much liquid out of the vegetables with a spatula as you can. Reserve both the vegetables and the liquid—you should have about 2 cups (500 ml)—and let cool. I prefer to refrigerate the liquid so I can skim the fat before using.

MIX THE FILLING   Tear the beef into bite-sized pieces into the bowl of a food processor. Blot the strained vegetables with paper towels and add them to the meat. Pulse in short bursts until chopped and well combined. Season to taste with salt, pepper, and freshly grated nutmeg.

For four to six servings, transfer half of the filling to a bowl or piping bag and refrigerate until ready to use. Pack the other half of the filling in a freezer-safe container and freeze for another day—it'll last for up to 3 months, though the sooner you use it, the better it'll taste. As for the braising liquid, I prefer to use all of it at once, but you can divide it into two containers and freeze one for later if you prefer.

TO SERVE   Bring the braising liquid to a simmer over medium-high heat in a medium sauté pan or large saucier. Season to taste with salt. Cook the pasta in well-salted water and, when tender, transfer it directly to the sauce, along with the 4 tablespoons cold butter. Continue cooking, swirling the pan constantly, until the butter melts and the pasta is well coated. Divide the pasta among bowls and serve.

PART FOUR

sauces
& more

Pasta enthusiasts come in two types: Those whose joy lies in kneading, rolling, and folding dough, and those who prefer to skip straight to the sauce.

For a long time, I was firmly rooted in the first group, probably because the sculptural nature of shaping pasta came more naturally to me, and because its slow rhythm soothed me. I'll also admit it was easy to eschew spending another hour at the stove, especially when butter and cheese are enough to make pasta taste great.

But a few years ago, things changed. I was a longtime vegetarian and found myself consumed by a craving that, no matter how much butter and cheese I ate, I just couldn't shake: a slow-cooked and deeply savory meat sauce. The craving persisted for weeks, until I finally decided to try my hand at a meatless ragù, challenging myself to conjure up something meaty enough to fool any carnivore (see page 317).

Instead of my usual need for speed, I took my time, chopping, slicing, and mincing with care. I reveled in the sound of sizzling vegetables and the satisfying hiss wine makes when deglazing a hot pan—I found the calm that I love so much about making pasta. Better yet, I realized I could use the extra cooking time wisely: While the sauce simmered, I rolled my dough into thin sheets and cut them into fat ribbons of pappardelle. And when it was done, embracing each strand in my bowl like an old friend, it was worth every moment.

Now I look forward to spending 20 minutes browning onions in my Dutch oven. But even if you're not as enthralled by sautéing vegetables as I am—or don't have that kind of time—know this: **Whether two ingredients or ten, quick-and-dirty or a full-day project, sauces do not need to be complicated.** As with all Italian (and Italian-inspired) cooking, simple is best, and with a few guidelines, you'll be creating restaurant-quality dishes in the comfort of your kitchen.

The recipes in this section are organized according to their star ingredients: tomato, vegetables and herbs, dairy, meat, and fish. Some are rooted in traditional Italian fare and others are my personal, more modern favorites. There's also a section dedicated to broths and soups, which is another common way fresh pasta is served.

One more thing: This might be a fresh pasta cookbook, but I strongly encourage you to dive into these recipes when you're looking for inspiration for the box of pasta in your pantry. In fact, some of the sauces are traditionally served with dried pasta, which I've noted where relevant, so you can be sure you're in for a satisfying meal either way.

before we start

pairing pasta & sauce

Pasta and sauce are made for each other. I'm not just talking about taste—I mean that pasta shapes are literally *designed* to capture sauce, from the concave domes of orecchiette to the dimpled bellies of scarpinocc. (Even tiny tortellini, served in broth, beg to be scooped up with a spoon.) This harmony is apparent not only in a shape's geometry, but also in the actual surface of the dough: rolling, dragging, pushing, and pulling creates texture, always in the name of enticing sauce.

But which pasta goes with which sauce? You might hear Italians (often loudly) insist that certain pasta shapes go with certain sauces (and vice-versa). But the truth is, "almost any kind of pasta goes reasonably well with almost any kind of sauce, and people who get all serious and talk about the importance of correct sauce pairing are probably overthinking." This is perhaps my favorite quote from any pasta book, from Oretta Zanini De Vita and Maureen B. Fant's *Pasta the Italian Way*. Pairing pasta and sauce is, first and foremost, personal. What you like is what you like, and don't let anyone else's opinion get in the way, especially in the comfort of your own home.

Tried and true Italian combinations blossomed out of regional traditions and local ingredients. Think of agnolotti del plin, the pinched parcels from Piedmont filled with leftover roasted meat and served in its braising liquid; thrifty pici dressed in tomatoes and a particular Tuscan garlic (all'aglione), or with fried stale breadcrumbs (con le briciole); and Ligurian trofie al pesto, hand-twisted spirals coated in flecks of sweet basil, an herb long ago introduced to the area by the Romans that was, even then, pounded into a paste by hand. These are dishes that were once cooked at home simply because that's what people had and they tasted good; now, they're entrenched in Italy's culinary canon and it's just how things are done.

Of course, every family has its own variations, and even the most protected dishes still court controversy. Take my favorite Roman pasta as an example: One might say cacio e pepe must be served with tonnarelli, a thin and chewy egg noodle, but another will prefer spaghetti, pici, bucatini, or even gnocchi. Bolognese ragù is served with tagliatelle ribbons, sure, but also tubular garganelli. Genovese pesto is just as traditional with trofie as it is with flat, linguine-like trenette.

Please don't mistake me: I am not dismissing the importance of tradition, nor the reality that these combinations are meritorious, exceptionally delicious, and worth eating. But I am saying that tagliatelle with Golden Saffron Sauce (page 301) makes for a tasty meal, too, and that there's still ample room for experimentation, with thousands of possibilities waiting to be uncovered.

If this spiel about the subjectivity and regionality of pasta-sauce pairings doesn't quite satisfy your need for direction—or you're struggling with how to tie a dish together—then let me try a more practical approach. There are three routes I might take when constructing a dish, and the first starts with **form**: If I know I want to make a particular pasta shape—let's say cavatelli—then I'll think about sauces, maybe a ragù or a robust vegetable sauce, that can snuggle into nooks and crannies. Another route starts with **flavor**: If I have beautiful summer basil on hand, then I'll think about which pasta shapes might suit a fresh and delicate pesto—thin corzetti coins, busiate spirals, or maybe foglie d'ulivo. The third route is the simplest and perhaps the most Italian in spirit, and it starts with **whatever's in the kitchen**: I'm not talking about

251

kitchen-sink pastas; focus instead on one or two ingredients. Got an onion, a tin of anchovies or sardines, and some all-purpose flour? Try pici (page 83) with anchovies and onions (page 331).

Here are a few principles that can help steer you toward a well-balanced dish:

- **DELICATE PASTAS PAIR WELL WITH DELICATE SAUCES.** Lighter sauces that require little-to-no cooking—herb, nut, and fresh tomato sauces—grab onto finer and thinner shapes without weighing them down. This rings true for small pastas, too, as described below.

- **BOLD PASTAS PAIR WELL WITH BOLD SAUCES (IN TEXTURE AND FLAVOR).** Hearty, rustic ragùs and vegetable sauces burrow into the tunnels and valleys of shapes like cavatelli, capunti, orecchiette, and garganelli particularly well. That's not to say smooth sauces are off limits. If it packs a punch—whether it's sweet roasted garlic or spicy Calabrian chilies—a silky sauce can hold its own while providing a welcome textural counterpoint.

- **SMALL PASTAS PAIR WELL WITH SOUPS AND BROTHS.** Pastine—a family of shapes that includes tiny dots, rings, squares, and stars—and similar shapes are frustrating, if not impossible, to eat without a spoon; tortellini, cappelletti, and other small filled pastas are similarly suited for broth. Little tubes like ditalini, broken spaghetti shards, and whisper-thin angel hair (capelli d'angelo) are usually served in broth, too, or in legume soups, as are maltagliati and other scrap-based pastas (page 79).

- **STUFFED PASTAS ARE ALL ABOUT THE FILLING, AND THE SIZE.** When it comes to stuffed pastas, the flavors on the inside inform the outside. Mild cheeses, potatoes, and greens suit more varied companions, from butter to tomatoes to meat; braised beef, mushrooms, and strong cheeses demand center stage, so simple butter sauces or broths will usually do. Larger, two-bite parcels—ravioli, tortelloni—are generally served in sauce, while smaller shapes are, as mentioned, served in broth.

- **ICYMI, MOST PASTAS PAIR WELL WITH MOST SAUCES.** Long strands like pici, fettuccine, tagliatelle, and pappardelle are especially versatile. They're great vehicles for meat and vegetables, and are also masters at soaking up creamy sauces, which coat their smooth surfaces beautifully. Strozzapreti and farfalle are other examples: their twists and folds can hold on to bits and pieces, while their firm bite is a delicious contrast to velvety sauces.

the marriage of pasta & sauce (la mantecatura)

Form, flavor, and tradition aside, there are other ways to create harmony between pasta and sauce. On the most basic level, **always mix pasta and sauce together** rather than spooning the sauce over the naked pasta on your plate. Nine times out of ten, this means briefly cooking the pasta in its sauce (after boiling, before serving) so each piece can soak up all the delicious flavors you worked so hard to create. Sometimes—when it comes to uncooked sauces like pesto—it means mixing the two together in a bowl to make sure everything's well-acquainted before digging in.

Think of marrying sauce and pasta like making a vinaigrette. When you're trying to combine oil and vinegar into a creamy, cohesive dressing, you have to mix—a lot, and with vigor. Thoroughly tossing pasta and sauce together will leave you with a luscious, balanced plate of food.

There's also a chemical process at work, and it has to do with **starch**. As pasta cooks, the starch in the flour melts into a sticky paste. This paste coats each piece of pasta and seeps into the cooking water, which is why it starts to look murky. It might not sound exciting, but it's actually crucial: Starch is pasta-sauce glue—the marriage officiant, if you will—and it helps the sauce adhere to the pasta's surface.

The usefulness of starch goes beyond the pasta itself, too. The starch-infused cooking water that's left behind can (and should!) be used to make sauces creamier. This can happen in a few ways. First, starch is a thickening agent, so letting a splash of starchy water bubble away in, let's say, a pan of butter, will ultimately leave you with a rich, syrupy glaze. Second, pasta water can loosen or stretch a sauce that's too thick or dry, which is particularly helpful with tomato and meat sauces. Third, and perhaps most magical of all, it can summon a sauce out of thin air, transforming raw ingredients like Pecorino cheese and pepper into creamy perfection. To put it simply, pasta water in the world of pasta-sauce matrimony is like telling a loved one a secret. It deepens the bond.

Here are other ways to create a more perfect union:

- **ADD MORE FAT.** Toss your pasta with a pat of butter or a glug of olive oil over low (or no) heat just before serving for especially creamy results.

- **SPRINKLE CHEESE INSIDE AND OUT.** Even if you're planning to shower your dish with Parmigiano-Reggiano at the table, incorporating cheese during the final tossing stage will fully distribute its flavor. Make sure your cheese is finely and freshly grated and add it off the heat to prevent clumping.

- **WARM THE BOWLS.** I know this is a lot to ask, but if you remember, heat your dishes in the oven on its lowest setting for 15 minutes prior to serving, or run them under hot water for a minute or two right before plating. If you're still reluctant but at all tempted by the Pecorino, Pepper & Lemon Sauce (page 298) or Butter & Parmesan Sauce (page 294), which I hope you are, please try it, just once. It'll keep these sauces from tightening, so your last bite is as luxurious as the first. (Skip this step for uncooked sauces and pasta salads.)

setting up for success

To bring pasta and sauce together as seamlessly as possible, position your pot of cooking water next to your pan or bowl of sauce. This way, you can quickly and easily lift the pasta from the pot, leaving no starch behind—and you won't have to worry about running out of cooking water again. Use a spider sieve or large slotted spoon to scoop up short-cut pastas, filled pastas, and gnocchi. For long pastas, I find it easiest to pull the strands into the bowl of the spider (or slotted spoon) with tongs. You can also use tongs alone, especially for sturdy dried pastas, but sometimes they can tear or break more delicate fresh pastas. If you want to go the extra mile, opt for an Italian-style pasta pot with a perforated insert or a pasta basket that's designed to sit inside the pot of water—just drop your pasta in the basket and lift it out when it's time for sauce.

If you do need to drain your pasta (and a couple of recipes suggest doing so), use a heatproof measuring cup or mug to scoop out at least 1 cup (240 ml) of cooking water beforehand, whether or not you think you'll need it. Which reminds me: When draining, **skip the rinse**. Spraying fresh water on cooked pasta will wash away the starch, making it harder for the sauce to cling to it. There's no need to worry about clumpy colander pasta if you transfer it to the sauce right away, while it's still hot.

tomato sauces

Few things bring me more joy than a ripe summer tomato basking in the sun on the kitchen counter. But for the other forty-four weeks of the year, I'll happily use what's in the can.

You've probably heard about San Marzano tomatoes. They're a variety of plum tomatoes revered in Italy due to their balance of sweetness, acidity, and intensity. What you might not know is that many of the Italian San Marzanos on the American market are... fake. Real San Marzanos must be 1) grown in a small area in southern Italy between Naples and Salerno; 2) harvested and processed in a particular way; and 3) labeled DOP (Denominazione d'Origine Protetta, or Protected Designation of Origin). The problem is that plenty of "San Marzano" tomatoes imported from Italy are labeled DOP because the designation isn't regulated in the United States. The good news is that all real Italian San Marzanos are sold peeled and whole (pomodori pelati), so you can rule out anything crushed or chopped (not to say crushed tomatoes are bad—they're not). The other good news is that there are great canned tomatoes on the market that aren't San Marzanos at all.

Why is this important? Because when you're making a tomato sauce, good-quality tomatoes—San Marzano or not—will make a noticeably better-tasting sauce. If you're looking for authentic Italian San Marzanos, opt for Rega, La Valle, DeLallo, Flora, Francesconi, La Fede, and Sclafani brands (to name a few). When you open the can, these tomatoes will be vibrant in color, bursting with juices, and easily cut with the side of a fork. If you're looking for other really good canned tomatoes, I recommend products from Bianco DiNapoli, grown and harvested in Northern California; Mutti, which has been cultivating tomatoes in Emilia-Romagna, Puglia, and Campania for over a century; and Pomì, a relative newcomer whose tomatoes are grown in Cremona, Parma, Piacenza, and Mantua.

Canned peeled whole tomatoes are a great all-purpose product that can be used to make many of the sauces in this book. But there's another pantry tomato that I find myself reaching for more regularly, and that's passata di pomodoro. "Passata" means "passed"—these tomatoes have been passed through a food mill and strained of all skins and seeds, leaving behind a velvety purée. It's traditionally made in late summer, at the height of tomato season, and barely cooked so you can count on fresh, bright flavors. It's sort of the halfway point between canned whole tomatoes and ready-to-eat marinara. I prefer smooth tomato sauces over chunkier versions, so if you're in the same boat, give it a try. Passata is always sold in glass jars or boxes. Mutti makes a great one, as does Pomì (look for "strained tomatoes"). Or, if you have a food mill, you can make your own either by simmering fresh tomatoes until they release their juices before milling, or simply milling your favorite canned tomatoes (juices included) straightaway.

To always be tomato-sauce ready, keep on hand whole peeled tomatoes, passata, and a tube of tomato paste, which adds richness and depth. (Mutti makes great tomato paste, too.) Try a few brands and find a reliable favorite. Know that when you're armed with good products, great tomato sauces come together quickly—rarely will anything need to simmer for more than 30 minutes. And once you know how simple they can be, you'll be empowered to whip up everything from a weeknight pomodoro to lasagne to meatballs in no time.

Cavatelli with All-Purpose Tomato Sauce

SERVES 4

enough for 22 ounces fresh pasta or 16 ounces dried pasta

Active time: 10 minutes
Total time: 30 to 45 minutes

PAIR IT WITH

Cavatelli (96) · "Classic" Ravioli (152) · Pici (83) ·
Malloreddus (102) · Potato Gnocchi (67) ·
Ricotta Gnocchi (60) · Tortelloni (172)

all-purpose tomato sauce, three ways

4 **garlic cloves**, peeled

6 tablespoons (85 grams) **unsalted butter** or ⅓ cup (80 ml) high-quality extra-virgin olive oil, divided

Fresh or canned tomatoes of choice (see variations opposite)

2 large sprigs **fresh basil**, plus torn or chopped basil for serving

Kosher salt and freshly ground black pepper

Finely grated **Parmigiano-Reggiano** or other hard grating cheese, for serving (optional)

I'm one of the many first introduced to the bliss of a butter-drenched tomato sauce by Marcella Hazan, but the combination is also a staple in Bologna, where it's known as burro e oro ("butter and gold"). This version is entirely adaptable to the season, what you have on hand, and how much body you want the sauce to have, from light (fresh tomatoes), to medium (fresh and canned tomatoes), to heavy (canned tomatoes). Whatever you choose, the sweetness of the butter balances the tomatoes' acidity and makes them taste more like themselves. (You can, of course, use olive oil instead, as is traditional in most parts of Italy, but make sure it's high-quality and somewhat mild in flavor or the sauce will be bitter.) For even more sweetness, cook half of a chopped yellow onion in the butter until softened before adding the garlic.

The sauce can be stored in an airtight container in the refrigerator for up to 5 days or in the freezer for up to 1 month.

PREPARE THE GARLIC   For just a hint of garlic flavor, crush the cloves; for more intensity, thinly slice them; for a heavy dose, mince or grate them.

In a Dutch oven or large sauté pan, melt 4 tablespoons of the butter or ¼ cup of the oil over medium heat. Add the garlic and cook until sizzling and fragrant, 3 to 5 minutes for whole or sliced cloves or 30 seconds for minced.

To cook, follow the instructions in the variations opposite.

Discard the basil and season the sauce to taste with salt and pepper.

TO SERVE   Cook your pasta of choice to your liking, then transfer it directly to the sauce (or drain it first and reserve 1 cup (240 ml) pasta cooking water). Add the remaining 2 tablespoons butter or oil and cook the pasta in the sauce over medium heat, stirring constantly, until the pasta is well coated, adding cooking water to loosen as needed. Turn off the heat and shower with Parmigiano-Reggiano if you'd like.

Divide the pasta among bowls and serve, topped with more grated cheese and basil.

1

all-purpose tomato sauce with fresh tomatoes

1½ pounds (680 grams) **small, sweet tomatoes** like cherry or Campari

Kosher Salt

Halve or quarter the tomatoes, depending on their size. In a medium bowl, toss the tomatoes with a big pinch of kosher salt. Allow to marinate for 20 minutes, stirring occasionally, so they release some of their juices and concentrate in flavor. Pour off the excess liquid.

After cooking the garlic, add the tomatoes, basil, and a big pinch of salt to the pot and cook over medium-low heat, stirring occasionally, until saucy, 10 to 15 minutes. Serve as directed.

2

all-purpose tomato sauce with fresh & canned tomatoes

12 ounces (340 grams) **small, sweet tomatoes** like cherry or Campari

12 ounces (340 grams) **tomato purée** (passata) or canned peeled whole or crushed tomatoes

Kosher Salt

Halve or quarter the fresh tomatoes, depending on their size. In a medium bowl, toss them with a big pinch of kosher salt. Allow to marinate for 20 minutes, stirring occasionally, so they release some of their juices and concentrate in flavor. Pour off the excess liquid.

After cooking the garlic, add the fresh tomatoes to the pot and cook, stirring occasionally, until jammy, 5 to 7 minutes. Add the canned tomatoes, basil, and a big pinch of salt, and cook, stirring occasionally, until slightly thickened, 15 to 20 minutes more. Serve as directed.

3

all-purpose tomato sauce with canned tomatoes

1 (24- or 26-ounce/680- or 750-gram) jar **tomato purée** (passata) or 1 (28-ounce/794-gram) can peeled whole or crushed tomatoes

After cooking the garlic, add the tomatoes, basil, and a big pinch of salt to the pot. Swirl some water into the empty tomato container to catch the residual juices and add that to the pot, too. If using whole peeled tomatoes, break them up with a wooden spoon or potato masher. Simmer at a low bubble until thickened, 15 to 20 minutes. (I like to do this while my water comes to a boil and the pasta cooks.) Serve as directed.

Foglie d'Ulivo with No-Cook Tomato & Basil Sauce

no-cook tomato & basil sauce

2¼ pounds (1 kg) **ripe tomatoes**

4 **garlic cloves**, finely chopped

1½ loosely packed cups (30 grams) **fresh basil** leaves, roughly torn, plus more for serving

Kosher salt

⅓ to ½ cup (80 to 120 ml) high-quality **extra-virgin olive oil**, plus more for serving

Finely grated **Parmigiano-Reggiano or Pecorino Romano**, for serving (optional)

When tomatoes are at their peak—and it's too hot to turn on the oven—this simple, no-cook sauce is what I come back to time and again. It's often called pomodoro crudo and served with very thin spaghetti, though you'll find many variations, including those with onions, capers, olives, and local cheese. In that spirit, don't hesitate to make this your own.

You can use any flavorful tomato here, from heirloom to plum to cherry. Remove the skins and seeds of the larger varieties if you'd like or keep it rustic and leave them intact (I prefer the latter). The pasta will soak up the garlicky tomato juices over time, meaning it makes for great (dare I say better?) leftovers and picnic fare.

TO PEEL AND SEED THE TOMATOES (OPTIONAL; FOR LARGER VARIETIES)
Bring a pot of water to a boil and fill a large bowl with ice water. With a paring knife, score the bottoms of the tomatoes with a small X, just piercing the skin. Drop them into the water and cook until the skin near the X starts to loosen, about 2 minutes. Use a slotted spoon to transfer them to the ice bath. When the tomatoes are cool, peel away the skins. Remove the pulp and seeds and roughly chop the flesh.

If you're using small tomatoes, halve or quarter them.

Combine the tomatoes, garlic, and basil in a large serving bowl. Season generously with salt, then drizzle in the oil. Stir to combine. Leave the sauce to sit, covered, for at least 1 hour, ideally in a warm, sunny place.

TO SERVE   Cook your pasta of choice to your liking—this is not a time for undercooking and finishing in the sauce.

Add the pasta to the sauce and stir to combine. Finish with another drizzle of oil, more basil, and a shower of cheese if you'd like. If you can bear it, let the pasta marinate in the sauce for 15 minutes before serving.

SERVES 4

enough for 22 ounces fresh pasta or
16 ounces dried pasta

Active time: 20 minutes
Total time: 30 minutes

PAIR IT WITH
Cavatelli (96) · Farfalle (140) · Potato Gnocchi (67) ·
Ricotta Gnocchi (60) · Sorpresine (138) ·
Spizzulus (104)

tomato-cream sauce
no-vodka vodka sauce

4 tablespoons (55 grams)
unsalted butter, divided

3 **garlic cloves**, minced

¼ teaspoon **red pepper flakes**

1 cup (240 ml) **heavy cream**

1 (4½-ounce/127-gram) tube
or 1 (6-ounce/170-gram) can
tomato paste

Kosher salt

2 tablespoons (30 grams)
mascarpone

1 ounce (30 grams) finely grated
Parmigiano-Reggiano, plus
more for serving

Torn or thinly sliced **fresh basil**, for
serving (optional)

Some of my earliest food memories take me back to a single place: the Cheesecake Factory. A night at our local mall's Cheesecake Factory wasn't quite as romantic as rolling fresh pasta at the heels of my imaginary Italian grandmother would have been, but it did elicit the same level of joy and wonder. Each dish served twelve (though I managed just fine on my own), was swimming in cream, and had copious amounts of grilled chicken. This sauce isn't quite like that, but it's inspired by the equally comforting penne alla vodka and brings back all the smiles and dairy-filled innocence of being ten years old.

You'll notice there's no alcohol in this recipe, but if you'd like to go the full mile, add ¼ cup (60 ml) of vodka, white wine, or even gin after the tomato paste. Whisk the tomato paste and alcohol together and simmer for about 3 minutes, then proceed as directed.

INFUSE THE CREAM In a small saucepan, melt 1 tablespoon of the butter over medium heat. Add the garlic and red pepper flakes and cook, stirring constantly, until fragrant, about 1 minute. Pour in the cream and bring to a bare simmer, stirring often with a flexible spatula to prevent scorching. Turn off the heat and infuse for 10 minutes.

In a Dutch oven or large sauté pan, warm the remaining 3 tablespoons butter over medium heat. Add the tomato paste and cook, using a whisk to break it up, until caramelized, 2 to 3 minutes.

Pour in the cream and whisk until smooth. Bring to a simmer, then turn off the heat. Season to taste with salt.

TO SERVE Cook your pasta of choice to your liking. When the pasta is almost done, return the sauce to medium heat. Add the mascarpone and ¼ cup (60 ml) pasta cooking water. Transfer the pasta directly to the sauce (or drain it first and reserve 1 cup (240 ml) pasta cooking water) and toss to coat, cooking 1 to 2 minutes more and adding more pasta water to loosen as needed.

Turn off the heat and stir in the cheese. Divide the pasta among bowls and serve, topped with more cheese and basil if you'd like.

Potato Gnocchi with Tomato-Cream Sauce

Pici with Slow-Roasted Tomato & Garlic Sauce

SERVES 4
*enough for 22 ounces fresh or
16 ounces dried pasta, plus leftovers*

Active time: 10 minutes
Total time: 1 hour 45 minutes

PAIR IT WITH
Cavatelli (96)
Fettuccine (131)
Pici (83)
Potato Gnocchi (67)
Ricotta Gnocchi (60)

slow-roasted tomato & garlic sauce

1½ pounds (680 grams) **cherry or similar small tomatoes**

2 medium **garlic heads**, the tops cut off crosswise to expose the cloves

Kosher salt and freshly ground black pepper

⅓ cup (80 ml) **extra-virgin olive oil**

2 tablespoons (30 grams) **unsalted butter**, for serving

1 ounce (30 grams) finely grated **Parmigiano-Reggiano** (optional)

Torn or thinly sliced **fresh basil**, for serving (optional)

MAKE IT VEGAN
Omit the butter and cheese.

When you're curled up on a cold winter day, this sauce will warm your soul and fill your kitchen with the irresistible aroma of roasted garlic. As the tomatoes bruise and burst, they concentrate into a rich, tangy-sweet jam that clings to any pasta beautifully. This recipe makes good use of end-of-season or out-of-season tomatoes, though I also love using canned cherry tomatoes—still sweet in the depths of winter—when I can find them (look for Mutti "ciliegini," which are available online and in some grocery stores). The sauce will keep in the refrigerator for 3 to 5 days and the freezer for several months.

Heat the oven to 375°F/190°C.

Add the tomatoes to a 9 x 13-inch baking dish and nestle the garlic, cut sides up, in the center. Season generously with salt and pepper, then pour over the oil, making sure all the garlic cloves are coated.

Cover the baking dish with aluminum foil and roast for 45 minutes. Increase the oven temperature to 425°F/220°C, uncover the baking dish, and continue to roast until the garlic is soft and caramelized and the tomatoes start to blister, 20 to 25 minutes more.

Cool slightly, then squeeze the softened garlic cloves into the tomatoes; discard the garlic skins. Transfer the mixture to a blender and purée until smooth.

TO SERVE Pour two-thirds of the sauce into a Dutch oven or large sauté pan (reserve the rest for another use). Cook your pasta of choice until just shy of your liking. When the pasta is almost done, return the sauce to medium heat and stir in about ¼ cup (60 ml) pasta cooking water, or enough to make the mixture creamy.

Transfer the pasta directly to the sauce (or drain it first and reserve 1 cup (240 ml) pasta cooking water), followed by the butter. Cook, stirring constantly, until the pasta is well coated, 1 to 2 minutes more, loosening with cooking water as needed. Turn off the heat and stir in the cheese, if using.

Divide the pasta among bowls and serve, topped with more cheese and fresh basil if you'd like.

PAIR IT WITH
Farfalle (140)
Orecchiette (108)
Strozzapreti (88)
Tagliolini (131)

tomato sauce with olives & fried capers

¼ cup plus 2 tablespoons (90 ml) **extra-virgin olive oil**, divided

¼ cup plus 2 tablespoons (60 grams) **capers in brine**, drained, divided

6 **garlic cloves**, thinly sliced

4 oil-packed **anchovy fillets**

¼ to ½ teaspoon **red pepper flakes**

½ cup (90 grams) **pitted black olives** like Gaeta or Kalamata, halved

2 tablespoons (30 grams) **tomato paste**

1 (24- or 26-ounce/680- or 750-gram) jar **tomato purée** (passata) or 1 (28-ounce/794-gram) can peeled whole or crushed tomatoes

Kosher salt and freshly ground black pepper

1 tablespoon finely chopped **fresh flat-leaf parsley**

1 tablespoon thinly sliced **fresh basil** leaves

Fresh burrata or a dollop of ricotta, for serving (optional)

MAKE IT VEGAN
Skip the anchovies.

Any dish that's an ode to pantry staples is a keeper in my book. This one's inspired by spaghetti alla puttanesca, a simple tomato sauce transformed into a savory powerhouse by anchovies, olives, and capers. The origins of puttanesca are murky—perhaps it's from Naples, or Ischia, or somewhere in between. The name literally means "in the style of prostitutes" since, legend has it, its enticing aroma was used to lure customers through the door (this is a myth, by the way). Here, fried capers add satisfying crunch; if you're feeling especially rebellious, top it off with a creamy cheese or throw in a can of oil-packed tuna for extra body.

FRY THE CAPERS   In a small skillet, heat ¼ cup of the oil over medium-high. Pat ¼ cup of the capers dry between paper towels—this will ensure they fry properly and don't sputter when they hit the heat. Add the capers to the oil and cook, shaking the pan often, until they burst and crisp up, 3 minutes. Tilt the pan and, with a slotted spoon, transfer the capers to a paper towel–lined plate.

In a Dutch oven or large sauté pan, warm the remaining 2 tablespoons oil over medium-low heat. Add the garlic, anchovies, and red pepper flakes. Cook, stirring often, until the garlic softens and the anchovies dissolve, 3 to 5 minutes. Stir in the remaining 2 tablespoons capers, the olives, and tomato paste. Cook until the paste caramelizes, 1 to 2 minutes.

Pour in the tomatoes—if using whole tomatoes, break them up with a wooden spoon or potato masher. Swirl some water into the empty tomato container to capture the residual juices and add it to the pan. Season with a large pinch of salt.

Bring the sauce to a simmer, then reduce the heat and cook at a low bubble, stirring occasionally, until slightly thickened, 15 to 20 minutes. Season to taste with salt and pepper.

TO SERVE   Cook your pasta of choice until just shy of your liking, then transfer it directly to the sauce (or drain it first and reserve 1 cup (240 ml) pasta cooking water). Toss and cook over medium heat until the pasta is well coated, 1 to 2 minutes. Turn off the heat and stir in the parsley and basil.

Divide the pasta among bowls. Serve, topped with the fried capers and your cheese of choice, if desired.

Orecchiette with Tomato Sauce with Olives & Fried Capers

*Tagliolini with Fiery
Calabrian Chili Sauce*

SERVES 4

enough for 22 ounces fresh pasta or
16 ounces dried pasta

Active time: 30 minutes
Total time: 1 hour

PAIR IT WITH

Cavatelli (96) · Orecchiette (108) ·
Pici (83) · Spizzulus (104) · Tagliolini (131)

fiery calabrian chili sauce

2 tablespoons (30 ml) **extra-virgin olive oil**

3 tablespoons (45 grams) **unsalted butter**, divided

½ medium **yellow onion**, finely chopped

Kosher salt and freshly ground black pepper

6 **garlic cloves**, 4 thinly sliced and 2 minced

1 (24- or 26-ounce/680- or 750-gram) jar **tomato purée** (passata)

1 tablespoon (15 grams) crushed **Calabrian chili pepper paste**, divided, plus more to taste

½ teaspoon **red pepper flakes**

½ loosely packed cup (10 grams) **fresh flat-leaf parsley**, finely chopped, divided

¾ ounce (20 grams) finely grated **Parmigiano-Reggiano**

MAKE IT VEGAN

Use a dairy-free butter alternative or olive oil and omit the cheese.

This one's for the spice lovers. It's inspired by a dish called spaghetti alla Corte d'Assise, which was first introduced to me by a friend and fellow pasta maker, Tina Prestia. As the story goes, it originated as a late-night creation of Calabrian chef Gaetano Agostino in 1958. Just as he was closing shop, a group of local judges walked into the restaurant and requested something spicy. He returned with an angry-red tomato sauce that satisfied even the pickiest among them. In appreciation, one of the judges dubbed the dish spaghetti alla Corte d'Assise, a reference to the Italian court that deals with the worst crimes and appropriate for such ruthless spice.

Traditionally, this sauce is made with fresh Calabrian chili peppers, a favorite variety in Italy that's fruity, spicy, and a little smoky. They're deep red in color and warm your tongue over time, which makes them ideal for layering into sauces. Here, I've used the paste version that comes in a jar, which can be found in many grocery stores and online (my favorite brand is Tutto Calabria). I suggest adding 1 teaspoon at a time throughout the cooking process so you can tailor the spice level to your liking.

In a large sauté pan or Dutch oven, combine the oil and 2 tablespoons of the butter over medium-low heat. Add the onion and season with salt and pepper. Cook, stirring occasionally, until soft and translucent, 5 to 7 minutes. Add the sliced garlic and cook, stirring often, until softened, 3 minutes.

Pour in the tomato purée, then swirl some water into the empty container to capture the residual juices and add that to the pan, too. Stir in half of the chili pepper paste and a large pinch of salt. Simmer over low heat, stirring occasionally, for 30 minutes. Taste the sauce throughout and add more pepper paste, a little at a time, until it reaches your desired spice level.

While the sauce simmers, in a small saucepan melt the remaining 1 tablespoon butter over medium-low heat. Stir in the minced garlic and red pepper flakes, and cook, stirring constantly, until fragrant, about 2 minutes. Turn off the heat and add half of the parsley.

Add the garlic mixture to the sauce and simmer for 5 minutes. Season to taste.

TO SERVE Cook your pasta of choice until just shy of your liking, then transfer it directly to the sauce (or drain it first and reserve 1 cup (240 ml) pasta cooking water). Toss and cook over medium heat until well coated, loosening with pasta cooking water as needed. Turn off the heat and stir in the cheese and remaining parsley. Divide the pasta among bowls and serve.

vegetable & herb sauces

～•••～

For all its association with meat and cheese, the Italian kitchen has always relied on "l'orto"—what grows in the garden—and there's no end to the ways in which Italian cooks have transformed these humble ingredients into pinnacles of flavor. Take pesto, where this section begins: the sweet, emerald sauce from Genoa that we all know and love gets a lot of airtime, but there are so many other combinations of herbs, vegetables, nuts, and cheeses that are showstoppers, too. "Pesto" simply means to "pound" or "crush" in Italian, so you'll find delicious variations across the peninsula, like those with tomatoes and citrus from Sicily.

Foraging, too, has strong roots in Italy. For a long time and for most communities, identifying edible plants and living off the land was essential to survival. In spring, tender herbs, greens, and vegetables like asparagus, fennel, and artichokes were ready for picking (and tossing with or tucking into pasta). By fall, when the air was cooler, the hunt for nuts and mushrooms, particularly the coveted porcini, began. Luckily, a renewed interest in where our food comes from (and when) is growing—so although now we have every vegetable at our fingertips year-round, I prefer to make many of these dishes when their main ingredients are at their peak (basil, eggplant, and zucchini just taste so much sweeter in summer!), not to mention their most affordable. Of course, don't let seasonality deter you: Make what you want when you want. I can assure you that some sauces, like the broccoli sauce on page 281 and the onion ragù on page 289, will hit the spot any day.

PAIR IT WITH

All hand-cut pastas (128) · All hand-formed pastas (80) ·
"Classic" Ravioli (152) · Corzetti Stampati (146) ·
Farfalle (140) · Lasagne (200) · Meyer Lemon & Herb Ricotta
Gnocchi (64) · Ricotta Gnocchi (60)

basil pesto

2 medium **garlic cloves**, peeled

3 tablespoons (35 grams) **pine nuts**

Coarse **sea salt or kosher salt**

2½ packed cups (60 grams) **fresh basil leaves**, rinsed under cold water and gently but thoroughly patted dry

1 ounce (30 grams) finely grated **Parmigiano-Reggiano**, plus more as desired

2 tablespoons (10 grams) finely grated **Pecorino Sardo or Romano**

⅓ cup (80 ml) mild-flavored **extra virgin-olive oil**, plus more as needed

Like Bolognese ragù, Genovese pesto is a sauce firmly rooted in its place of origin, and the recipe is loved and protected with equal vigor. Liguria is home to especially sweet, tender varieties of basil, particular types of garlic, and delicate olive oils, and the pine nuts are sourced from nearby Pisa, where they're especially buttery. But even if these special ingredients are out of reach, a delicious basil pesto still awaits. Opt for small basil leaves (the potted plants available at many grocery stores are a good option) and a mild-flavored olive oil that'll let their sweetness shine. If you have some extra time and a mortar and pestle, I'd highly recommend giving the traditional method a try—the result is strikingly rich, and the scent of basil perfuming your kitchen makes it totally worth the extra effort.

IN A FOOD PROCESSOR   Pop the food processor blade in the freezer while you prepare the ingredients. This will help prevent the basil leaves from discoloring.

Roughly chop the garlic cloves, then add them to the bowl of the food processor. Sprinkle in the pine nuts and a pinch of salt and pulse together until well combined and paste-like, about 10 seconds.

Scrape down the sides of the bowl and add the basil and cheeses. Pulse in short bursts, no more than a couple seconds at a time, until finely minced, scraping down the sides of the bowl as needed. Transfer the mixture to a bowl and slowly stream in the oil, mixing constantly, until creamy. Adjust the seasoning to taste.

IN A MORTAR & PESTLE   If your mortar is on the small side, make a half batch.

Add the garlic and a pinch of coarse salt to the mortar. Pound the garlic into a sticky paste, rotating the pestle in a circular motion against the sides of the mortar to break it down. Sprinkle in the pine nuts and continue the motion until they too break down into a fine paste.

Follow with the basil, adding a large handful at a time. This takes a bit of patience; I find gently crushing and rotating the leaves against the walls of the mortar is most effective. Add a pinch of salt to help break them down if needed until the mixture becomes vibrant green with very small flecks of basil. Muddle in the cheeses, then slowly drizzle in the oil, stirring constantly, until emulsified.

TO SERVE   Cook your pasta of choice to your liking and transfer it directly to a large, heatproof (preferably metal) mixing bowl (or drain it first and reserve 1 cup (240 ml) pasta cooking water). Spoon the pesto over the pasta and toss well until luscious and creamy, loosening with pasta cooking water as needed. Divide among bowls and serve.

To store, transfer the pesto to an airtight container and cover with a thin layer of olive oil. Refrigerate for up to 3 days or freeze for up to 3 months.

1) *Whole Wheat Busiate with Tomato & Almond Pesto*
2) *Ricotta Gnocchi with Kale & Arugula Pesto*
3) *Corzetti della Valpolcevera with Red Pesto*
4) *Corzetti Stampati with Ligurian Walnut Sauce*

tomato & almond pesto

pesto alla trapanese

½ cup (85 grams) **blanched almonds**

1½ pounds (680 grams; about 8 medium) ripe **plum tomatoes** like Roma

3 **garlic cloves**, peeled

Kosher salt

1 packed cup (25 grams) **fresh basil** leaves

1½ ounces (40 grams) finely grated **Pecorino Sardo or Romano**

¼ cup (60 ml) **extra-virgin olive oil**

MAKE IT VEGAN

Omit the cheese and serve with Toasted Breadcrumbs (page 354).

This pesto from Trapani, on the western coast of Sicily, takes the cake for me. Called pesto alla Trapanese, it has all the complexity of its Ligurian cousin with added freshness from summer tomatoes. Look for tomatoes that are firm to the touch but have a little give (if good plum varieties aren't available, swap in whatever medium-sized tomatoes look best). Make this pesto in a food processor as described or, if time allows, in a mortar and pestle according to the instructions on page 271—after breaking down the basil, muddle in the tomatoes in batches, then stir in the cheese and olive oil.

This sauce is typically served with busiate (page 106), which also hail from Trapani, so you know the two are a match made in heaven.

TOAST THE NUTS   Heat the oven to 375°F/190°C. Spread the almonds on a small foil-lined sheet pan. Toast in the oven until golden and fragrant, watching closely, 8 to 10 minutes. Let cool.

PREPARE THE TOMATOES   Bring a pot of water to a boil and fill a large bowl with ice water. With a paring knife, score the bottoms of the tomatoes with a small X, just piercing the skin. Drop them into the water and cook until the skin near the X starts to loosen, about 2 minutes. Use a slotted spoon to transfer them to the ice bath. When the tomatoes are cool, peel away the skins, then cut them in half and scoop out the seeds. Pat the flesh dry and cut into large pieces.

MAKE THE PESTO   Add the garlic, almonds, and a pinch of salt to the bowl of a food processor and pulse until the nuts are well chopped and gravel-like. Add the basil, cheese, and tomatoes. Pulse in short bursts until the ingredients are combined but the sauce still has texture. Transfer to a bowl and stir in the oil. Season to taste, adding more cheese if you'd like. Let the pesto stand at room temperature for 15 minutes.

TO SERVE   Cook your pasta of choice to your liking and transfer it directly to a large, heatproof (preferably metal) mixing bowl (or drain it first and reserve 1 cup (240 ml) pasta cooking water). Spoon most of the pesto over the pasta and toss well until luscious and creamy. Add more pesto and loosen with cooking water as needed until the pasta is well coated. Divide among bowls and serve, finished with more oil and grated cheese. Reserve any remaining pesto for another use.

citrus & pistachio pesto

1 **navel orange**

1 **lemon**

2 **garlic cloves**, peeled and crushed

2 tablespoons (20 grams) **capers in brine**, drained (optional)

2 tablespoons (20 grams) **pine nuts**

⅓ cup (50 grams) **shelled raw or lightly salted pistachios**

2 cups (45 grams) **fresh basil** leaves

1 ounce (30 grams) finely grated **Parmigiano-Reggiano**

¼ cup (60 ml) **extra-virgin olive oil**

Kosher salt

Pesto agli agrumi, another sauce from Sicily, is supremely refreshing thanks to juicy segments of orange and lemon. Almonds are sometimes used here, but I've included a mix of pine nuts and pistachios for sweetness and color. The flavors pair wonderfully with seafood and a glass of white wine al fresco.

Pop your food processor blade in the freezer while you prepare the ingredients. This will help prevent the basil from discoloring.

PREPARE THE CITRUS   Grate the zests of the orange and lemon into a medium bowl. Cut the ends off both fruits so they stand upright, then cut away the peel and the white pith. Using a sharp knife, segment the orange by cutting between the segment walls—catch any juice on your cutting board and remove any seeds. Repeat with half of the lemon (save the rest for another use). Add the segments and juice to the bowl. Stir in the garlic and capers and let marinate for 15 minutes.

MAKE THE PESTO   Add the nuts to the bowl of the food processor and pulse until coarsely chopped. Add the basil and citrus mixture. Pulse in short bursts, no more than a couple seconds at a time, until well combined but still with some texture. Transfer to a bowl and fold in the cheese, then slowly stream in the oil, mixing constantly, until creamy. Season to taste with salt.

TO SERVE   Cook your pasta of choice to your liking and transfer it directly to a large, heatproof (preferably metal) mixing bowl (if draining, reserve 1 cup (240 ml) pasta cooking water). Spoon most of the pesto over the pasta and toss well until luscious and creamy. Add more pesto and loosen with cooking water as needed until the pasta is well coated. Divide among bowls and serve, topped with more cheese if you'd like. Reserve any remaining pesto for another use.

PAIR IT WITH

All Basil Pesto pairings, especially Cavatelli (96),
Corzetti della Valpolcevera (92),
Farfalle (140), and Fettuccine (131)

red pesto
pesto rosso

¼ cup (42 grams) **blanched almonds**

2 ounces (55 grams; about ¼ packed cup) **sun-dried tomatoes** packed in oil

2 **garlic cloves**, roughly chopped

2 teaspoons **fresh rosemary** leaves

3½ ounces (100 grams) **roasted red peppers**

¾ ounce (20 grams) finely grated **Pecorino Romano**

1 teaspoon crushed **Calabrian chili pepper paste**, plus more to taste (optional)

¼ cup (60 ml) **extra-virgin olive oil**

Kosher salt and freshly ground black pepper

Smoky, spicy, sweet—this pesto has it all. It's also entirely customizable: Swap the almonds for pine nuts, the rosemary for basil, or the Pecorino for Parmigiano-Reggiano. Opt for oil-packed sun-dried tomatoes if you can (they're a little less salty) and if you want to make your own roasted red peppers, two medium-sized peppers will do (see page 318 for instructions).

You can serve the sauce straight out of the food processor, but it's even better the next day and the day after that. It'll keep in an airtight container in the refrigerator for up to 5 days.

TOAST THE NUTS   Heat the oven to 375°F/190°C. Spread the almonds on a small foil-lined sheet pan. Toast in the oven until golden and fragrant, watching closely, 8 to 10 minutes. Let cool.

SOAK THE TOMATOES (IF YOU NEED TO)   While the almonds toast, taste the sun-dried tomatoes. If they're very salty, put them in a small bowl and cover with ½ cup (120 ml) boiling water to draw out some of the salt.

MAKE THE PESTO   Add the almonds, garlic, and rosemary to the bowl of a food processor. Pulse, scraping down the sides and bottom of the bowl as needed, until finely chopped and a coarse paste forms. If you soaked the tomatoes, drain and rinse them. Add the tomatoes and peppers to the food processor and pulse until well combined—the mixture should be creamy but still have some texture. Transfer the pesto to a bowl and stir in the cheese and chili pepper paste (add more of either to your liking). Slowly stream in the oil, mixing constantly, until creamy. Season to taste with salt and pepper.

TO SERVE   Cook your pasta of choice to your liking and transfer it directly to a large, heatproof (preferably metal) mixing bowl (or drain it first and reserve 1 cup (240 ml) pasta cooking water). Spoon the pesto over the pasta and toss well until luscious and creamy, loosening with cooking water as needed. Divide among bowls and serve.

SERVES 4
MAKES ABOUT 1 CUP (250 GRAMS)

Active time: 15 minutes
Total time: 25 minutes

PAIR IT WITH
*All Basil Pesto pairings, especially Capunti (100), Cavatelli
(96), Orecchiette (108), and Ricotta Gnocchi (60)*

kale & arugula pesto

½ cup (55 grams) **raw walnuts**

2 ounces (55 grams; about ½ bunch) **Tuscan (lacinato) kale**

2 medium **garlic cloves**, roughly chopped

Kosher salt

2 ounces (55 grams; about 2 cups) **baby arugula**

Juice of ½ **lemon**, plus more to taste

½ cup (120 ml) mild-flavored **extra-virgin olive oil**, divided

1 ounce (30 grams) finely grated **Parmigiano-Reggiano**, plus more for serving

Here's a pesto you can enjoy in the cooler months when heartier greens are at their peak. Kale and arugula in equal parts round out the pepperiness and bitterness of the other, and a squeeze of lemon pulls them together. Toss it with pasta, of course, or dollop it onto other grains, sandwiches, and roasted vegetables.

TOAST THE NUTS   Heat the oven to 375°F/190°C. Spread the walnuts on a small foil-lined sheet pan. Toast in the oven until golden and fragrant, watching closely, 8 to 10 minutes. Let cool.

PREPARE THE KALE   Remove the stems and ribs from the kale and reserve for another use. Roughly chop the leaves.

MAKE THE PESTO   Add the walnuts, garlic, and a pinch of salt to the bowl of a food processor. Pulse, scraping down the sides and bottom of the bowl as needed, until they form a coarse paste. Add the kale, arugula, lemon juice, another pinch of salt, and half of the oil. Pulse until the greens are finely chopped and the mixture is creamy but still has some texture.

Transfer the pesto to a bowl and fold in the cheese. Slowly stream in the remaining oil, mixing constantly, until creamy. Season to taste with salt and add more cheese and/or lemon juice if you'd like.

TO SERVE   Cook your pasta of choice to your liking and transfer it directly to a large, heatproof (preferably metal) mixing bowl (or drain it first and reserve 1 cup (240 ml) pasta cooking water). Spoon the pesto over the pasta and toss well until luscious and creamy, loosening with cooking water as needed. Divide among bowls and serve with more grated cheese.

PAIR IT WITH
Agnolotti (177) · Caramelle (182) · "Classic" Ravioli (152) ·
Corzetti Stampati (146) · Ossola-Style Chestnut ·
Squash & Potato Gnocchi (66) · Ricotta Gnocchi (60) ·
Sweet Potato Gnocchi (70) · Tortelloni (172)

sage & hazelnut pesto

½ cup (70 grams) **raw hazelnuts**

¼ cup (60 ml) **extra-virgin olive oil**, plus more as needed

¼ cup (5 grams; about 15 large leaves) **fresh sage** leaves, roughly chopped

2 **garlic cloves**, thinly sliced

1 teaspoon **honey**, plus more to taste

¾ ounce (20 grams) finely grated **Parmigiano-Reggiano**

2 tablespoons (10 grams) finely grated **Pecorino Romano**

Kosher salt and freshly ground black pepper

Sage packs a punch, but this sauce is far more subtle than it seems. A touch of honey tempers its usual earthiness and, when the hazelnuts meet a splash of hot pasta water, they transform into a rich and creamy dressing.

TOAST THE NUTS   Heat the oven to 375°F/190°C. Spread the hazelnuts on a small foil-lined sheet pan. Toast in the oven until golden and fragrant, watching closely, 8 to 10 minutes. When cool enough to handle, bundle the hazelnuts in a clean dishcloth and rub them together vigorously to remove most of the skins.

COOK THE SAGE AND GARLIC   In a small skillet, warm the oil over medium-low heat. Add the sage and garlic and cook, stirring occasionally, until sizzling and fragrant but not browned, about 5 minutes. Let the mixture bubble for a minute or two, stirring often, then turn off the heat and let cool slightly.

MAKE THE PESTO   Add the hazelnuts to the bowl of a food processor and pulse until chopped into a coarse sand consistency. Add the garlic-sage mixture, along with the honey, and pulse into a coarse paste, scraping down the sides of the bowl as needed. Transfer to a bowl and stir in the cheeses, then loosen with another tablespoon or two of oil. Season to taste with salt and pepper and add more honey if you'd like.

TO SERVE   Cook your pasta of choice to your liking and transfer it directly to a large, heatproof (preferably metal) mixing bowl (or drain it first and reserve 1 cup (240 ml) pasta cooking water). Spoon the pesto over the pasta and toss well until luscious and creamy, loosening with plenty of cooking water until the pasta is well coated. Divide among bowls and serve, finished with more grated cheese.

Active time: 15 minutes
Total time: 25 minutes

PAIR IT WITH
*Cappelletti (168) • "Classic" Ravioli (152) •
Corzetti della Valpolcevera (92) • Corzetti Stampati (146) •
Fettuccine (131) • Potato Gnocchi (67) • Strozzapreti (88) •
Tagliatelle (131) • Tortelloni (172)*

ligurian walnut sauce

salsa di noci

1 cup (100 grams) **raw walnuts**

½ cup (70 grams) **pine nuts**

1 slice (30 grams) **stale white bread**, crusts removed

½ cup (120 ml) **milk**, plus more as needed

2 **garlic cloves**, roughly chopped

2 tablespoons (30 ml) **extra-virgin olive oil**

1 tablespoon **fresh marjoram or oregano**, or a few sage leaves, plus more to taste

¼ cup (60 grams) **full-fat ricotta**

Kosher salt and freshly ground black pepper

4 tablespoons (55 grams) **unsalted butter**, for serving

1½ ounces (45 grams) finely grated **Parmigiano-Reggiano**, for serving

What this sauce lacks in looks, it makes up tenfold in flavor. Known as salsa di noci (walnut sauce), it's another Ligurian pesto served with many of the region's fresh pastas, particularly corzetti (page 000) and herb-filled pasta pockets called pansotti. I first made a version of this recipe with food historian Karima Moyer-Nocchi, who also taught me how to make the corzetti della Valpolcevera (page 92) that accompanied it. The sauce is rich, creamy, and intensely satisfying, not to mention you can whip it up in the time it takes to boil water.

TOAST THE NUTS   Heat the oven to 375°F/190°C. Spread the walnuts and pine nuts on a small foil-lined sheet pan. Toast in the oven until golden and fragrant, watching closely, 8 to 10 minutes.

SOAK THE BREAD   While the nuts toast, place the bread in a small bowl. Pour over the milk and soak until soft and saturated, 5 minutes.

MAKE THE PESTO   Add the bread (and residual milk), nuts, garlic, oil, herbs, and ricotta to the bowl of a food processor. Pulse until the mixture is well combined and has a coarse-creamy consistency. Scrape down the sides of the bowl and add a splash more milk to loosen as needed. Season to taste with salt and pepper and add more herbs if you'd like.

TO SERVE   Cook your pasta of choice to your liking. Reserve 1 cup (240 ml) of pasta cooking water. In a Dutch oven or large skillet, melt the butter over medium heat. Transfer the pasta to the butter, toss to coat, and turn off the heat. Add half of the sauce, all the Parmigiano-Reggiano, and ¼ cup (60 ml) cooking water to the pasta. Toss vigorously, adding more sauce and cooking water as needed until the pasta is well coated. Divide among bowls and serve, topped with more grated cheese and black pepper.

Whole Wheat Orecchiette with Broccoli Sauce

SERVES 4

enough for 22 ounces fresh pasta or 16 ounces dried pasta

Active time: 20 minutes
Total time: 30 minutes

PAIR IT WITH

Capunti (100) • Cavatelli (96) •
Farfalle (140) • Fettuccine (131) • Foglie d'Ulivo (110) •
Orecchiette (108) • Ricotta Gnocchi (60) •
Strozzapreti (88)

broccoli sauce

Kosher salt

1 pound (450 grams; 1 large or 2 small heads) **broccoli**

¼ cup (60 ml) **extra-virgin olive oil**

½ medium **yellow onion**, finely chopped

Freshly ground black pepper

4 **garlic cloves**, thinly sliced

¼ teaspoon **red pepper flakes**

1½ ounces (40 grams) finely grated **Pecorino Romano**, plus more for serving

Juice of ½ **lemon**

MAKE IT VEGAN
Skip the Pecorino.

Pasta with broccoli is a staple in the Italian south, particularly Calabria, and in Rome. Like the best weeknight dishes, its ingredient list is short and it's on the table in no time. Cooking the broccoli and pasta in the same pot isn't just convenient—it makes for a harmonious eating experience that might make you, like me, question everything you know about this humble vegetable. Don't be afraid of overcooking the broccoli here; the more it falls apart, the creamier the sauce will be.

Bring a large pot of water to a boil and season it generously with salt. Break the broccoli into small florets, then trim and peel away the tough outer layer of the stalk and cut it into bite-sized pieces. When the water is boiling, add the broccoli and cook until tender, about 7 minutes.

While the broccoli cooks, warm the oil over medium heat in a large sauté pan or Dutch oven. Add the onion, along with a pinch of salt and pepper, and cook until softened, stirring often, about 5 minutes. Stir in the garlic and red pepper flakes and cook for 2 minutes more.

With a slotted spoon, transfer the broccoli and a splash of its cooking water directly to the pan with the onion (reserve the cooking water). Reduce the heat to medium-low. If using fresh pasta, continue to cook the broccoli in the pan for 5 minutes, using a wooden spoon to break it down further; if using dried pasta, skip to the next step.

Add your pasta of choice to the broccoli cooking water and cook until just shy of your liking. Keep breaking down the broccoli while the pasta cooks, stirring often. Season to taste.

TO SERVE Transfer the pasta directly to the sauce, along with ½ cup (120 ml) pasta cooking water (if you need to drain the pasta first, make sure to reserve a little more cooking water than you might need). Continue cooking, stirring constantly, until the pasta is well coated, 1 to 2 minutes. Turn off the heat and stir in the cheese and lemon juice.

Divide the pasta among bowls and serve, topped with lots of black pepper and more grated cheese.

SERVES 4

enough for 22 ounces fresh pasta or 16 ounces dried pasta

Active time: 20 minutes
Total time: 30 minutes

PAIR IT WITH

All hand-cut pastas (128) • Cavatelli (96) • Farfalle (140) •
Garganelli (142) • Pici (83)

fried zucchini sauce

1½ pounds (680 grams; about 4 small) **zucchini**, sliced into thin coins

1¾ ounces (50 grams) finely grated **provolone piccante**

1¾ ounces (50 grams) finely grated **caciocavallo**

1¾ ounces (50 grams) finely grated **Parmigiano-Reggiano**

¼ cup (60 ml) **extra-virgin olive oil**

2 large **garlic cloves**, peeled and crushed

Kosher salt and freshly ground black pepper

2 tablespoons (30 grams) cold **unsalted butter**

Torn or sliced **fresh basil** leaves, for serving

This sauce is inspired by spaghetti alla Nerano, a dish born in a small fishing town halfway between Sorrento and the Amalfi Coast. It was invented in 1952 by Maria Grazia at her eponymous restaurant, and the original recipe remains a closely guarded secret. In Nerano, the zucchini are smaller, sweeter, and paler in color than what you'll find in most grocery stores, and the cheese of choice is buttery, semi-aged provolone del Monaco. But even when I tuck into a plate of this less traditional version, Amalfi doesn't seem so far away.

I like to prep the cheeses in a food processor using the fine grater attachment. If you can't find caciocavallo (a sharp, spicy, soft, and springy cheese that's more powerful than mozzarella and tamer than provolone), split the difference with more provolone and Parmigiano-Reggiano.

Spread the zucchini slices across a paper towel–lined sheet pan and pat dry. Mix the grated cheeses together in a small bowl.

In a large nonstick sauté pan, heat the oil over medium-high. Add the garlic and fry, stirring often, until tinged gold around the edges, about 2 minutes. Remove the garlic from the pan and set aside.

Arrange half of the zucchini slices in the pan and fry, flipping occasionally, until tender and some of the pieces start to caramelize, 5 to 7 minutes (you're not looking for crispy here). Turn down the heat if the zucchini brown too quickly.

Transfer the zucchini to a paper towel–lined plate and season liberally with salt and pepper. Add another splash of oil to the pan and repeat with the remaining slices. Turn off the heat and let the pan cool slightly, then drain off the excess oil and set the pan aside.

Add the reserved garlic and half of the fried zucchini slices to a blender or food processor and purée until smooth.

Cook your pasta of choice until just shy of your liking. While the pasta cooks, return the pan used to fry the zucchini to medium heat. Add the zucchini purée and remaining fried slices, along with ½ cup (120 ml) pasta cooking water. Bring to a bare simmer and season to taste.

Transfer the pasta directly to the sauce (or drain it first and reserve 1 cup (240 ml) pasta cooking water) and toss until well coated, adding more cooking water to loosen as needed. Turn off the heat. Stir in the butter and

three-quarters of the cheeses, one handful at a time, reserving the rest for serving. Mix vigorously until melted and emulsified, adding more cooking water as needed.

Divide the pasta among bowls and serve, topped with the basil, remaining grated cheese, and lots of black pepper.

ABOVE
Cavatelli with Fried Zucchini Sauce

Chestnut Pappardelle with
Wild Mushroom Sauce

PAIR IT WITH

Agnolotti (177) · "Classic" Ravioli (152) · Farfalle (140) · Garganelli (142) · Pappardelle (131) · Potato Gnocchi (67) · Ricotta Gnocchi (60) · Tagliatelle (131) · Tortelloni (172)

wild mushroom sauce

1½ pounds (680 grams) **mixed fresh mushrooms** like chanterelle, maitake, oyster, cremini, and royal trumpet, cleaned

2 tablespoons (30 ml) **extra-virgin olive oil**

5 tablespoons (70 grams) **unsalted butter**, divided

Kosher salt and freshly ground black pepper

1 **shallot**, minced

5 **garlic cloves**, thinly sliced

¼ cup (60 ml) **dry white wine** like Pinot Grigio

1½ cups (360 ml) **low-sodium vegetable or chicken stock**

1 cup (240 ml) **heavy cream**

1½ teaspoons roughly chopped **fresh thyme**

1 scant teaspoon minced **fresh rosemary**

1 ounce (30 grams) finely grated **Parmigiano-Reggiano**, plus more for serving

1 large **lemon**, zested and juiced

In the fall, when I can get my hands on great mushrooms, cooking always feels like a treat. This dish takes advantage of the season's hypnotic shapes and textures to create something luxurious that's entirely achievable on a weeknight.

PREPARE THE MUSHROOMS   Trim and slice larger ones like cremini and royal trumpet; halve or quarter chanterelles, leaving small ones whole; tear maitake and oyster mushrooms into large pieces.

In a Dutch oven or large sauté pan, heat the oil and 2 tablespoons of the butter over medium-high. Add the mushrooms, stir to coat, then cook undisturbed until they release their juices, about 7 minutes.

Reduce the heat to medium and stir more frequently until the mushrooms are golden around the edges, 10 to 12 minutes. If the bottom of the pan gets dark, add a splash of stock or water to deglaze. Season to taste with salt and pepper.

Add the shallot and garlic. Cook until softened and fragrant, stirring frequently, about 3 minutes. Pour in the wine. Reduce it almost entirely, 1 to 2 minutes, scraping up the browned bits from the bottom of the pan. Add the stock and simmer, stirring occasionally, until thickened and reduced by two thirds, 10 to 12 minutes.

Reduce the heat to medium-low. Stir in the cream and herbs and simmer until slightly thickened, about 5 minutes. Season to taste.

TO SERVE   Cook your pasta of choice to your liking, then transfer the pasta directly to the sauce, along with ¼ cup (60 ml) pasta cooking water (if you need to drain the pasta first, make sure to reserve a little more cooking water than you might need). Add the remaining 3 tablespoons butter and toss until the pasta is well coated. Turn off the heat and stir in the cheese, lemon juice, and half of the lemon zest. Toss again until creamy, adding more cooking water to loosen as needed.

Divide the pasta among bowls and serve, finished with more grated cheese, the remaining lemon zest, and black pepper.

PAIR IT WITH

Capunti (100) · Cavatelli (96) ·
Farfalle (140) · Orecchiette (108) · Spizzulus (104) ·
Strozzapreti (88)

sweet & sour eggplant sauce with burrata

½ cup plus 1 tablespoon (135 ml) **extra-virgin olive oil**, divided, plus more for serving

3 tablespoons (45 ml) **red or white wine vinegar**, divided

1 teaspoon **granulated sugar**

1 teaspoon **kosher salt**, plus more to taste

Freshly ground black pepper

1½ pounds (680 grams) **globe, Italian, or Japanese eggplants**, cut into 1-inch cubes

1 large **red onion**, sliced into ½-inch-thick wedges

1½ pounds (680 grams) **cherry tomatoes**, divided

4 **garlic cloves**, thinly sliced

½ cup (90 grams) **pitted green olives**, preferably Castelvetrano, halved

3 tablespoons (30 grams) **capers in brine**, drained and patted dry

¼ teaspoon **red pepper flakes**

¼ cup (45 grams) **pine nuts**, toasted in the oven or a dry pan

Fresh basil leaves, for serving

4 ounces (115 grams) **burrata or cubed fresh mozzarella**, for serving

Caponata is a sweet and tangy Sicilian staple that transforms the often-underrated eggplant into the star of the show. There are dozens of caponata variations, each spotlighting local ingredients from Palermo to Catania. In many recipes, large cubes of eggplant are fried, then cooked down with celery, onions, tomatoes, capers, and olives (sometimes bell peppers, sometimes raisins, too) and enriched with sugar and vinegar. The result is a briny spread-meets-stew that's equally delicious as a topping for crusty bread as it is a side dish for fish.

Here, the vegetables are roasted together slowly until their juices intermingle into a jewel-toned dressing. And, like the original, this sauce is best served pasta-salad style at room temperature or cold the next day.

Heat the oven to 325°F/165°C. Whisk together ½ cup of the oil, 2 tablespoons of the vinegar, the sugar, salt, and pepper to taste in a small bowl until the sugar dissolves. Pour the mixture onto a sheet pan.

Add the eggplant, onion, and two thirds of the tomatoes to the pan. Stir to coat in the olive oil and vinegar mixture. Roast the vegetables until soft and jammy, about 1 hour and 45 minutes, stirring every 20 to 30 minutes.

While the vegetables roast, warm the remaining 1 tablespoon oil in a small saucepan over medium heat. Add the garlic, olives, and capers and cook, stirring frequently, until the garlic turns golden at the edges, about 3 minutes. Remove from the heat and stir in the red pepper flakes.

When the vegetables are done, stir in the remaining 1 tablespoon vinegar and adjust seasoning to taste. Fold in the garlic/olive/caper mixture.

Halve the remaining tomatoes and add them to a medium bowl. Toss with a sprinkle of salt and set aside.

TO SERVE Cook your pasta of choice to your liking. Reserve 1 cup (240 ml) pasta cooking water, then drain (but don't rinse!) the pasta. Return the pasta to the pot and scrape in the roasted vegetables. Loosen the sauce with some of the reserved pasta water and season to taste. Drain off the liquid from the salted tomatoes and add them to the pasta with half of the pine nuts.

Serve the pasta at room temperature, either on a platter or in bowls, topped with the remaining pine nuts, the basil, and burrata. Cut into the cheese and finish with a drizzle of extra-virgin olive oil.

Capunti with Sweet & Sour Eggplant Sauce with Burrata

Tagliatelle with Braised Onion Ragù

PAIR IT WITH

*Cappelletti (168) • "Classic" Ravioli (152) •
Garganelli (142) • Pappardelle (131) • Potato Gnocchi (67) •
Ricotta Gnocchi (60) •
Tagliatelle (131) • Tortelloni (172)*

braised onion ragù

6 tablespoons (85 grams) **unsalted butter**, divided

2¼ pounds (1 kg; about 4 medium) **yellow onions**, thinly sliced into half moons

Kosher salt

3 **garlic cloves**, thinly sliced

¼ cup (60 grams) **tomato paste**

½ cup (120 ml) **dry white wine** like Pinot Grigio

A pinch of **ground cloves**

2 **bay leaves**

3 cups (720 ml) **low-sodium vegetable or chicken stock**, plus more as needed

Freshly ground black pepper

1 teaspoon high-quality **balsamic vinegar or balsamic reduction** (page 356)

Finely grated **Parmigiano-Reggiano** and **fresh thyme**, for serving

MAKE IT VEGAN

Swap the butter for a dairy-free alternative, skip the Parmigiano.

This sauce is loosely inspired by a Bolognese dish called il friggione, a flavorful combination of slow-cooked onions and tomatoes. You'll find il friggione served with meat, as a side dish, and as an antipasto—but, of course, it works well with pasta, too. Like most oniony dishes, the key to this one is time: Traditionally, the onions are marinated in sugar for a couple of hours before being cooked down for many more. This version is entirely untraditional, but the jammy, tomatoey essence is there, and it pairs particularly well with the roasted garlic and rosemary filling on page 222.

In a Dutch oven or large, heavy-bottomed sauté pan, melt 4 tablespoons of the butter over medium heat. Add the onions, season with salt, and stir to coat. Cook until the onions are soft but not browned, stirring occasionally, 5 to 10 minutes.

Add the garlic and cook until fragrant, 1 minute. Stir in the tomato paste and cook until caramelized, 1 to 2 minutes. Pour in the wine and simmer for 2 to 3 minutes, scraping up any browned bits from the bottom of the pan. Add a small pinch of cloves, the bay leaves, and the stock. Bring to a simmer, then reduce to a low bubble. Cook, stirring occasionally, until the liquid is absorbed and the mixture is jammy, 1½ to 2 hours. If needed, stir in additional stock, ½ cup (120 ml) at a time, to prevent burning. Remove and discard the bay leaves. Season to taste with salt and pepper.

Stir in the remaining 2 tablespoons butter and the balsamic. Turn off the heat.

TO SERVE Cook your pasta of choice to your liking. While the pasta cooks, return the onions to medium heat. Stir in a little pasta cooking water until saucy. Transfer the pasta directly to the sauce (if you need to drain it first, reserve a little extra cooking water in case you need it) and cook, tossing frequently, until well coated, 1 to 2 minutes.

Divide the pasta among bowls and serve with Parmigiano-Reggiano and a scattering of fresh thyme.

butter, cream & cheese sauces

~ ɛ ɛ ɛ ~

Snow-capped mountains, medieval castles, and sprawling forests aren't usually what first come to mind when you think of Italy, but that's exactly what you'll find in many of the country's northernmost regions. Explore Piedmont, Lombardy, Friuli-Venezia Giulia, Trentino-Alto Adige, and the Val d'Aosta, and you might think you've stepped into neighboring Switzerland, Austria, France, or Slovenia instead. Set against the backdrop of the Alps, where livestock have grazed and shepherds have flourished for centuries, the cuisine is perhaps less surprising: Rich, melty cheeses, fresh cream, and plenty of butter are its backbone, along with hearty vegetables, stews, and meats. Pasta takes a back seat here; instead, polenta, rice, and potatoes are preferred—stick-to-your-ribs mountain food.

Only a few recipes in this section are traditional Italian fare. The rest (and most cream-based pasta dishes) are more modern inventions. Still, they're all exceptionally delicious, quick to prepare, and work particularly well with egg-based and stuffed pastas, as well as gnocchi.

how to make a simple butter sauce

What's the difference between melted butter and a butter *sauce*? The answer is, perhaps unsurprisingly, pasta cooking water. Gradually and vigorously mixing butter into a small amount of pasta water yields a silky, glaze-like coating that's saucy instead of greasy, and it's this emulsion that graces most plates of stuffed pasta in today's restaurants (in classic French cooking, both the sauce and technique are called *beurre*

monté). This method works particularly well with smaller portions of pasta since you need plenty of space in the pan for mixing. Just make sure to use unsalted butter so you have more control over the seasoning, especially because the pasta cooking water is already salted.

1. Add ¼ cup (60 ml) pasta cooking water to a skillet or saucier and bring to a lively simmer over medium-high heat. Let it bubble for a few moments.

2. Reduce the heat to low. Add 4 tablespoons (55 grams) cold unsalted butter, 1 tablespoon at a time, and whisk or stir constantly until the butter melts and the sauce thickens.

3. Add your cooked pasta and swirl the pan until it's well coated.

4. If the glaze gets too thick, add another splash of pasta water and swirl. If it separates, turn off the heat, add more butter, and swirl. And if you want to increase the amount of sauce, continue to add more pieces of butter.

5. Serve immediately and drizzle more sauce on top.

NOTE: You can also add the pasta to the pan with the simmering water before adding the butter and proceed as directed, making sure to keep the pan/pasta moving continuously.

how to make brown butter

Brown butter looks, smells, and tastes complex, but it couldn't be simpler to make. Use it as a sauce, as an ingredient in pasta fillings, or for sweet and savory recipes beyond this book to add a nutty, caramel undertone to any dish. Make a large batch and keep it in the fridge (for up to 2 weeks) or freezer (for up to 3 months) so you'll always have this liquid gold at your fingertips.

1. Add your preferred amount of unsalted butter to a small saucepan. Cook over medium-low heat, stirring often, until the milk solids separate, foam, and just start to turn golden, about 5 to 7 minutes. Keep an eye on it!

2. Remove from the heat and continue to stir—the residual heat of the pan will deepen the color. When it's your desired shade of amber, transfer to a heatproof bowl or container to stop the cooking.

Whipped Ricotta Agnolotti with a Simple Butter Sauce

Egg Yolk Raviolo (Uovo in Raviolo)
with Butter & Sage Sauce

PAIR IT WITH

*All gnocchi (59) · All stuffed pastas (150) ·
Fettuccine (131) · Garganelli (142) ·
Tagliatelle (131)*

butter & sage sauce
burro e salvia

¾ cup (170 grams; 1½ sticks)
unsalted butter

16 **fresh sage leaves**, or more if
you'd like

Kosher salt

Freshly grated **Parmigiano-
Reggiano**, for serving

It's amazing the depth of flavor you can create with two ingredients in less than 10 minutes. Basting sage in hot, foaming butter not only infuses the sauce with its floral fragrance, it crisps the leaves into crackling, lace-like chips that impart welcome textural contrast.

In a large sauté pan or skillet, melt the butter over medium heat. Add the sage and fry until crisp and dark around the edges, swirling the pan often to coat the leaves in the butter, about 3 minutes. Remove from the heat and transfer the sage to a paper towel–lined plate.

TO SERVE Cook your pasta of choice to your liking. When the pasta is almost done, return the butter to medium heat. Scoop out ¾ cup (180 ml) pasta cooking water and add it to the butter. Whisk or stir the sauce constantly until emulsified.

If the pasta can comfortably fit in your pan, transfer it directly to the sauce with a spider sieve or slotted spoon (or drain it first and reserve 1 cup (240 ml) pasta cooking water). Simmer, stirring or swirling the pan often, until the sauce thickens and the pasta is well coated, about 2 minutes. Turn off the heat and shower the pasta with Parmigiano-Reggiano. Swirl again until creamy, loosening with more cooking water as needed.

If there's too much pasta to fit in the pan, simmer the sauce until slightly thickened, about 2 minutes. Transfer the pasta to a serving platter or bowl and pour the sauce on top, making sure all the pasta is coated.

Serve topped with grated Parmigiano-Reggiano and the fried sage.

SERVES 4

*enough for 22 ounces fresh pasta or
16 ounces dried pasta*

Active time: 15 minutes
Total time: 15 minutes

PAIR IT WITH

*Farfalle (140) · Fettuccine (131) ·
Pappardelle (131) · Pici (83) · Potato Gnocchi (67) ·
Tagliatelle (131)*

butter & parmesan sauce
alfredo's alfredo

6 ounces (170 grams)
Parmigiano-Reggiano, plus
more for serving

¾ cup (170 grams; 1½ sticks) cold
unsalted butter

Kosher salt

Fettuccine Alfredo, one of the most popular pasta dishes in the United States by a mile, was born in Rome in 1914. Chef Alfredo di Lelio first served it at his restaurant Alfredo's after, according to some, it had been one of the only dishes his wife, Ines, enjoyed regularly during a difficult pregnancy. The combination of pasta, butter, and Parmigiano-Reggiano wasn't new: Alfredo's recipe was an ultra-rich version of an Italian classic with various names—fettuccine al burro, fettuccine burro e Parmigiano, or pasta in bianco ("white pasta"). The decadent sauce soon became a favorite among visiting members of the Hollywood elite who, upon returning to the United States, popularized it with a few changes. Because access to high-quality butter and cheese was limited stateside, the addition of heavy cream soon made an appearance to lend similar richness. Later, other stabilizers and thickeners were introduced to make the sauce ready for supermarket shelves. (Needless to say, the dish never took off in Italy, but that doesn't mean it isn't delicious!)

Alfredo's original version included an eye-watering amount of butter and cheese: half a pound of each for every pound of pasta. I've made it (a little) lighter while keeping its essence intact. There's no need to splurge on highly aged Parmigiano-Reggiano here; opt for something younger, which will melt more easily and have a milder flavor. Grana Padano is a good substitute.

Note
Freshly grated cheese is key to a creamy, emulsified sauce, so avoid anything pre-grated, which might have additives. Using the smallest star-shaped holes of a box grater creates the most surface area for the cheese to melt, which will help prevent clumping.

Grate the cheese on the smallest holes of a box grater and add it to a large, heatproof (preferably metal) mixing bowl. Cut the butter into small cubes and add it to the bowl.

TO SERVE Cook your pasta of choice to your liking. Using tongs, a spider sieve, and/or a slotted spoon, transfer the pasta directly from the pot to the bowl (or drain it first and reserve 1 cup (240 ml) pasta cooking water).

Pour ½ cup (120 ml) pasta cooking water into the bowl on top of the pasta, then immediately start tossing everything together vigorously—and I mean *vigorously*—until the butter and cheese melt into a creamy sauce. If it starts to look dry, add more cooking water; it's better for the sauce to be a little loose since it will tighten as it cools. Season to taste with salt—though you might not need any.

Divide the pasta among bowls and serve topped with more grated cheese.

Black Pepper Fettuccine with Butter & Parmesan Sauce

compound butters

"Compound butter" sounds fancier than it is, probably because you'll usually find one slowly melting over a ribeye at a white tablecloth steakhouse. But compound butters are just softened butter mixed with savory or sweet flavorings. And although it's certainly delicious on your favorite proteins, adding a few pantry staples to a stick of butter will make for an instant pasta upgrade, too. Garlic and herbs are always a crowd-pleaser, but the combinations are endless: sharp cheeses, spicy chilies, sweet black garlic, briny anchovies...dare I say truffles?

Here are a few of my favorite combinations. These butters can be chilled, sliced, and stored in the refrigerator for 1 to 2 weeks and in the freezer for up to 3 months so you always have something special on hand.

TO SERVE Refrigerate the butter while you cook the pasta of your choice to your liking; cold butter will emulsify into a sauce more readily. When the pasta is almost ready, transfer ½ cup (120 ml) pasta cooking water from the pot to a large nonstick sauté pan over medium-high heat. Bring the water to a simmer, then transfer the pasta to the pan (or drain it first and reserve 1 cup (240 ml) pasta cooking water). Let the water thicken slightly, then turn off the heat and add the butter. Swirl the pan constantly until the butter melts and the pasta is well coated, loosening with more pasta water as needed. Season to taste.

TO STORE Cut a 12-inch-long sheet of parchment paper and transfer the butter mixture to the center. Pull the top of the parchment over the butter and, pinning the edge that's closest to you to the work surface, use a bench scraper or other straightedge to push and tuck the parchment around the butter into a tight log. Roll the rest of the parchment around the butter, then twist the ends in opposite directions to seal (like a candy wrapper). Refrigerate until firm.

TO FREEZE Slice the chilled butter log into 8 pieces and freeze in a freezer-safe bag. Let the frozen butter stand at room temperature for about 30 minutes before tossing with pasta.

parmesan-garlic butter

Makes ½ cup; serves 2 to 4
Active time: 10 minutes
Total time: 10 minutes

½ cup (115 grams)
unsalted butter, softened at
room temperature

4 **garlic cloves**, grated

1½ ounces (42 grams) finely
grated **Parmigiano-Reggiano**

½ loosely packed cup (10 grams)
fresh flat-leaf parsley

¼ teaspoon **kosher salt**,
plus more to taste

Add the ingredients to a small
food processor and pulse until
the parsley is finely chopped and
the mixture is well combined.
(Alternatively, finely chop
the parsley by hand and mix
everything together in a bowl.)
Adjust seasoning to taste.

lemon-chive butter

Makes ½ cup; serves 2 to 4
Active time: 10 minutes
Total time: 10 minutes

½ cup (115 grams)
unsalted butter, softened at
room temperature

Grated zest of 1 **lemon**

1 teaspoon **lemon juice**

2 tablespoons minced
fresh chives

¼ teaspoon **kosher salt**,
plus more to taste

Add the ingredients to a small
food processor and pulse until
well combined (or mix everything
together in a bowl). Adjust
seasoning to taste.

spicy tomato-anchovy butter

Makes ¾ cup; serves 2 to 4
Active time: 15 minutes
Total time: 15 minutes, plus cooling

1 tablespoon (15 ml)
extra-virgin olive oil

4 fillets **oil-packed anchovies**

2 **garlic cloves**, grated

3 tablespoons (45 grams)
tomato paste

1 tablespoon (15 grams) crushed
Calabrian chili pepper paste,
plus more to taste

½ cup (115 grams)
unsalted butter, softened at
room temperature

Kosher salt to taste

Warm the oil in a small saucepan
over medium heat. Add the
anchovies and cook, stirring
constantly, until dissolved. Add
the garlic and cook, stirring, until
fragrant, 30 seconds. Add the
tomato paste and pepper paste
and cook, stirring, for 2 minutes.
Transfer to a bowl and let cool
completely.

Add the anchovy-tomato mixture
and butter to a small food
processor and pulse until well
combined. Season to taste with
salt.

PAIR IT WITH

*All hand-cut pastas (128) • Capunti (100) •
Cavatelli (96) • Farfalle (140) • Pici (83) •
Potato Gnocchi (67)*

pecorino, pepper & lemon sauce

3½ ounces (100 grams) **Pecorino Romano**

1 **lemon**

2 teaspoons (6 grams) **whole black peppercorns**

2 tablespoons (30 grams) **unsalted butter**

Kosher salt

¼ cup (60 ml) **heavy cream**

Cacio e pepe—one of Rome's "big four," along with gricia, carbonara, and amatriciana—is my favorite pasta dish. There, I said it. It's also a sauce that can be technically challenging. Because it consists solely of Pecorino Romano and black pepper, traditional cacio e pepe is easier to make with starch-heavy pasta water—best achieved with longer-cooking dried pasta—which helps keep the sauce creamy instead of clumpy. So I've decided to take the building blocks of cacio e pepe on a little field trip. Here, a shot of citrus provides brightness, and butter and cream, although entirely untraditional, emulsify the sauce with a fraction of the effort (and the starch). I tend to reserve this dish for a date night in, so this recipe serves two, with plenty of sauce for drizzling.

Finely grate the Pecorino on the smallest holes of a box grater and add it to a bowl. Grate the zest of half of the lemon and juice it all.

Heat a large nonstick skillet over medium-high and toast the peppercorns until fragrant, shaking the pan often, 3 to 5 minutes. Transfer to a mortar and pestle or spice grinder and crush until semi-fine.

In the same nonstick skillet, melt the butter over medium heat and add three-quarters of the pepper. Cook, stirring often, until the butter starts to foam. Turn off the heat and set aside.

TO SERVE Bring a large pot of water to a boil and season it generously with salt. Cook your pasta of choice until just shy of your liking (if using dried pasta, 1 to 2 minutes before al dente).

When the pasta is almost ready, add ¼ cup (60 ml) pasta cooking water to the bowl with the Pecorino and stir into a thick paste.

Place the skillet with the butter and pepper over high heat. Transfer the pasta and ½ cup (120 ml) pasta cooking water to the pan and toss until the water thickens, 1 to 2 minutes. (If you need to drain the pasta first, reserve 1 cup (240 ml) pasta cooking water.) Reduce the heat to medium-low and stir in the cream. Let it bubble for a few moments until thickened once more.

Turn off the heat and add the Pecorino paste. Stir vigorously until the cheese melts and the sauce becomes creamy. Loosen with more pasta water if needed—it's better for the sauce to be a little loose since it will tighten as it cools. Stir in the lemon zest and juice. Divide the pasta among bowls and serve immediately with a sprinkle of the remaining pepper.

Pici with Pecorino, Pepper & Lemon Sauce

*Four-Cheese Caramelle with
Golden Saffron Sauce*

PAIR IT WITH

Agnolotti (177) · Capunti (100) · Caramelle (182) ·
Cavatelli (96) · "Classic" Ravioli (152) · Farfalle (140) ·
Pappardelle (131) · Tortelloni (172)

golden saffron sauce

A generous pinch (about ½ teaspoon) **saffron threads**

½ cup (120 ml) **hot, but not boiling, water**

½ cup (120 ml) **dry white wine** like Pinot Grigio

4 tablespoons (55 grams) cold **unsalted butter**, cut into tablespoons, divided

½ cup (120 ml) **heavy cream**

Kosher salt

Aleppo pepper, for serving

This vibrant and luxurious sauce is just as ready to perk up a post-work weeknight as it is a date night. Saffron is, of course, the star, magically transforming more humble ingredients into glossy gold. When paired with a bright white wine and a hint of heat, its sweet, floral flavor makes for a surprisingly light meal.

With your fingers or a mortar and pestle, gently crush the saffron threads to break them up and release their flavor and add to a small bowl. Pour over the hot water and steep for 15 minutes.

Meanwhile, add the wine to a large sauté pan or Dutch oven. Bring to a simmer over medium-high heat and cook until the liquid reduces by half, about 3 minutes.

Reduce the heat to medium. Swirl in 2 tablespoons of the butter, one tablespoon at a time, stirring constantly to emulsify. Follow with the cream and the saffron and its liquid. Stir to combine and simmer briefly until thickened, 2 minutes. Season to taste with salt and turn off the heat.

TO SERVE Cook your pasta of choice to your liking. When it's almost ready, return the sauce to medium heat. Transfer the pasta directly to the sauce (or drain it first and reserve 1 cup (240 ml) pasta cooking water), along with the remaining 2 tablespoons butter. Toss until the butter melts and the pasta is well coated, loosening with cooking water as needed. Adjust seasoning to taste.

Divide the pasta among bowls and serve with a sprinkle of Aleppo pepper.

PAIR IT WITH

*Capunti (100) · Corzetti della Valpolcevera (92) ·
Farfalle (140) · Potato Gnocchi (67) ·
Spizzulus (104)*

roasted garlic & miso sauce

2 large **garlic heads**, the tops cut off crosswise to expose the cloves

1 tablespoon (15 ml) **extra-virgin olive oil**

Kosher salt and freshly ground black pepper

2 tablespoons (35 grams) **white miso paste**

4 tablespoons (55 grams) **unsalted butter**, divided

½ cup (120 ml) **heavy cream**

Finely chopped fresh flat-leaf parsley and minced fresh rosemary, for serving

---

MAKE IT VEGAN

Swap the cream for an unflavored dairy-free alternative like oat milk.

Fermented Japanese miso paste lends a level of complexity to this sauce that is deeply savory, a little tangy, and a touch sweet—think buttery, salty garlic bread in pasta form. And yes, you read it right: there are two whole heads of garlic.

Heat the oven to 400°F/205°C.

Arrange the garlic heads, cut sides up, on individual pieces of aluminum foil. Drizzle with the oil and season with salt and pepper. Tightly wrap each head and place directly on the middle oven rack or a sheet pan. Roast until tender and caramelized, about 45 minutes.

When the garlic is cool enough to handle, squeeze the softened cloves into a small bowl. Mash with a fork until smooth, then add the miso and combine into a paste. Set aside.

In a Dutch oven or large sauté pan, melt 2 tablespoons of the butter over medium heat. Add the garlic and miso mixture, breaking it up with a whisk until homogenous. Remove from the heat.

TO SERVE Cook your pasta of choice to your liking. While the pasta cooks, return the miso mixture to medium heat. Add ¼ cup (60 ml) pasta cooking water to the pan and whisk to combine. Follow with the cream and stir until uniform and glossy. Simmer briefly to thicken and season to taste with salt and pepper. If the sauce gets very thick, loosen it with more pasta cooking water.

Transfer the pasta directly to the sauce (or drain it first and reserve 1 cup (240 ml) pasta cooking water), along with the remaining 2 tablespoons butter. Toss until the butter melts and the pasta is well coated, loosening with cooking water as needed.

Divide the pasta among bowls and serve topped with the fresh herbs.

Spizzulus with Roasted Garlic & Miso Sauce

Garganelli with Smoky Pumpkin Sauce

PAIR IT WITH

All hand-cut pastas (128) •
Farfalle (140) • Garganelli (142) •
Pici (83) • Ricotta Gnocchi (60)

smoky pumpkin sauce

4 tablespoons (55 grams)
unsalted butter, divided

12 **fresh sage leaves**

4 **garlic cloves**, minced

1¼ cups (280 grams) **pumpkin
purée**

¾ cup (180 ml) **vegetable stock**

¾ teaspoon **smoked paprika**

½ teaspoon **chili powder**

½ teaspoon **chipotle chili powder**

Whole **nutmeg**

Kosher salt

⅓ cup (80 ml) **heavy cream**

¾ ounce (20 grams) finely grated
Parmigiano-Reggiano

Here's a sauce to make all autumn long, especially when you have that last bit of pumpkin purée left over from a holiday pie. Don't be fooled, though: this isn't giving off any pumpkin spice latte vibes. It's smoky, spicy, and plenty savory.

In a small skillet, melt 2 tablespoons of the butter over medium heat. Add the sage and fry, shaking the pan often, until darkened and crisp, about 2 minutes. Transfer to a paper towel–lined plate.

In a large sauté pan or Dutch oven, melt the remaining 2 tablespoons butter over medium heat. Add the garlic and cook until fragrant, stirring constantly, 30 seconds.

Stir in the pumpkin, stock, smoked paprika, chili powder, chipotle powder, a generous grating of nutmeg, and a pinch of salt. Simmer the sauce until slightly thickened, stirring occasionally, 5 to 7 minutes. Stir in the cream and simmer until thickened, about 3 minutes. Season to taste and turn off the heat.

TO SERVE Cook your pasta of choice to your liking. When it's almost ready, reheat the sauce over medium. Transfer the pasta directly to the sauce (or drain it first and reserve 1 cup (240 ml) pasta cooking water) and toss until the pasta is well coated. Turn off the heat and stir in the cheese. Loosen with cooking water as needed and adjust the seasoning to taste.

Divide the pasta among bowls and serve topped with the fried sage.

MAKE IT VEGAN

Swap the cream for an unflavored dairy-free alternative like oat milk; swap the Parmigiano-Reggiano for a vegetarian version or nutritional yeast, or omit it entirely.

PAIR IT WITH

*Cavatelli (96) • Farfalle (140) • Ossola-Style Gnocchi (66) •
Pici (83) • Potato Gnocchi (67) • Sweet Potato Gnocchi (70) •
Tagliatelle (131)*

four-cheese sauce
quattro formaggi

¾ cup (180 ml) **heavy cream**

1 **garlic clove**, peeled and smashed

4 sprigs **fresh rosemary, thyme, sage, or a mix**

2 ounces (55 grams) **rind-free Taleggio**, cut into small cubes

2 ounces (55 grams) **rind-free Fontina, Gruyère, Comté, or Emmental**, cut into small cubes

2 ounces (55 grams) **Gorgonzola Dolce, Roquefort, or other sweet blue cheese**, broken into small pieces

2 ounces (55 grams) finely grated **Parmigiano-Reggiano**

Whole nutmeg

Freshly ground white or black pepper

Kosher salt

Four-cheese pasta, or pasta ai quattro formaggi, is northern Italy's mac and cheese: easy to make and always on hand. It's a pantry dish, made from the odds and ends of whatever's in the house, which are usually melty Alpine varieties like Fontina and Taleggio. What I love about this dish is that there are no rules, no flour or other thickening agents, and it's really just an excuse to eat fondue. The cheeses here are traditional, but I encourage you to experiment with any combination of aged, funky, tangy, and buttery varieties you prefer.

Add the cream, garlic, and herbs to a large saucier or saucepan. Bring to a gentle simmer over medium heat, stirring often to prevent scorching. Turn off the heat and let the mixture steep for 10 minutes. Discard the aromatics.

Return the cream to low heat. Add the Taleggio and whisk constantly until fully melted. Add the Fontina, whisk until smooth, and repeat with the Gorgonzola. Turn off the heat and whisk in the Parmigiano-Reggiano. Season to taste with nutmeg, pepper, and salt if it needs it.

TO SERVE   Cook your pasta of choice to your liking. When it's almost ready, return the sauce to low heat. Transfer the pasta directly to the sauce (or drain it first and reserve 1 cup (240 ml) pasta cooking water) and toss until the pasta is well coated—don't worry if the sauce is a bit loose; it'll tighten as it cools.

Divide the pasta among bowls and serve with more grated nutmeg if you'd like. To reheat this dish, loosen the sauce with some cooking water and keep the heat low.

Sweet Potato Gnocchi with Four-Cheese Sauce

PAIR IT WITH

*Cavatelli (96) • Capunti (100) • "Classic" Ravioli (152) •
Corzetti della Valpolcevera (92) • Potato Gnocchi (67) •
Scarpinocc (166) • Spizzulus (104)*

caramelized onion cheese sauce

6 tablespoons (85 grams) **unsalted butter**, divided

3 medium **yellow onions**, halved and sliced into ¼-inch half-moons

Kosher salt

¼ cup (60 ml) **aged sherry vinegar or balsamic vinegar**

Freshly ground black pepper

1 cup (60 grams) **toasted breadcrumbs**, page 354

1 teaspoon stripped **fresh thyme**, roughly chopped

1½ teaspoons minced **fresh rosemary**, from about 1 large sprig

2 tablespoons (20 grams) **all-purpose flour**

1½ cups (360 ml) **whole milk**

3½ ounces (100 grams) grated **mild white cheddar**

2½ ounces (70 grams) grated **aged white cheddar**

2½ ounces (70 grams) grated **Gruyère, Gouda, Comté, or Emmental**

This dish is everything I want from comfort food (butter, cheese) while also being a little unexpected. It's mac and cheese with grown-up flair, and I'd firmly put it into "project cooking" territory—not for being difficult (it isn't), but for its time commitment. The key? Don't rush the onions. Caramelized onions take time, and they're worth every second.

FOR THE CARAMELIZED ONIONS   In a Dutch oven or large, heavy-bottomed sauté pan, melt 4 tablespoons of the butter over medium-high heat. Add the onions and stir until thoroughly coated. Cook, stirring frequently, until the onions are soft and translucent, 15 minutes, then season generously with salt. Reduce the heat to medium-low and continue cooking, stirring every few minutes, until golden—this can take anywhere from 30 to 60 minutes, depending on your stovetop.

Once the onions start to stick to the bottom of the pan, reduce the heat to low and stir them frequently to prevent burning. If needed, deglaze the pan with a bit of water. Continue to cook, stir, and scrape until the onions are jammy and a rich, deep brown.

When the onions are done, increase the heat to medium and pour in the vinegar. Cook, stirring frequently, until the sharpness has dissipated, 2 to 3 minutes. Season to taste with salt and pepper. Transfer the onions to a bowl.

FOR THE BREADCRUMBS   Make the toasted breadcrumbs and stir in the thyme and rosemary while still warm (if using leftover breadcrumbs, gently reheat them in a dry skillet, add the herbs, and stir until fragrant, about 1 minute).

In the same vessel you used for the onions, melt the remaining 2 tablespoons butter over medium heat. Add the flour and whisk to combine into a paste, scraping up any browned bits from the bottom of the pan. Continue whisking for 1 to 2 minutes until the mixture smells nutty and starts to loosen.

Add the milk in a thin, steady stream, or a splash at a time, and whisk vigorously to combine. The mixture will get very thick at first but will thin out significantly once all the milk is added. Continue to cook, whisking frequently, until the sauce begins to bubble, then reduce the heat to low and stir until it thickens and coats the back of a spoon, another minute or two.

Reduce the heat to low. Add the cheeses in 3 or 4 increments, whisking thoroughly after each addition. Remove from the heat and stir in the caramelized onions. Season to taste.

TO SERVE Cook your pasta of choice to your liking. While the pasta cooks, reheat the sauce over medium-low and stir frequently. Add ¼ cup (60 ml) pasta cooking water and stir until smooth and saucy.

Transfer the pasta directly to the sauce (or drain it first and reserve 1 cup (240 ml) pasta cooking water) and stir to combine, loosening with more cooking water as needed. Divide the pasta among bowls and serve with plenty of breadcrumbs and black pepper.

meaty sauces

I didn't think I'd be writing this section. For the past decade, I haven't eaten meat at all, and it's only recently that I started indulging in a taste here and there on holidays and special occasions. What's more, I abide by Jewish kosher laws, which, among other things, means no pork and no mixing of meat and dairy—so quite a few Italian staples are off the table.

Although I rarely indulge in eating meat, I was surprised to find myself especially excited to test these recipes. It felt like I was being initiated into a secret society of Italian cooking that had for so long been out of reach. I also found that my dietary parameters made for an exhilarating challenge, and what I'd once considered restrictive suddenly became an important way to honor both Italian tradition and my own heritage.

Some of these recipes are written using meat alternatives, which is what you'll find me eating on a more regular basis. For traditional dishes that incorporate non-kosher animal products, these are noted in the recipes' introductions should you prefer to use them. Finally, most of these sauces only get better with time, so don't hesitate to make them in advance. They can be stored in the refrigerator for up to 3 days or in the freezer for up to 3 months.

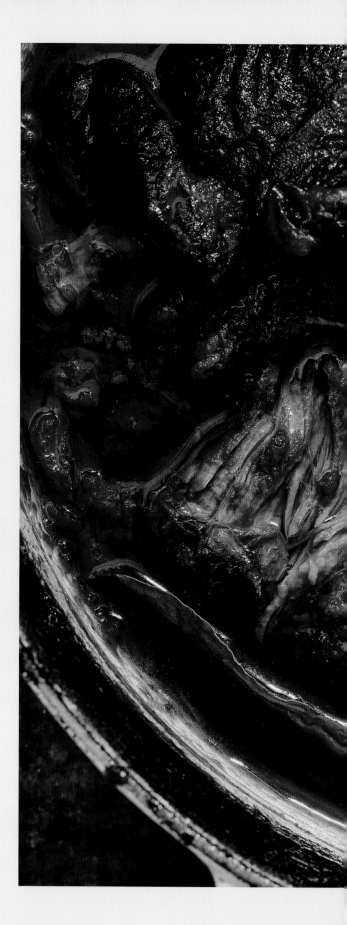

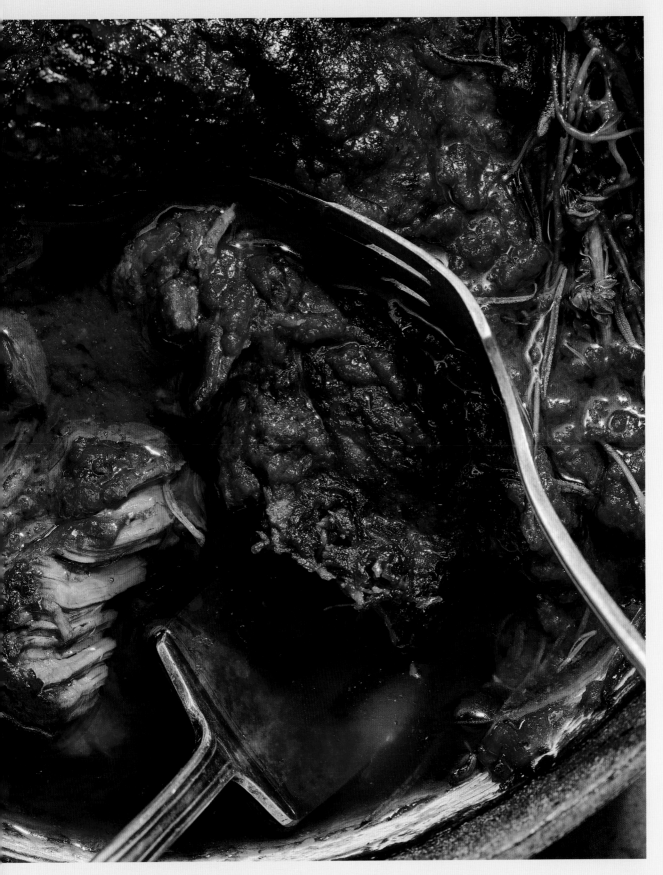

Port-Braised Lamb Ragù with Shallots & Rosemary

SERVES 4

enough for 22 ounces fresh pasta or 16 ounces dried pasta

Active time: 45 minutes
Total time: 2 hours 15 minutes

PAIR IT WITH

Cavatelli (96) • Foglie d'Ulivo (110) •
Orecchiette (108) • Malloreddus (102) •
Spizzulus (104)

sausage, saffron & fennel ragù

¼ teaspoon (a generous pinch) **saffron threads**

½ cup (120 ml) hot (but not boiling) **water**

2 tablespoons (30 ml) **extra-virgin olive oil**

½ **yellow onion**, finely chopped

½ small **fennel bulb**, finely chopped

Kosher salt and freshly ground black pepper

3 **garlic cloves**, minced

12 ounces (340 grams) uncooked **sweet Italian or fennel-flavored sausage**, any casings removed

¾ cup (180 ml) dry **white wine** like Pinot Grigio

1 (24- or 26-ounce/680- or 750-gram) jar **tomato purée** (passata) or 1 (28-ounce/794-gram) can peeled whole tomatoes

1 **bay leaf**

Finely grated **Pecorino Romano**, for serving (optional)

Torn **fresh basil** leaves, for serving

This is a perfect late-summer meat sauce when you're looking for something light but cooler temperatures are on the horizon. Bright and tangy, with floral undertones from the fennel and saffron, it's inspired by malloreddus alla campidanese, a Sardinian dish that celebrates the region's famous fennel-spiked pork sausage.

For those who abstain from eating pork like I do, sweet Italian-style sausages made with beef are a good substitute. And if you can't find anything with fennel, add 1 teaspoon fennel seeds to the sauce when browning the meat.

STEEP THE SAFFRON   With your fingers or with a mortar and pestle, gently crush the saffron threads to break them up and release their flavor and add to a small bowl. Pour over the hot water and steep for 15 minutes.

In a Dutch oven or large nonstick sauté pan, warm the oil over medium-low heat. Add the onion and fennel and season with salt and pepper. Cook until softened but not browned, stirring occasionally, about 10 minutes. Add the garlic and cook until fragrant, stirring constantly, 30 seconds.

Push the vegetables to one side of the pot and add the meat. Flatten it into a patty with a wooden spoon or spatula and allow to cook undisturbed until golden, 3 to 5 minutes. Flip the meat, break it into small pieces, and cook until no longer pink, about 3 minutes more.

Mix the meat and vegetables together. Increase the heat to medium-high and pour in the wine, scraping up any browned bits from the bottom of the pot, and simmer 2 to 3 minutes. Stir in the tomatoes, then swish some water around the empty container to catch the residual juices and add it to the pot. (If using whole tomatoes, use a wooden spoon to break them up.) Add the bay leaf, saffron and its liquid, and a pinch of salt and pepper.

Bring to a simmer, then reduce to a low bubble and cook for 1½ hours, stirring occasionally. If the sauce starts to look dry, add a splash of water. Discard the bay leaf and season to taste.

TO SERVE   Cook your pasta of choice until just shy of your liking. Ladle ½ cup (120 ml) pasta cooking water into the sauce, then transfer the pasta directly to the pot (or drain it first and reserve 1 cup (240 ml) pasta cooking water). Toss to combine and cook until the pasta is well coated, 1 to 2 minutes, adding more cooking water to loosen as needed. Divide the pasta among bowls and serve topped with grated cheese, if using, and basil.

Saffron Malloreddus with Sausage, Saffron & Fennel Ragù

Ricotta Gnocchi with The Meatiest Meatless Ragù

PAIR IT WITH

Garganelli (142) · Lasagne (200) · Maltagliati (79) ·
Pappardelle (131) · Potato Gnocchi (67) · Ricotta Gnocchi (60) ·
Tagliatelle (131) · Tortelloni (172)

the meatiest meatless ragù

4 tablespoons (55 grams) **unsalted butter**, divided, plus more for serving

12 to 16 ounces (340 to 450 grams) **plant-based ground beef alternative** like Impossible or Beyond Meat

1 small **yellow onion**, finely chopped

½ **fennel bulb or 1 peeled carrot**, finely chopped

2 **celery stalks**, finely chopped

Kosher salt and freshly ground black pepper

4 **garlic cloves**, minced

2 tablespoons (30 grams) **tomato paste**

1½ tablespoons (30 grams) **white miso paste**

¾ cup (180 ml) **dry red wine** like Sangiovese or Chianti

1 tablespoon (15 grams) fish-free **Worcestershire sauce**

1 cup (240 ml) **vegetable stock**, plus more as needed

½ cup (120 ml) **whole milk**

Finely grated **Parmigiano-Reggiano**, for serving (optional)

In Tuscany, there's a dish called sugo finto, meaning "fake sauce," which was born out of peasant kitchens where meat was an unaffordable luxury. It's a bright combination of vegetables, wine, and tomatoes, and a delicious sauce in its own right—but like a quinoa burger, it doesn't quite satisfy my meaty cravings.

This is another "fake sauce," inspired by the technique of Bolognese and using umami-forward ingredients that are guaranteed to pack a punch. I've served this to many rooms of unsuspecting meat-eaters—when asked if anyone could guess the "secret" ingredients, lamb was the most common suggestion. All of that is to say: I love it. You'll love it. Your meat-eating friends will love it, too.

In a Dutch oven or large nonstick sauté pan, melt 2 tablespoons of the butter over medium heat. Add the ground beef alternative and cook, stirring frequently, until mostly browned, 5 to 7 minutes. If it verges on burning, add a splash of water to loosen it from the bottom of the pot. Transfer to a bowl.

Return the pot to medium heat and add the remaining 2 tablespoons butter. Add the onion, fennel (or carrot), and celery and season with salt and pepper. Cook until soft and translucent, stirring occasionally, 10 to 15 minutes.

Add the garlic and cook until fragrant, 30 seconds. Stir in the tomato and miso pastes, mashing the miso with the side of a spatula to melt it down. Cook, stirring frequently, until the tomato paste caramelizes, 1 to 2 minutes. If the vegetables start to brown, turn down the heat and add a splash of water to deglaze.

Return the "meat" to the pan and mix with the vegetables. Increase the heat to medium-high and add the wine and Worcestershire. Simmer for 2 minutes, scraping up any browned bits from the bottom of the pot. Add the stock, bring to a simmer, then reduce the heat to low. Cook the sauce at a low bubble, stirring occasionally, for 1 hour. If it looks dry at any point, add more stock.

Stir in the milk and simmer, stirring occasionally, for 45 minutes more. Season to taste with salt and pepper.

TO SERVE Cook your pasta of choice to your liking. Transfer it directly to the sauce, along with another knob of butter and ¼ cup (60 ml) pasta cooking water (if you need to drain the pasta first, reserve a little more cooking water than you might need). Toss until the pasta is well coated, loosening with more cooking water as needed. Divide the pasta among bowls and serve with grated cheese if you'd like.

SERVES 4

enough for 22 ounces fresh pasta or
16 ounces dried pasta

Active time: 1 hour
Total time: 4 hours

PAIR IT WITH

Garganelli (142) · Lasagne (200) ·
Maltagliati (79) · Pappardelle (131) · Potato Gnocchi (67) ·
Tagliatelle (131) · Tortelloni (172)

casual bolognese

2 tablespoons (30 ml) extra-virgin **olive oil or unsalted butter**

1 small **yellow onion**, very finely chopped

Kosher salt and freshly ground black pepper

1 medium **carrot**, peeled and very finely chopped

2 **celery stalks**, very finely chopped

1 pound (450 grams) **ground beef**

3 heaping tablespoons (50 grams) **tomato paste**

¾ cup (180 ml) **dry red or white wine** like Sangiovese, Chianti, or Pinot Grigio

1½ cups (360 ml) **low-sodium beef or chicken stock**, plus more as needed

1 cup (240 ml) **tomato purée** (passata)

½ cup (120 ml) **whole milk** (or, to keep it kosher, dairy-free alternative like oat milk)

Whole nutmeg (optional)

Finely grated **Parmigiano-Reggiano**, for serving (optional)

There's a lot of debate around Bolognese meat sauce, simply referred to as "ragù" in its home city. Some recipes insist on six or seven hours of cooking; others demand three types of meat and even gelatin to take it to its highest level. I'll be the first to admit that Bolognese is relatively new to me. Pork is a hallmark of Bologna's cuisine, and for a long time I assumed its famous meat sauce must include pork products. So I just didn't think to make it.

There is, perhaps unsurprisingly, an official recipe registered with Bologna's Chamber of Commerce, and it includes pancetta (cured pork belly) as the base. But every Bolognesi cook has their own version of this sauce, each following a similar style but varying widely in the specifics. Start with your fat of choice—butter, olive oil, and/or that rendered pancetta—and a soffritto (finely chopped onion, carrot, and celery). Next add the meat, usually ground beef, but sometimes pork and/or veal. Pour in some wine, red or white, and then the tomato: this can be paste, passata, or canned whole tomatoes, though always less than the proportion of meat—this is a meat sauce, after all. Stir in some milk at the beginning or end, or none at all. Simmer low and slow.

The first time I made Bolognese I was expecting my world to shift. I'd read so many recipes and heard so many arguments about this sauce that, keeping almost entirely to the traditional method, I was ready to become a changed woman. The sauce was good—my plate was licked clean—but it was just that... good meat sauce. At first I was a little confused. But then I realized that really good meat sauce is exactly what Bolognese is meant to be.

This recipe is a reminder that Bolognese is a simple, casual affair—something that takes time but can easily be put together on a weekend afternoon, usually with ingredients you already have. It's also a reminder that its comfort lies in its subtlety. If you couldn't tell, I'm usually one for a zing of garlic and a handful of herbs, but here it's worth using a little restraint. I should also mention that this ragù, as with most, tastes better the next day, and the day after that, so make it ahead or double the recipe and freeze half for your very appreciative future self.

Warm the oil in a Dutch oven or large, heavy-bottomed saucepan over medium-low heat. Add the onion and a pinch of salt and pepper. Cook, stirring occasionally, until soft and translucent, about 10 minutes. Add the carrot, celery, and another pinch of salt and pepper, and cook until very soft, 10 minutes more.

Push the vegetables to the side of the pot and increase the heat to medium. Add the meat and season it generously, then use a wooden spoon to break it into small pieces. Cook until no longer pink and most of its liquid has evaporated, 10 to 15 minutes, stirring often.

Stir in the tomato paste and mix with the meat and vegetables. Cook for 1 to 2 minutes. Pour in the wine and simmer until mostly evaporated, 2 to 3 minutes, scraping up any browned bits from the bottom of the pot.

Add the stock and tomato purée and bring to a simmer. Reduce the heat to low and cook, uncovered, at a low bubble for 2 to 2½ hours, until most of the liquid has reduced. Stir the sauce occasionally and add more stock if it looks dry.

Stir in the milk (or alternative) and a generous grating of nutmeg, if using. Simmer for 20 to 30 minutes more. Season to taste with salt and pepper.

TO SERVE Cook your pasta of choice to your liking. Transfer it directly to the sauce, along with ¼ cup (60 ml) pasta cooking water (if you need to drain the pasta first, reserve a little more cooking water than you might need). Toss to combine and continue to cook the pasta in the sauce until well coated, 1 to 2 minutes, loosening with more cooking water as needed. Divide the pasta among bowls and serve topped with grated cheese, if you'd like.

PAIR IT WITH

*Cavatelli (96) ·
Corzetti della Valpolcevera (92) ·
Garganelli (142) · Orecchiette (108) · Pappardelle (131) ·
Pici (83) · Spizzulus (104) · Tagliatelle (131)*

roasted red pepper & vegetarian sausage ragù

2 large **red bell peppers**

½ cup (120 ml) **vegetable stock**

3 tablespoons (45 ml) **extra-virgin olive oil**, divided

12 ounces (340 grams) **plant-based sausage** (I like Beyond Meat Hot Italian sausages—use something that crumbles), any casings removed and torn into pieces

½ **yellow onion**, finely chopped

Kosher salt

4 **garlic cloves**, minced

1 tablespoon (15 grams) **tomato paste**

½ cup (120 ml) **dry white wine** like Pinot Grigio

1 teaspoon **smoked paprika**

1 teaspoon **Aleppo pepper or red pepper flakes**

⅓ cup (80 ml) **heavy cream**

Freshly ground black pepper

This ragù is one of the dishes that got me hooked on the power of a good sauce, and you'd never know it comes together in just over an hour. Smoked paprika and plenty of garlic provide slow-cooked–level depth that make it hard to stop eating. Plus, the creaminess comes (mostly) from the roasted peppers, so, although it tastes decadent, it's lighter than it looks.

This recipe is vegetarian as written, but for the omnivore, use your favorite spicy or sweet Italian sausage.

ROAST THE PEPPERS   Set the oven broiler to high. Cut the peppers in half lengthwise. Remove the stems and seeds, then arrange the halves cut sides down on a foil-lined sheet pan. Broil the peppers for 25 minutes, rotating the pan halfway through, or until the skins are almost completely blackened. Alternatively, if you have a gas stovetop, carefully char the whole peppers directly over the flame, using tongs to rotate them.

Transfer the peppers to a bowl and cover tightly with plastic wrap or a dishcloth. Let steam for 10 minutes. When the peppers are still warm but cool enough to handle, remove the skins (they should peel off easily). Then transfer them to a blender and add the stock. Purée until smooth.

In a large nonstick sauté pan, heat 2 tablespoons of the oil over medium-high. Add the sausage and use a spatula or wooden spoon to break it up into small pieces. Cook, stirring frequently, until mostly browned, 5 to 7 minutes. If it verges on burning, add a splash of water to loosen it from the bottom of the pan. Transfer to a bowl.

Reduce the heat to medium and add the remaining 1 tablespoon oil. Add the onion and a pinch of salt. Cook until softened, stirring occasionally, 3 to 5 minutes. Stir in the garlic and cook until fragrant, 30 seconds. Add the tomato paste and cook, stirring frequently, for another minute until caramelized.

continues

Spizzulus with Roasted Red Pepper & Vegetarian Sausage Ragù

Return the sausage to the pan. Increase the heat to medium-high and add the wine. Stir to combine, scraping up any browned bits from the bottom of the pan, and simmer until the wine reduces by half, 2 to 3 minutes.

Reduce the heat to medium-low and stir in the red pepper purée, spices, and a pinch of salt. Simmer, stirring occasionally, until the sauce thickens, 5 to 7 minutes. Stir in the cream and simmer for 2 minutes more. Turn off the heat and season to taste.

TO SERVE Cook your pasta of choice to just shy of your liking. Return the sauce to medium heat and transfer the pasta directly to the pan, along with ¼ cup (60 ml) pasta cooking water (if you need to drain the pasta first, reserve a little more cooking water than you might need). Toss to combine and cook until the pasta is well coated, 1 to 2 minutes, adding more cooking water to loosen as needed. Divide the pasta among bowls and serve.

SERVES 4

*enough for 22 ounces fresh pasta or
16 ounces dried pasta*

Active time: 1½ hours
Total time: 4½ hours, plus marinating

PAIR IT WITH

*Corzetti della Valpolcevera (92) •
Garganelli (142) • Pappardelle (131) • Tagliatelle (131) •
Potato Gnocchi (67)*

port-braised lamb ragù with shallots & rosemary

2½- to 3-pound (1.1- to 1.5-kg) **bone-in lamb shoulder roast**

Kosher salt and freshly ground black pepper

6 sprigs **fresh rosemary**, divided

6 sprigs **fresh thyme**, divided

4 **garlic cloves**, coarsely chopped

Extra-virgin olive oil

1 pound (450 grams; 8 to 10 large) **shallots**, thinly sliced

2 tablespoons (30 grams) **tomato paste**

2 cups (500 ml) **ruby port**

1 cup (240 ml) **low-sodium chicken stock**, plus more as needed

1½ cups (360 ml) **tomato purée** (passata)

2 **bay leaves**

Braised meat and sweet red wine are two staples of Jewish tables. In the fall, during the High Holy Days, you'll find fork-tender brisket bathed in onions; in the spring, at the Passover seder, it's customary to drink four cups of wine—always Manischewitz in my house—throughout the night. This ragù pays homage to those festive meals shared with family, friends, and friends of friends. As the lamb cooks low and slow, the shallots and wine melt together into a sweet, aromatic sauce that softens the meat's usual gaminess.

If a bone-in lamb shoulder isn't an option, use the same amount of beef brisket, preferably second cut, or 1½ to 2 pounds (875 grams) boneless lamb shoulder, excess fat trimmed, and cut it into 1½-inch cubes. If using boneless shoulder, reduce the braising time to 2 to 2½ hours.

THE NIGHT BEFORE, PREPARE THE LAMB Pat the lamb dry with paper towels, then season it generously all over with salt and pepper. Use a sharp knife to score the fat side in a crisscross pattern. Place the meat, fat side up, in a deep container or baking dish and scatter half of the rosemary, half of the thyme, and all the garlic on top and bottom. Cover and refrigerate overnight.

Let the lamb stand at room temperature for 1 hour, then wipe away the herbs and garlic (remove as much as you can so they don't burn when browning the meat). Tie the remaining rosemary and thyme sprigs together with butcher's twine if you have some. Heat the oven to 325°F/160°C.

Coat the bottom of a large Dutch oven with a little oil and turn the heat to medium-high. Carefully add the lamb, fat side down, and sear until browned and a crust forms, about 6 minutes. Flip the meat and cook until golden, 3 to 5 minutes more, reducing the heat as needed to prevent scorching. Transfer to a plate. Turn off the heat and move the pot to the side to cool for a moment.

Add the shallots to the pot, season with salt and pepper, and return the heat to medium-low. Cook, stirring often and scraping up any browned bits from the bottom of the pot, until very tender and jammy, about 15 minutes.

continues

Pappardelle with
Port-Braised Lamb Ragù

Add the tomato paste and cook, stirring, until caramelized, about 2 minutes. Increase the heat to medium-high. Pour in the port and simmer until slightly reduced, about 5 minutes, again scraping up any browned bits from the bottom of the pot.

Stir in the stock and tomato purée, then return the meat to the pot, fat side up. Nestle the tied herbs and bay leaves around the lamb. Bring to a simmer, then turn off the heat and cover.

Roast the lamb in the oven, checking on it and basting the top every hour or so, until very tender, about 3 hours (for smaller roasts, check around 2 hours 45 minutes). If the pot looks dry, add more stock.

When it's done, remove the herbs and bay leaves and transfer the meat to a cutting board. Allow to rest, tented with foil, for 15 minutes. Pull the meat from the bone (remove the fat) and shred it with two forks. Add it back to the pot and mix everything together. Season to taste—you might not need any salt.

Note: Depending on the cut of meat, this recipe can make a lot of sauce, so scoop some out and reserve for another use if needed.

TO SERVE Cook your pasta of choice to your liking. Warm the sauce over medium heat, transfer the pasta directly to the ragù (or drain it first and reserve 1 cup (240 ml) pasta cooking water), and toss to combine. Continue to cook the pasta in the sauce until well coated, 1 to 2 minutes, using cooking water to loosen as needed. Divide the pasta among bowls and serve.

fish sauces

The importance of seafood in Italian cooking is no secret—the country is a peninsula, after all. But seeing the myriad ways in which the same ingredients are used is no less exciting. Pasta with anchovies, for example, will look different depending on who you ask and where you are. In Venice, you'll find them cooked down with onions and vinegar; in Sicily, with breadcrumbs, tomatoes, and saffron. In Tuscany, sea bass is the star of a light and aromatic ragù; in Liguria, it's roasted and tucked into ravioli with wild herbs.

Clams, mussels, shrimp, and squid make regular appearances in Italy's pasta dishes, as do other fish byproducts like colatura (an Italian-style fish sauce, made with fermented anchovies) and bottarga (cured tuna or mullet roe). You'll likely notice their absence here: Shellfish are prohibited under kosher laws and, although I love colatura and bottarga, they're expensive ingredients that can be difficult to find. Instead, these recipes rely heavily on tinned and other readily available fish. When it comes to the can, brands like Ortiz, Scalia, Rustichella D'Abruzzo, and Agostino Recca are a good bet for anchovies; Fishwife, Ortiz, and Matiz Gallego are my preference for sardines; and I'll usually reach for Ortiz (again!) and Tonnino oil-packed tuna.

These are the sauces I gravitate toward when I'm exhausted after a long week; the recipes work exceptionally well with dried pasta. They're also what I choose when I'm looking for a stress-free meal to please a crowd—orecchiette with spicy anchovies and garlic confit (page 335) was the only dish that never left the supper club menu.

*Citrus-Scented Tagliolini with
White Fish Ragù*

PAIR IT WITH

Farfalle (140)
Fettuccine (131)
Sorpresine (138)
Tagliolini (131)

white fish ragù with lemon & capers

¼ cup (60 ml) **extra-virgin olive oil**

1 **shallot**, thinly sliced

Kosher salt

6 **garlic cloves**, thinly sliced

¼ cup (40 grams) **capers in brine**, drained

1 **lemon**, half zested and juiced and half cut into wedges for serving

½ cup (120 ml) **dry white wine** like Pinot Grigio

2 cups (340 grams) **Sungold tomatoes**, halved

1 pound (450 grams) **boneless, skinless flaky white fish**, preferably sea bass (not Chilean)

Freshly ground black pepper

2 tablespoons (30 grams) **unsalted butter**

2 tablespoons (5 grams) finely chopped **fresh flat-leaf parsley**

With warm summer air comes beautiful fresh fish, and this quick ragù reminds me of meals enjoyed along the Italian coast. Sea bass (branzino) reigns in many seaside towns, particularly in Tuscany and Liguria, and its sweetness shines brightest when prepared simply. Serve this sauce with thin but sturdy strands like tagliolini and spaghetti. If you can't find sea bass, another flaky white fish like grouper, halibut, cod, bream, or snapper will work, too.

In a Dutch oven or large sauté pan, warm the oil over medium heat. Add the shallot and a pinch of salt, and cook until softened but not browned, 3 to 5 minutes. Add the garlic, capers, and lemon zest, and cook, stirring occasionally, until the garlic softens, 3 to 5 minutes more.

Pour in the wine and simmer until reduced by half, 2 to 3 minutes. Add the tomatoes and cook, stirring occasionally, until they break down and become jammy, 5 to 7 minutes. Season to taste and turn off the heat.

TO SERVE   Cut the fish into 2-inch pieces and season generously with salt and pepper. Start cooking your pasta of choice to your liking. When it's almost done—this will be almost immediate for some fresh pastas—return the sauce to medium-low heat and pour in ½ cup (120 ml) pasta cooking water. Add the fish, cover the pot, and cook until almost cooked through, about 2 minutes, depending on the fish.

Transfer the pasta directly to the sauce (or drain it first and reserve 1 cup (240 ml) pasta cooking water), along with the butter, lemon juice, and parsley. Toss gently until the pasta is well coated and the fish is slightly broken up and cooked through. Serve with lemon wedges for squeezing.

SERVES 4

*enough for 22 ounces fresh pasta or
16 ounces dried pasta*

Active time: 30 minutes
Total time: 1 hour 15 minutes

PAIR IT WITH

All hand-cut pastas (128)
Farfalle (140)
Garganelli (142)
Sorpresine (138)

slow-roasted salmon & crème fraîche sauce with peas

For the salmon

1 **navel orange**, thinly sliced

1 **lemon**, thinly sliced

A handful of **fresh dill fronds**

Kosher salt and freshly ground black pepper

1 pound (450 grams) **boneless salmon fillet**

½ cup (120 ml) **extra-virgin olive oil**

For the sauce

2 tablespoons (30 grams) **unsalted butter**

1 **shallot**, minced

1 cup (130 grams) fresh or thawed frozen **green peas**

Kosher salt and freshly ground black pepper

4 ounces (115 grams) **crème fraîche**

4 ounces (115 grams) **mascarpone**

1 **lemon**, half zested and juiced and half cut into wedges for serving

¾ ounce (20 grams) finely grated **Parmigiano-Reggiano**

Chopped **fresh herbs** like dill, chives, tarragon, and/or mint, for serving

Slow-roasting is a low-effort, high-reward technique that yields exceptionally juicy results. Bathed in olive oil, citrus, and herbs, salmon takes on gentle, bright flavors that—alongside tangy crème fraîche—round out its richness. Both skinless and skin-on salmon will work; for skin-on, roast the fish skin side down, then remove the skin when flaking it into pieces. If you're short on time, swap in 6 ounces (170 grams) hot- or cold-smoked salmon.

FOR THE SALMON   Heat the oven to 300°F/160°C. Arrange the orange, lemon, and dill along the bottom of a baking dish just large enough to hold the fish. Sprinkle with salt and pepper. Pat the salmon dry, then season it generously. Lay the fish over the aromatics and pour the oil on top, making sure the fish and the bottom of the dish are completely coated.

Roast the salmon for 30 minutes. Remove it from the oven and, carefully tilting the baking dish, spoon some of the oil over the fish. Return it to the oven until just cooked through and very tender, about 15 minutes more. Cool slightly, then flake it into large pieces with a fork and transfer to a plate (discard any skin). Spoon more of the citrus oil on top and set aside.

FOR THE SAUCE   In a Dutch oven or large sauté pan, melt the butter over medium heat. Add the shallot and cook, stirring occasionally, until softened, about 3 minutes. Add the peas, season with salt and pepper, and cook until vibrant and just tender, 1 to 2 minutes for thawed frozen peas and a bit longer for fresh. Turn off the heat. Stir in the crème fraîche and mascarpone until smooth. Season to taste.

TO SERVE   Cook your pasta of choice to your liking. When the pasta is almost done, return the sauce to medium-low heat and stir in ¼ cup (60 ml) pasta cooking water, or enough to make the mixture saucy. Fold in the salmon.

Transfer the pasta directly to the sauce (if you need to drain it first, reserve 1 cup (240 ml) of cooking water) and gently toss to combine. Turn off the heat and add the lemon juice and zest and Parmigiano-Reggiano. Toss again until the pasta is well coated, adding more cooking water to loosen as needed.

Divide the pasta among bowls. Serve, finished with the herbs, lots of black pepper, and lemon wedges for squeezing.

Farfalle with Slow-Roasted Salmon & Crème Fraîche Sauce with Peas

329

Whole Wheat Pici with Anchovy & Onion Sauce

PAIR IT WITH

*Busiate (106) · Capunti (100),
Fettuccine (131) · Malloreddus (102) · Orecchiette (108) ·
Pici (83) · Tagliatelle (131)*

anchovy & onion sauce with breadcrumbs

2 tablespoons (30 ml) **extra-virgin olive oil**

4 tablespoons (55 grams) **unsalted butter**, divided

2 medium **yellow or white onions**, thinly sliced into half-moons

Kosher salt and freshly ground black pepper

1 ounce (25 grams; 6 to 8 fillets) **oil-packed anchovies**

½ cup (120 ml) **dry white wine** like Pinot Grigio

1 (4.2-ounce/120-gram) tin **oil-packed sardines**, drained and bones removed

1 **lemon**, zested and juiced

1 loosely packed cup (20 grams) **fresh flat-leaf parsley**, finely chopped

⅔ cup (40 grams) **toasted breadcrumbs**, page 354, plus more for serving

In Venice, you'll come across bigoli in salsa, a thick spaghetti-like pasta, often made with whole wheat or buckwheat flour, coated in a rich mix of anchovies and onions. It's one of the region's signature dishes, but, unsurprisingly, there are dozens of variations. Some use salt-cured anchovies while others prefer oil-packed or sardines; some add a dash of vinegar to balance the sweetness of the onions, and others accentuate it with a pinch of cinnamon.

Travel south to Sicily and you'll find pasta c'anciove e ca muddica, another anchovy-based dish that's full of texture thanks to crunchy breadcrumbs and wild fennel, as well as pasta con le sarde, which features raisins, pine nuts, and saffron—remnants of the region's Arabic influence—alongside oily fresh sardines.

This sauce is inspired by all of them. It also includes butter, an ingredient found in none, but one that I find softens the flavor of the fish (plus, is there anything better than onions cooked in butter?), though feel free to skip the sardines if you don't have any. Pair it with whole wheat pici (page 83, for the dough) to mimic the effect of bigoli and add a deliciously nutty, rustic dimension.

In a Dutch oven or large sauté pan, warm the oil and 2 tablespoons of the butter over medium heat. Add the onions, season with salt and pepper, and cook, stirring often, until very soft but not browned, 15 to 20 minutes. Reduce the heat as needed.

Add the anchovies and cook, stirring, until dissolved, then cook 2 to 3 minutes longer. Pour in the wine and simmer for 2 minutes, scraping up any browned bits from the bottom of the pan. Turn off the heat.

TO SERVE Cook your pasta of choice until just shy of your liking. When the pasta is almost ready, return the sauce to medium-high heat and add ¾ cup (180 ml) pasta cooking water. Simmer until slightly thickened. Season to taste.

Transfer the pasta directly to the sauce (or drain it first and reserve 1 cup (240 ml) pasta cooking water), along with the remaining 2 tablespoons butter, the sardines, lemon zest and juice, most of the parsley, and the breadcrumbs. Toss to combine and cook, stirring constantly, until the pasta is well coated and the sardines flake into pieces, 1 to 2 minutes. Loosen with more pasta cooking water as needed.

Divide the pasta among bowls and serve topped with the rest of the parsley and breadcrumbs.

PAIR IT WITH

Busiate (106) · Farfalle (140) · Sorpresine (138) ·
Strozzapreti (88) · Tagliolini (131)

pantry tuna & tomato sauce

3 **garlic cloves**, minced

½ loosely packed cup (10 grams) **fresh flat-leaf parsley**, finely chopped

1 tablespoon (about 6 large leaves) thinly sliced **fresh basil**

¼ cup plus 2 tablespoons (90 ml) **extra-virgin olive oil**, divided

½ teaspoon **red pepper flakes**

2 tablespoons (40 grams) **tomato paste**

2 (5-ounce/142-gram) cans **tuna in olive oil**, drained

½ cup (120 ml) **dry red wine** like Sangiovese or Chianti

1 (28-ounce/794-gram) can **peeled whole or crushed tomatoes** or 1 (24-ounce/680-gram) jar tomato purée (passata)

Kosher salt and freshly ground black pepper

I first stumbled upon this recipe in Edda Servi Machlin's *The Classic Cuisine of the Italian Jews*, a treasure of a book that's now out of print. It's a twist on pasta al tonno, a quick and satisfying meal built from pantry staples—dried pasta, canned tomatoes, and tinned tuna—with a pop of garlic and parsley for freshness. In Machlin's version, an unexpected and generous pour of red wine gives the dish an added savory, almost gamey punch.

I've made a few adjustments to Machlin's original recipe, which is usually prepared with spaghetti. She recalls first enjoying it with an old friend in Livorno, a stunning city in Tuscany that overlooks the Tyrrhenian Sea. But even if you can't make it to the Italian coast, I encourage you to give this one a try—it'll hit the spot as a dinner for one, eaten straight from the pan, or as the centerpiece of any gathering.

Mix the garlic and herbs together in a small bowl.

In a large sauté pan or Dutch oven, warm ¼ cup (60 ml) of the oil over medium heat. Stir in half of the garlic-herb mixture and the red pepper flakes. Cook, stirring frequently, until sizzling and fragrant, 1 to 2 minutes.

Add the tomato paste and cook, stirring, until caramelized, 1 to 2 minutes. Add the tuna and use a spatula or wooden spoon to break it up in the pan. Cook for another minute, stirring often.

Increase the heat to high. Pour in the wine and simmer until it reduces by half, about 2 minutes. Add the tomatoes and a large pinch of salt, then swish some water into the empty container to catch the residual juices and add that to the pan, too. If using whole tomatoes, use a wooden spoon or potato masher to break them up.

Reduce the heat to a low simmer. Cook the sauce until slightly thickened, stirring occasionally, about 25 minutes. Season to taste.

TO SERVE Cook your pasta of choice to your liking. Transfer the pasta directly to the sauce (or drain it first and reserve 1 cup (240 ml) of cooking water), along with the remaining garlic-herb mixture. Toss to combine and cook until the pasta is well coated, 1 to 2 minutes, loosening the sauce with more pasta water as needed. Divide the pasta among bowls and serve.

Strozzapreti with Pantry Tuna & Tomato Sauce

Whole Wheat Orecchiette with Spicy Garlic & Anchovy Sauce with Broccoli

SERVES 4

*enough for 22 ounces fresh pasta or
16 ounces dried pasta*

Active time: 25 minutes
Total time: 25 minutes

PAIR IT WITH
*Cavatelli (96) · Capunti (100) · Malloreddus (102) ·
Orecchiette (108) · Potato Gnocchi (67) ·
Ricotta Gnocchi (60)*

spicy garlic & anchovy sauce with broccoli

½ cup (120 grams) **garlic confit**, with residual oil, page 355

1 (2-ounce/55 gram) tin **oil-packed anchovies**

1 pound (450 grams) **broccoli**, cut into bite-sized florets, or broccolini, trimmed and cut into ½-inch pieces

2 tablespoons (30 grams) crushed **Calabrian chili pepper paste**, plus more to taste

Kosher salt and freshly ground black pepper

2 tablespoons (30 grams) cold **unsalted butter**

1 ounce (30 grams) finely grated **Parmigiano-Reggiano**

Juice of 1 **lemon**, plus more to taste

Toasted breadcrumbs, page 354, for serving

I could eat this dish every day and, at one point, I did. The first time I made it was with Bronwen Kinzler-Britton, an excellent chef and friend from my pasta production days at Misi. We hovered over the stove of her tiny Brooklyn apartment—tasting, adjusting, laughing as we went—until it hit just the right balance of savory, spicy, tangy, and sweet. We ate it from mismatched mugs and later it became the signature dish we served to countless groups of supper club diners.

The power of this sauce lies in its foundation: an entire tin of anchovies melted down with buttery cloves of garlic confit. But don't let the anchovies scare you. You'll forget they're in there or remember only because of the deliciously deep, underlying savoriness. Serve it with orecchiette if you can—the little ears are, as Bronwen would say, "perfect vessels" for this sauce's bits and pieces—and keep the garlic confit oil within arm's reach for drizzling.

Add the garlic confit and a splash more garlic oil to a Dutch oven or large sauté pan. Mash it into a rough paste with a fork, then warm it over medium heat. Once it starts to sizzle, add the anchovies and their oil and cook, mashing with a wooden spoon or spatula and stirring often, until they dissolve and the mixture is cohesive, about 5 minutes.

Stir in the broccoli and chili pepper paste and season with salt and pepper. Cook, stirring continuously, until the broccoli is vibrant green and just shy of crisp-tender, 2 to 3 minutes. If the bottom of the pan starts to get dark, add a splash of water to deglaze. Remove from the heat.

TO SERVE Cook your pasta of choice to your liking. Return the sauce to medium heat and add the pasta, butter, and ¼ cup (60 ml) pasta cooking water (if you need to drain the pasta first, reserve 1 cup (240 ml) of cooking water). Stir until the butter melts and the pasta is well coated. Turn off the heat and add the cheese, mixing until melted, followed by the lemon juice. Season to taste with salt, pepper, and more chili pepper paste.

Divide the pasta among bowls and serve drizzled with garlic confit oil and sprinkled with breadcrumbs.

broths
& soups

You can never go wrong with serving pasta in sauce—a preparation known as "pasta asciutta," meaning dry pasta. But if you walk the streets of Bologna searching for tortellini, you'll usually find them dancing in a bowl of rich, soul-soothing brodo, or broth. Italian broths are clear, in taste and in appearance, more akin to consommé than stock. Other pastas in this book served in brodo are sorpresine (page 138), garganelli (page 142), and cappelletti (page 168), as well as pasta scraps like quadrettini and quadrucci (page 79). Minestre— hearty soups and brothy stews, often brimming with beans and other legumes—are also a vehicle for pasta, and lagane (page 86) and maltagliati (page 79) are typically served this way.

Once you start making broths it's hard to stop. They're a great way to use vegetable trimmings and other offcuts, and they're a panacea for any ailment, no matter the season. Here you'll find a broth for every time of year, and a few hearty soups that are mainstays of my rotation. As always, I encourage you to get creative with ingredients you already have.

Parmesan Broth

PAIR IT WITH
Cappelletti (168) • Cavatelli (96) • Farfalle (140) •
Garganelli (142) • Maltagliati (79) • Ricotta Gnocchi (60) •
Sorpresine (138) • Spizzulus (104)

tomato broth

2¼ pounds (1 kg; about 5 cups) **small sweet tomatoes** like cherry, San Marzano, or Campari

2 tablespoons (30 ml) **extra-virgin olive oil**, plus more for serving

2 **shallots**, roughly chopped

2 large **oil-packed anchovy fillets**, roughly chopped

4 **garlic cloves**, peeled and crushed

3 tablespoons (45 grams) **tomato paste**

½ cup (120 ml) **dry white wine** like Pinot Grigio

6 cups (1.4 liters) **cold water**

2 large sprigs **fresh basil**

Kosher salt

If you're looking for a twist on tomato sauce, you've found it in this jewel-toned broth. Its underlying sweetness reminds me of Spaghetti-Os, so serve it with cheese- or greens-filled pastas, little dumplings, or short-cut pieces for a full dose of childhood comfort.

If you're using small tomatoes, halve them; if they're on the larger side, quarter them.

In a medium pot or Dutch oven, warm the oil over medium heat. Add the shallots and cook, stirring occasionally, until softened but not browned, 3 to 5 minutes. Add the anchovies and garlic and cook, stirring, until the anchovies dissolve, about 2 minutes. Stir in the tomato paste and cook until caramelized and darkened in color, 1 to 2 minutes.

Add the tomatoes and cook, stirring often, until they release their juices and become jammy, about 10 minutes. Use the side of a spatula or wooden spoon to mash them into a pulp.

Pour in the wine and simmer until slightly reduced, about 3 minutes. Add the water, basil, and a big pinch of salt. Bring to a boil, then immediately reduce to a simmer and cook, uncovered, for 20 minutes.

Strain the broth through a fine-mesh sieve into a heatproof bowl or container, pressing as much liquid as possible from the tomato pulp with a spatula. Season to taste. The broth can be refrigerated for up to 3 days or frozen for up to 3 months.

TO SERVE   Cook your pasta of choice—about 2½ ounces (75 grams) per serving—in well-salted boiling water until tender or to your liking. When the pasta is almost ready, bring the broth to a simmer and taste for seasoning. Divide the pasta among bowls and immediately ladle the hot broth on top. Serve, finished with your favorite olive oil.

Cavatelli in Tomato Broth

Summer Corn & Basil Cappelletti
in Corn Broth

PAIR IT WITH
*Agnolotti del Plin (177) · Cappelletti (168) · Maltagliati (79) ·
Ricotta Gnocchi (60) · Sorpresine (138)*

corn broth

2 large **Parmigiano-Reggiano rinds**

4 large **corn cobs,** kernels removed and reserved for another use (like the filling on page 230)

1 **yellow onion,** unpeeled, halved, and root trimmed

2 large **garlic cloves,** peeled and crushed

6 sprigs **fresh parsley**

1 **bay leaf**

1 tablespoon (10 grams) **whole black peppercorns**

12 to 16 cups (2.8 to 3.8 liters) **cold water**

Kosher salt

In the height of summer, you'll find me making all sorts of corn-flavored pasta. But what to do with all those leftover cobs? This broth puts them to good use, extracting every last bit of their sweetness. Serve it with fresh corn-filled pastas or pop it in the freezer for a winter day when you need a dose of sunshine the most.

Wipe the Parmigiano-Reggiano rinds clean and grate off the top layer of the exterior.

Add the cheese rinds, corn cobs, onion, garlic, parsley, bay leaf, and peppercorns to a large heavy-bottomed pot or Dutch oven. Add enough cold water to cover and a big pinch of salt. Bring to a boil, then immediately reduce the heat to a bare simmer.

Cook the broth, uncovered, until golden and reduced by about half, 2 to 2½ hours, stirring occasionally to prevent the cheese rinds from sticking to the pot. When it's done, strain through a fine-mesh sieve into a heatproof bowl or container, pressing as much liquid as possible from the vegetables and cheese rinds with a spatula. If using the broth on its own, season to taste; if reserving as an ingredient for other soups, leave it as is.

TO STORE, transfer the broth to a heatproof container and cool it quickly (submerge it in an ice bath if you can). Refrigerate for up to 3 days, or freeze for up to 3 months.

TO SERVE Bring the broth to a gentle boil. Add your pasta of choice—about 2½ ounces (75 grams) per serving—and cook, stirring often, until just shy of tender. Then turn off the heat, cover, and let stand for 2 minutes. Divide among bowls and top with black pepper.

PAIR IT WITH
Agnolotti del Plin (177) • Cappelletti (168) •
Garganelli (142) • Hand-cut pastas (128) cut into smaller
pieces • Maltagliati (79) • Sorpresine (138)

parmesan broth

5 large **Parmigiano-Reggiano rinds**

2 tablespoons (30 ml) **extra-virgin olive oil**

2 **garlic heads**, cut in half crosswise to expose the cloves

1 **yellow onion**, unpeeled, halved, and root trimmed

1 large **carrot**, trimmed, roughly peeled, and cut into large pieces

2 **celery stalks**, trimmed and cut into large pieces

5 sprigs **fresh thyme**

5 sprigs **fresh parsley**

2 **bay leaves**

2 teaspoons (6 grams) **whole black peppercorns**

12 to 16 cups (2.8 to 3.8 liters) **cold water**

Kosher salt

This broth is an ode to the wise, aged "king of cheeses." And if there's one thing I've learned when it comes to Parmigiano-Reggiano, it's to never throw away the rind—because even the scraps can transform a simple pot of water into something rich and complex. Serve this broth with any small pasta or use it in place of other stocks for soups, beans, braises, and sauces. I rarely make it the same way twice (sometimes I add leeks, other times I skip the celery), so use whatever vegetables and aromatics you like. When the broth is ready, pan-fry the softened rinds for a savory snack.

If you don't have wedges of Parmesan on hand, you can find the rinds already packaged in some grocery stores and many cheese shops. Store them tightly wrapped in the refrigerator for several months or in the freezer for even longer.

Wipe the cheese rinds clean and grate off the top layer of the exterior. To prevent the rinds from sticking to the bottom of the pot, wrap them in cheesecloth and tie a knot at the top (you can skip this step but make sure to stir the broth occasionally).

In a large heavy-bottomed pot or Dutch oven, heat the oil over medium-high. Add the garlic and onion, cut sides down, and cook until slightly caramelized, 2 to 3 minutes.

Add the rinds, carrot, celery, herbs, bay leaves, and peppercorns to the pot, as well as enough cold water to cover and a big pinch of salt. Bring to a boil, then immediately reduce to a bare simmer.

Cook the broth, uncovered, until golden and reduced by about half, 2 to 2½ hours. When it's done, strain through a fine-mesh sieve into a heatproof bowl or container, pressing as much liquid as possible from the vegetables and cheese rinds. If using the broth on its own, season to taste; if reserving as an ingredient for other soups or braises, leave it as is.

To store, transfer the broth to a heatproof container and cool it quickly (submerge it in an ice bath if you can). Refrigerate for up to 3 days or freeze for up to 3 months.

TO SERVE Bring the broth to a gentle boil. Add your pasta of choice—about 2½ ounces (75 grams) per serving—and cook, stirring often, until just shy of tender. Then turn off the heat, cover, and let stand for 2 minutes. Divide among bowls.

Sorpresine in Italian Meat Broth

SERVES 4
MAKES ABOUT 2 QUARTS (2 LITERS)

Active time: 10 minutes
Total time: 3½ hours

PAIR IT WITH
Agnolotti del Plin (177) · Cappelletti (168) ·
Garganelli (142) · Hand-cut pastas (128) cut into smaller
pieces · Maltagliati (79) · Sorpresine (138)

italian meat broth
brodo di carne

2½ to 3 pounds (1.2 to 1.4 kg)
mixed meat like brisket, short
ribs, and/or chicken bones,
thighs, legs, or wings

2 **carrots**, trimmed, roughly
peeled, and cut into large
pieces

2 **celery stalks**, trimmed and cut
into large pieces

1 **yellow onion**, unpeeled, halved,
and root trimmed

5 sprigs **fresh parsley**

16 cups (3.8 liters) **cold water**

Kosher salt

Italian meat broth is a simple affair—just add everything to the pot. There's
no roasting of bones or caramelization here, so the result is clear, light, and a
perfect backdrop for pasta. Tough cuts like brisket and short ribs benefit most
from this low-and-slow method (and make sure to throw a few bones in there,
too). Serve it piping hot with tortellini or cappelletti, of course, but also any
small pasta like garganelli, sorpresine, maltagliati, or quadrettini. Enjoy the
leftover meat on its own or use it in pasta fillings, meatballs, salads, or slather
it in salsa verde.

Add the meat, vegetables, and parsley to a large heavy-bottomed pot or
Dutch oven, as well as enough cold water to cover, and a big pinch of salt.
Bring to a boil, then immediately reduce to a bare simmer. Cook the broth,
uncovered, until reduced by half, about 3 hours, skimming off any scum that
rises to the surface.

When the broth is ready, remove the meat with tongs and reserve for
another use. Carefully ladle the broth through a fine-mesh sieve into a
heatproof bowl or container. If using the broth on its own, season to taste; if
reserving as an ingredient, leave it as is.

To store, transfer the broth to a heatproof container and cool it quickly
(submerge it in an ice bath if you can). Refrigerate for up to 3 days—skim the
fat off the top once it's cool if you'd like—or freeze for up to 3 months.

TO SERVE Bring the broth to a gentle boil. Add your pasta of choice—about
2½ ounces (75 grams) per serving—and cook, stirring often, until just shy
of tender. Then turn off the heat, cover, and let stand for 2 minutes. Divide
among bowls.

PAIR IT WITH
Cappelletti (168) · Cavatelli (96) · "Classic" Ravioli (152) ·
Farfalle (140) · Hand-cut pastas (128) cut into smaller pieces
· Lagane (86) · Maltagliati (79) · Sorpresine (138)

grandma ruthe's chicken soup

1½ pounds (680 grams) **chicken bones with some meat left on them** (a leftover roast chicken carcass works great)

1 **yellow onion**, unpeeled, halved, and root trimmed

3 **carrots**, trimmed, roughly peeled, and sliced into thick rounds

2 **parsnips**, trimmed, roughly peeled, and sliced into thick rounds

2 stalks **celery**, trimmed and thickly sliced

5 sprigs **fresh parsley**

Kosher salt

Fresh dill, for serving (optional)

My mom's mom, Ruthe, was exactly how you might picture a Jewish grandmother. Short but not small, cropped blonde hair that may or may not have been her own, and, when not in the kitchen, asking you what you wanted to eat. I actually don't remember her making this soup—my memories instead revolve around a custardy, almost-raw but extremely delicious challah French toast—but it was always a staple of my mom's holiday table. Apparently the secret to this soup is the parsnips, which add subtle sweetness—I'm not a fan of parsnips, but I am a fan of this soup, so I take my mom's word for it.

Chicken soup's reputation precedes it and this one checks all the boxes. Sipped alone, wisps of steam curling under your nose, it calms the nerves and soothes a cold. Served with pasta (I'd suggest simple noodles like maltagliati or lagane, or ravioli-like parcels filled with meat called kreplach), it becomes a nourishing, celebratory meal. Enjoy it with family, of course, or share it with friends and they'll quickly feel like family, too.

Add the chicken, onion, carrots, parsnips, and celery to a large heavy-bottomed pot or Dutch oven. Cover with cold water by 2 to 3 inches.

Bring to a boil, then immediately turn the heat down to a bare simmer. Cover the pot and cook for 2 hours, checking occasionally and skimming off any scum that rises to the surface. Add the parsley and a generous pinch of salt. Simmer the soup, uncovered, for 1 hour more.

Let the soup cool slightly, then remove the chicken. Pull the meat off the bones and add it back to the pot. Discard the onion and parsley. (If you prefer, after removing the chicken and onion, strain the soup through a sieve and return the other vegetables to the pot.) Season to taste.

To store, transfer the soup to a heatproof container and cool it quickly (submerge it in an ice bath if you can). Refrigerate for up to 3 days—skim the fat off the top once it's cool if you'd like—or freeze for up to 3 months.

TO SERVE Bring the soup to a gentle boil. Add your pasta of choice—about 2½ ounces (75 grams) per serving—and cook, stirring often, until just shy of tender. Then turn off the heat, cover, and let stand for 2 minutes. Divide among bowls and serve with fresh dill, if you'd like.

Sausage & Spinach Ravioli in Grandma Ruthe's Chicken Soup

Lagane in Chickpea Soup with Harissa & Rosemary

SERVES 4

*Enough for 12 ounces of fresh pasta or
8 ounces of dried pasta*

*Active time: 30 minutes
Total time: 45 minutes*

PAIR IT WITH

*Capunti (100) • Cavatelli (96) • Hand-cut pastas (128)
cut into smaller pieces • Lagane (86) • Maltagliati (79) •
Orecchiette (108)*

chickpea soup
with harissa & rosemary

¼ cup (60 ml) **extra-virgin olive oil**

2 **garlic cloves**, thinly sliced

1 teaspoon minced **fresh rosemary** (from about 1 medium sprig)

1 tablespoon (15 grams) **tomato paste**

1 tablespoon (15 grams) **harissa**, or more depending on your spice preference

2 (15-ounce) cans **chickpeas**

4 cups (1 liter) **vegetable or chicken stock, or water**, plus more as needed

Kosher salt and freshly ground black pepper

12 ounces (340 grams) **fresh pasta or** 8 ounces (225 grams) **dried pasta** of choice

1½ ounces (45 grams) finely grated **Pecorino Romano**

Salsa verde, page 357, for serving (optional, but recommended)

MAKE IT VEGAN
Omit the cheese.

Pasta with chickpeas (pasta e ceci) is Italian comfort food at its best: warm, starchy, and cheap. Like the Jewish affinity for chicken soup, every family has their own version of this dish, and the results range from brothy to saucy. Small dried soup pastas like ditalini are often used, as are fresh maltagliati and lagane. This version is mostly traditional, though of course the addition of harissa is not, nor is serving it with a spoonful of salsa verde. I like the color and peppery flavor the harissa adds, but if you'd like to keep it classic, use a pinch of red pepper flakes and double the tomato paste instead. The zingy salsa verde, while optional, is truly delicious, not to mention it makes for a beautiful plate of food.

In a Dutch oven or medium pot, warm the oil over medium heat. Add the garlic and rosemary and cook, stirring often, until soft, sizzling, and fragrant, about 3 minutes. Stir in the tomato paste and harissa and cook, stirring, 1 minute more. Turn off the heat.

Add one can of chickpeas and their liquid to the pot. Crush the beans with a potato masher or the back of a fork, or blend until smooth with an immersion blender. Return the pot to medium heat and add the rest of the chickpeas and their liquid, as well as the stock. Season generously with salt and pepper.

If using fresh pasta, simmer the soup, uncovered, until slightly thickened, 15 to 20 minutes, stirring occasionally. Then turn up the heat to a gentle boil, add your pasta of choice, and cook, stirring constantly, until tender.

If using dried pasta, bring the soup to a gentle boil and immediately add your pasta of choice. Reduce the heat to a simmer and cook, stirring often, until the pasta is al dente or cooked to your liking.

When the pasta is done, turn off the heat and wait until the bubbles subside. Add the cheese and mix vigorously until incorporated. Season to taste. Divide the soup among bowls and top with a spoonful of salsa verde, if using.

Note: The soup will continue to thicken as it cools, so if you prefer a brothy consistency, gently reheat the leftovers with more stock or water.

PAIR IT WITH

*Capunti (100) · Cavatelli (96) · Hand-cut pastas (128)
cut into smaller pieces · Lagane (86 ·
Maltagliati (79) · Orecchiette (108)*

white bean soup with parmesan & kale

1 **Parmigiano-Reggiano rind**

¼ cup (60 ml) **extra-virgin olive oil**

½ **red onion**, finely chopped

Kosher salt and freshly ground black pepper

2 **garlic cloves**, thinly sliced

1 tablespoon finely chopped **fresh sage**

1 teaspoon minced **fresh rosemary**, from 1 medium sprig

2 (15-ounce) cans **white beans** like butter or cannellini, drained and rinsed

1 large bunch (about 10 ounces; 285 grams) **hearty greens** like kale, chard, or mustard greens, any tough stems/ribs removed and leaves roughly torn into pieces

4 cups (1 liter) **low-sodium vegetable broth or Parmesan Broth** (page 342), plus more as needed

12 ounces (340 grams) **fresh pasta or** 8 ounces (225 grams) **dried pasta** of choice

1 ounce (30 grams) finely grated **Parmigiano-Reggiano**, plus more for serving

1 **lemon**, half juiced and half cut into wedges, for serving

This dish is a little bit soup, a little bit stew, and a little bit gravy. As the beans fall apart and absorb the broth, a hearty Parmesan-flavored cream emerges, ideal for enveloping rustic egg-dough offcuts like maltagliati and quadrucci, as well as semolina dumplings like cavatelli and orecchiette, not to mention small dried pastas. Canned beans make it a weeknight-friendly winter meal but you can, of course, use cooked dried beans instead.

Wipe the Parmigiano-Reggiano rind clean and grate off the top layer of the exterior.

In a Dutch oven or medium pot, warm the oil over medium heat. Add the onion, season with salt and pepper, and cook, stirring occasionally, until soft and translucent, 5 to 7 minutes. Turn the heat down a little and add the garlic. Cook until soft and fragrant, 3 to 5 minutes. Stir in the herbs and cook for 1 minute.

Add the beans, then use the back of a spoon to crush some of them against the side of the pot. Add the greens and stir until mostly wilted. Add the broth, cheese rind, and a generous pinch of salt and pepper. Bring to a lively simmer.

If using fresh pasta, simmer the soup, uncovered, until slightly thickened, about 15 minutes, stirring occasionally. Then turn up the heat to a gentle boil, add your pasta of choice, and cook, stirring constantly, until tender.

If using dried pasta, bring the soup to a gentle boil and immediately add your pasta of choice. Reduce the heat to a simmer and cook, stirring often, until the pasta is al dente or cooked to your liking. The soup will be thick and gravy-like; if preferred, add more stock or water to loosen it.

When the pasta is done, turn off the heat. Add the Parmigiano-Reggiano and stir vigorously to combine. Add the lemon juice and season to taste.

Divide the soup among bowls and serve with more grated cheese and lemon wedges for squeezing.

Maltagliati in White Bean Soup with Parmesan & Kale

toppings
&
condiments

Sometimes a dish needs a little extra something. Here
are a few mainstays of my pantry that add crunch,
sweetness, and tang when I'm searching for balance.

Toasted Breadcrumbs

toasted breadcrumbs
pangrattato

5¼ ounces (150 grams; about 4 slices) **stale bread**, torn into large pieces

1 to 2 tablespoons (15 to 30 ml) **extra-virgin olive oil**

Kosher salt

Some might call it "poor man's Parmesan," but crunchy toasted breadcrumbs are an exceptional addition to many pasta dishes. This version is a blank canvas: stir in red pepper flakes, grated cheese, lemon zest, and/or minced fresh herbs like parsley, rosemary, and thyme—when the crumbs are golden and still warm—for extra kick. Here are a few methods, depending on the ingredients and time you have.

Heat the oven to 350°F/175°C.

Add the bread to the bowl of a food processor and pulse into coarse crumbs. Transfer to a sheet pan. Drizzle with the oil and sprinkle with salt, then mix with your hands until the crumbs are lightly coated. Spread them out in a thin layer.

Bake the breadcrumbs until crisp and deeply golden, about 20 minutes, stirring and rotating the pan halfway through. Adjust the seasoning to taste and let cool completely.

IF YOU ONLY HAVE FRESH BREAD Tear or cut the bread into large pieces. Bake at 350°F/175°C until dried out but not browned, about 15 minutes. Let cool, then proceed with the recipe above.

IF YOU'RE SHORT ON TIME In a large skillet, warm 2 tablespoons of olive oil over medium-high heat. Add 1 cup homemade, panko, or unseasoned breadcrumbs and a generous pinch of salt. Stir until completely coated.

Cook, stirring occasionally, until the crumbs begin to brown, about 3 minutes, then stir constantly until evenly toasted and deeply golden, 2 to 4 minutes more (if they start to darken too quickly, turn down the heat). Turn off the heat and adjust the seasoning to taste. Transfer to a sheet pan or bowl and let cool.

The toasted breadcrumbs can be stored in an airtight container in a cool, dry place for up to 1 week or in the freezer for several months.

VARIATION

Pan-Fried Garlic Breadcrumbs: When the oil is hot, add 1 to 2 smashed garlic cloves and cook, turning occasionally, until golden around the edges, about 3 minutes. Discard the garlic, add the breadcrumbs and salt, and proceed as directed.

MAKES
about 2 cups (450 grams)

garlic confit

1½ cups (170 grams, or about 5 heads' worth) **peeled garlic cloves**

1 to 1½ cups (240 to 360 ml) mild-flavored **extra-virgin olive oil**, plus more as needed

Garlic poached gently in oil gives you all the benefits of roasting—sweet, buttery, and spreadable—with the added perk of garlic-infused oil, which is perfect for drizzling over bread or folding into marinades and dips. Don't be afraid to double the recipe; you won't be able to take your hands off it.

Add the garlic to a small, heavy-bottomed saucepan. Pour over enough oil to cover the cloves completely. Turn the heat to medium-low and cook until a steady stream of tiny bubbles rises to the surface, about 10 minutes. Immediately reduce the heat to its lowest setting and cook at a bare simmer until the cloves are completely tender, 30 to 40 minutes. The garlic might turn golden in some areas but it should not brown. Check every so often to make sure the oil isn't spitting and getting too hot—if it is, remove the saucepan from the heat for a few moments to cool down, then continue cooking. When it's done, let cool.

Spoon the garlic into a glass canning jar or other airtight container, then pour the oil over it. To store, close the container tightly and refrigerate for up to 2 weeks, making sure to replenish the oil as needed so the garlic remains covered.

balsamic reduction

1 cup (240 ml) **balsamic vinegar**

Aged balsamic vinegar from its homeland in Modena is liquid gold and I keep my stash tucked safely away in the satin-lined box it came in. True balsamic vinegar pours a little like syrup, and it's sweet and sour in equal measure. This reduction doesn't have all the complexity or delicacy of the real thing, but it's similar in texture and can still transform a dish, particularly when drizzled over rich, butter-slicked stuffed pastas. To take the flavor to the next level, add 2 to 3 tablespoons of ruby port to the mix.

Add the vinegar to a small saucepan. Bring to a rapid simmer over medium heat, then reduce to medium-low and cook at a low bubble, stirring occasionally, until thickened, about 15 minutes. When it's ready, it should coat the back of a metal spoon.

Remove from the heat and let cool (it will continue to thicken). The reduction can be stored in an airtight container in the refrigerator for up to 3 months. If it hardens or becomes too thick, gently reheat with a spoonful of water to loosen.

salsa verde

1 small bunch **fresh flat-leaf parsley**, leaves and tender stems

1 large bunch **fresh basil**, leaves and tender stems

1 small bunch **fresh mint**, leaves only

2 **garlic cloves**, roughly chopped

1 tablespoon (10 grams) **capers in brine**, drained

4 **oil-packed anchovy fillets**

⅓ cup (55 grams) **pitted green olives**, preferably Castelvetrano

1 small **green chili pepper** like serrano or jalapeño, halved, seeded, and cut into pieces (optional)

Zest and juice of ½ **lemon**, plus more to taste

¼ cup (60 ml) **extra-virgin olive oil**, plus more as needed

Kosher salt

Like pesto, salsa verde is a bright, herbaceous "green sauce" that's more of a genre than a recipe. This version is less traditional, but it's equally excellent served with fish, spread on a sandwich, drizzled on raw or roasted vegetables, slathered on meat, or eaten by the spoonful. I also use it as a light pasta sauce, a bright, briny condiment well suited to summer barbecues and picnics in the park.

In the bowl of a food processor, combine the herbs, garlic, capers, anchovies, olives, half of the chili pepper, and the lemon zest and juice. Pulse a few times until everything is roughly chopped. With the machine running, slowly stream in the oil until the mixture is saucy but still has some texture, scraping down the sides of the bowl as needed.

Season to taste with salt, then add more of any of the ingredients to your liking—if you want it spicier, add the rest of the chili pepper; if you want it brinier, add more capers—and pulse to combine.

To store, transfer to an airtight container, cover with a thin layer of olive oil, and refrigerate for up to 5 days.

acknowledgments

Although my name is on the cover, this book has been made possible by many, many others. I'll do my best to thank them here:

First and foremost, to my husband, Adam, without whom I might never have had the courage to become a cook. Thank you for your unwavering support, always-honest feedback, and willingness to taste-test, even when the result isn't so delicious. This is a team effort, and you are my team.

To my family, and especially my parents, for fostering my fascination with food from a very young age. Thank you for your dedication to our Jewish heritage, which brought meaning to the dinner table and sparked my desire to get in the kitchen, and for our family trips, which expanded my culinary horizons and kept me curious.

To Andrianna deLone, my agent and my friend, for guiding me through a process I knew nothing about, answering the phone when I needed it most, and testing recipes just *one more* time. I dedicate the Fiery Calabrian Chili Sauce to you (and Sean!).

To my editor, Michael Szczerban, and assistant editor, Thea Diklich-Newell, for your infectious passion for pasta and excitement about this project from day one. Mike, thank you for making this crazy idea cookable, reminding me of the long game when I got bogged down in the details, and giving gnocchi another try. And to the entire Voracious and Little, Brown team for transforming a messy Word document into a beautiful book. Thank you all for your keen eye and attention to detail, and for humoring my indecisiveness even when timing was tight.

To Nico Schinco, for the most spectacular images that bring this thing to life in a way I never thought possible, and for believing in me long ago. Thank you to Judy Kim, for styling each plate so beautifully and with such care, and Maeve Sheridan, the Queen of Props, a true beacon of joy and a new lifelong friend. And thank you to Rachel Gorman Senesac and Veronica Spera for your speed and diligence in the kitchen—you made an impossible shot list possible.

To the wonderful brands that generously donated ingredients of the highest quality: Vital Farms, Molino Pasini, Regalis Foods, and Kerrygold. A special thank you to Vital Farms for sponsoring the accompanying video production, a dream of mine from the beginning and one that I know will help readers feel more confident in making pasta.

To my recipe testers, Michael Zeolla, Karishma Pradham, Stacy Jargowsky, and Emilie Pullar, thank you for taking the time to make sure each recipe was as accurate and accessible as possible. Michael, thank you for working through the kinks with me, even at 11 o'clock at night.

To those who shaped my love of pasta making in its infancy and took a chance on me — chef Missy Robbins, Bronwen Kinzler-Britton, and the Misi pasta production team; Brian Mommsen and the Resident team; Brinda Ayer, Patrick Moynihan, and the Food52 team, and so many others. And, of course, my fellow pasta makers I've met over the years through social media, for so generously sharing your knowledge and always pushing me forward, particularly Enrica Monzani, Karima Moyer-Nocchi, Nina Napolitano, Tina Prestia, and Giulia Scarpaleggia, whose work inspired some of the recipes in this book.

Last, but certainly not least, to the Pasta Social Club community, for inviting me into your kitchens and making pasta with me, whether online or in person, and for giving my recipes a try. Everything I do is inspired by and created for you. This book is for you, too, and I hope you enjoy it.

Chestnut Maltagliati

index

Note: Page references in *italics* indicate photographs.

A

Agnolotti & Agnolotti del Plin, *176,* 177–81, *179*

all-purpose flour
about, 24, 26
brand used, 16
substituting 00 flour with, 24

almonds
Red Pesto (Pesto Rosso), *272,* 276
Tomato & Almond Pesto (Pesto alla Trapanese), *273,* 274

alternative flours. *See also specific types*
brands of, 16, 24
combining with durum or soft wheat, 24
types of, 24

anchovies
Anchovy & Onion Sauce with Breadcrumbs, *330,* 331
Salsa Verde, 357
Spicy Garlic & Anchovy Sauce with Broccoli, *334,* 335
Spicy Tomato–Anchovy Butter, 297
Tomato Broth, 338, *339*
Tomato Sauce with Olives & Fried Capers, 264, *265*

Arugula & Kale Pesto, *273,* 277

Asparagus & Spring Pea Filling with Mint, 229

B

Balsamic Reduction, 356

basil
Basil Pasta Dough, 38
Basil Pesto, *269,* 270–71

Citrus & Pistachio Pesto, *250,* 275
Eggplant & Burrata Filling, 233
No-Cook Tomato & Basil Sauce, *258,* 259
Salsa Verde, 357
Sorrento-Style Baked Gnocchi with Tomatoes and Mozzarella (Gnocchi alla Sorrentina), 203
Summer Corn & Basil Filling, *216,* 230
Tomato & Almond Pesto (Pesto alla Trapanese), *273,* 274

beans
Chickpea Soup with Harissa & Rosemary, *348,* 349
White Bean Soup with Parmesan & Kale, 350, *351*

Besciamella, 202

beef
Braised Beef & Caramelized Cabbage Filling, 243–44
Casual Bolognese, *311,* 312–13
Italian Meat Broth (Brodo di Carne), *344,* 345

beets
Pink Vegetable Purée, 55

bench scraper, 14

bicycle pastry cutter (bicicleta), 14

black pepper
Black Pepper Pasta Dough, 46, *47*
Black Pepper & Pecorino Filling, 219
Pecorino, Pepper & Lemon Sauce, 298, *299*

Bolognese, Casual, *311,* 312–13

Bolognese-Style Meat Lasagne, 200

box grater, 15

breadcrumbs
Anchovy & Onion Sauce with Breadcrumbs, *330,* 331

Pan-Fried Garlic Breadcrumbs, 354
Toasted Breadcrumbs (Pangrattato), *353,* 354

broccoli
Broccoli Sauce, *280,* 281
Spicy Garlic & Anchovy Sauce with Broccoli, *334,* 335

broths
Corn Broth, *340,* 341
Italian Meat Broth (Brodo di Carne), *344,* 345
Parmesan Broth, 342–43
Tomato Broth, 338, *339*

Busiate, 106–7, *107*

butter. *See also* butter, cream, and cheese sauces
brands used, 16
browned, preparing, 291
compound, about, 296
Lemon-Chive Butter, 297
Parmesan-Garlic Butter, 297
for pasta dough, 25
Spicy Tomato–Anchovy Butter, 297

butter, cream, and cheese sauces
Butter & Parmesan Sauce (Alfredo's Alfredo), 294, *295*
Butter & Sage Sauce (Burro e Salvia), *292,* 293
Caramelized Onion Cheese Sauce, 308–9, *309*
Four-Cheese Sauce (Quattro Formaggi), 306, *307*
Golden Saffron Sauce, *300,* 301
making a simple butter sauce, 290
Pecorino, Pepper & Lemon Sauce, 298, *299*
Roasted Garlic & Miso Sauce, 302, *303*
Smoky Pumpkin Sauce, *304,* 305

C

Cabbage, Caramelized, & Braised Beef Filling, 243–44

Calabrian chili pepper paste, 17

Fiery Calabrian Chili Sauce, *266,* 267

Spicy Garlic & Anchovy Sauce with Broccoli, *334,* 335

Spicy Tomato–Anchovy Butter, 297

capers

Tomato Sauce with Olives & Fried Capers, 264, *265*

White Fish Ragù with Lemon & Capers, *326,* 327

Cappelletti, 168–71, *171*

Capunti, 100–101, *101*

Caramelle, 182–85, *185*

Cavatelli, 96–99, *99*

cheese, 17. *See also* butter, cream, and cheese sauces; Parmigiano-Reggiano; ricotta

Alpine Cheese Fondue Filling, *224,* 225

Any-Greens Filling, 226, *227*

Asparagus & Spring Pea Filling with Mint, 229

Autumn Squash Lasagne, 201

Besciamella for Autumn Squash Lasagne, 202

Besciamella for Cheesy Spinach Lasagne, 202

Black Pepper & Pecorino Filling, 219

Braised Shallot & Grana Padano Filling, 236–37

Cheesy Spinach Lasagne, *11,* 201

Eggplant & Burrata Filling, 233

Four-Cheese Filling, 215

Four-Cheese Sauce (Quattro Formaggi), 306, *307*

Fried Zucchini Sauce, 282, *283*

Honeymoon Cheese & Herb Filling, 221

Pecorino, Pepper & Lemon Sauce, 298, *299*

Portofino-Style Pesto Lasagne, 201

rinds, saving for soups and broths, 17

Roasted Salmon & Mascarpone Filling, 240

Smoked Salmon Filling, 240

Sorrento-Style Baked Gnocchi with Tomatoes and Mozzarella (Gnocchi alla Sorrentina), 203

Summer Corn & Basil Filling, *216,* 230

Sweet & Sour Eggplant Sauce with Burrata, 286, *287*

chestnut flour

Chestnut Pasta Dough, 49

Ossola-Style Chestnut, Squash & Potato Gnocchi Dough, 66

chicken

Grandma Ruthe's Chicken Soup, 346, *347*

Italian Meat Broth (Brodo di Carne), *344,* 345

Chickpea Soup with Harissa & Rosemary, *348,* 349

chives

Lemon-Chive Butter, 297

Mashed Potato & Chive Filling, 232

Citrus-Scented Pasta Dough, 50

"Classic" Ravioli, 152–57, *154*

Colorful Egg Pasta Dough, 54

Colorful Flour & Water Pasta Dough, *53,* 54

Confit, Garlic, 355

cookie cutters, 15

corn

Corn Broth, *340,* 341

Summer Corn & Basil Filling, *216,* 230

Corzetti della Valpolcevera, 92–94, *95*

Corzetti della Valpolcevera Dough, 37

Corzetti Ravioli, 148–49, *149*

corzetti stamp, 15

Corzetti Stampati, 146–47, *147*

cream. *See also* butter, cream, and cheese sauces

Alpine Cheese Fondue Filling, *224,* 225

Tomato-Cream Sauce (No-Vodka Vodka Sauce), 260, *261*

Wild Mushroom Sauce, *284,* 285

Crème Fraîche & Slow-Roasted Salmon Sauce with Peas, 328, *329*

D

digital kitchen scale, 13

00 (double-zero) flour

about, 23, 26

Almost All-Yolk Pasta Dough, *44,* 45

Black Pepper Pasta Dough, 46, *47*

brands used, 16

Chestnut Pasta Dough, 49

Citrus-Scented Pasta Dough, 50

Colorful Egg Pasta Dough, 54

Italian brands, 23–24

Parsley-Speckled Pasta Dough, 46, *47*

pizza flour, note about, 24

Red Wine Pasta Dough, 50

Soft Wheat & Water Pasta Dough, 37

Sour Cream & Rye Pasta Dough, *48,* 49

Standard Egg Pasta Dough, 45

substituting all-purpose flour for, 24

Vegan "Egg" Pasta Dough, 45

White Wine Pasta Dough, 50, *51*

Whole Wheat Egg Pasta Dough, 45

durum wheat. *See also* semolina

about, 23, 26

lack of substitute for, 32

Dutch oven, 15

E

egg pasta dough

about, 42

Almost All-Yolk Pasta Dough, *44,* 45

Black Pepper Pasta Dough, 46, *47*

Chestnut Pasta Dough, 49

Citrus-Scented Pasta Dough, 50

Colorful Egg Pasta Dough, 54

Gluten-Free Egg Pasta Dough, 57

Parsley-Speckled Pasta Dough, 46, *47*

Red Wine Pasta Dough, 50

Sour Cream & Rye Pasta Dough, *48,* 49

Standard Egg Pasta Dough, 45

suggested rest time, 32

Vegan "Egg" Pasta Dough, 45

White Wine Pasta Dough, 50, *51*

Whole Wheat Egg Pasta Dough, 45

eggplant

Eggplant & Burrata Filling, 233

Sweet & Sour Eggplant Sauce with Burrata, 286, *287*

eggs. *See also* egg pasta dough

Egg Yolk Ravioli (Uovo in Ravioli), 159–61, *292*

impact on dough texture, 24

large, for recipes, 16

equipment
    for cooking and sauces, 15
    for fillings, 14–15, 213
    for pasta dough, 13–14
    for shaping pasta, 14–15

F
Farfalle, 140–41, *141*
fats, for pasta dough, 25, 26
Fennel, Sausage & Saffron Ragù, 314, *315*
ferretto, 14
fettuccine
    how it is served, 128
    Tagliolini, Tagliatelle, Fettuccine & Pappardelle, *130,* 131–35
fillings
    Alpine Cheese Fondue Filling, *224,* 225
    Any-Greens Filling, 226, *227*
    Asparagus & Spring Pea Filling with Mint, 229
    Black Pepper & Pecorino Filling, 219
    Braised Beef & Caramelized Cabbage Filling, 243–44
    Braised Shallot & Grana Padano Filling, 236–37
    Eggplant & Burrata Filling, 233
    equipment for, 213
    Four-Cheese Filling, 215
    Honeymoon Cheese & Herb Filling, 221
    ideal texture, 212
    Mashed Potato & Chive Filling, 232
    Mushroom, Garlic & Thyme Filling, *216,* 231
    pairing with sauces, 213
    Roasted Garlic & Rosemary Filling, 222
    Roasted Salmon & Mascarpone Filling, 240
    runny, how to fix, 212
    Sausage & Spinach Filling, 245
    seasoning, note on, 212
    Smoked Salmon Filling, 240
    Smoky Caramelized Onion Filling, 239
    Spinach & Ricotta Filling, *217,* 218
    storing, 213
    Summer Corn & Basil Filling, *216,* 230
    tools for, 15
    Whipped Ricotta Filling, 214, *217*

    Winter Squash & Brown Butter Filling, *216,* 234–35
fish. *See* anchovies; fish sauces; salmon
fish sauces
    Anchovy & Onion Sauce with Breadcrumbs, *330,* 331
    Pantry Tuna & Tomato Sauce, 332, *333*
    Slow-Roasted Salmon & Crème Fraîche Sauce with Peas, 328, *329*
    Spicy Garlic & Anchovy Sauce with Broccoli, *334,* 335
    White Fish Ragù with Lemon & Capers, *326,* 327
flour and water pasta dough
    about, 34
    Basil Pasta Dough, 38
    Colorful Flour & Water Pasta Dough, *53,* 54
    Corzetti della Valpolcevera Dough, 37
    Durum Wheat & Water Pasta Dough, 37
    Foglie d'Ulivo Dough, 37
    Gluten-Free Flour & Water Pasta Dough, 57
    Orecchiette Dough, 37
    Pici Dough, 37
    Saffron Pasta Dough, 41
    Soft Wheat & Water Pasta Dough, 37
    suggested rest time, 32
    Whole Wheat & Water Pasta Dough, 38
flours. *See also* 00 (double zero); semolina
    all-purpose, 16, 24, 26
    alternative, 16, 24
    durum wheat, 23, 26, 32
    fresh, 16
    gluten-free, 24, 26
    soft wheat, 23–24
    whole-grain, 16, 24, 26
flour/sugar shaker, 14
Foglie d'Ulivo, 110–13, *113*
Foglie d'Ulivo Dough, 37
food processor, 15, 30, 213
fresh flours, 16

G
Garganelli, 142–44, *145*
garganelli board/comb (pettina), 15

garlic
    Garlic Confit, 355
    Mushroom, Garlic & Thyme Filling, *216,* 231
    Pan-Fried Garlic Breadcrumbs, 354
    Parmesan-Garlic Butter, 297
    Roasted Garlic & Miso Sauce, 302, *303*
    Roasted Garlic & Rosemary Filling, 222
    Slow-Roasted Tomato & Garlic Sauce, *262,* 263
    Spicy Garlic & Anchovy Sauce with Broccoli, *334,* 335
gluten, in wheat flour, 25
gluten-free flours. *See also specific types*
    about, 26
    types of, 26
    working with, 24
gluten-free pasta dough
    about, 56
    Gluten-Free Egg Pasta Dough, 57
    Gluten-Free Flour & Water Pasta Dough, 57
    Gluten-Free Potato Gnocchi Dough, 69
    rolling, note about, 117
    shaping, note about, 80
    working with, 24, 26
gnocchi
    about, 186
    cooking, note about, 205
    Delicate Gnocchi Method, 192–95
    short- and long-term storage, 207
    Sorrento-Style Baked Gnocchi with Tomatoes and Mozzarella (Gnocchi alla Sorrentina), 203
    Standard Gnocchi Method, 188–91, *191*
    Stuffed Gnocchi (Gnocchi Ripieni), 196, *197*
gnocchi dough
    Gluten-Free Potato Gnocchi Dough, 69
    Meyer Lemon & Herb Ricotta Gnocchi Dough, 64
    Ossola-Style Chestnut, Squash & Potato Gnocchi Dough, 66
    Potato Gnocchi Dough, 67–69, *68*
    preparing, 59
    Pumpkin & Ricotta Gnocchi Dough, 65

Ricotta Gnocchi Dough, 60–63,
63
serving sizes, 10
Sweet Potato Gnocchi Dough,
70–73, *71*
gnocchi or cavarola board, 14
graters, 15
greens
Any-Greens Filling, 226, *227*
Cheesy Spinach Lasagne, *11,* 201
Green Vegetable Purée, 55
Kale & Arugula Pesto, *273,* 277
Sausage & Spinach Filling, 245
Spinach & Ricotta Filling, *217,* 218
White Bean Soup with Parmesan &
Kale, 350, *351*

H
hand-cut pastas
how they are served, 128
making pasta nests with, 133
short- and long-term storage, 207
Tagliolini, Tagliatelle, Fettuccine &
Pappardelle, *130,* 131–35
types of, 128
hand-formed pastas
Busiate, 106–7, *107*
Capunti, 100–101, *101*
Cavatelli, 96–99, *99*
Corzetti della Valpolcevera, 92–94,
95
Foglie d'Ulivo, 110–13, *113*
gluten-free, note about, 80
Lagane, 86, *87*
Malloreddus, 102–3, *103*
Orecchiette, *36,* 108–9
Pici, *82,* 83–85
short- and long-term storage,
207
Spizzulus, 104–5, *105*
Strozzapreti, 88–90, *91*
Harissa & Rosemary, Chickpea Soup
with, *348,* 349
Hazelnut & Sage Pesto, 278
herbs. *See also* vegetable and herb
sauces; *specific herbs*
flavoring dough with, 26
Herb-Laminated Pasta Sheets, *120,*
121–23
Honeymoon Cheese & Herb Filling,
221
Meyer Lemon & Herb Ricotta
Gnocchi Dough, 64

I
ingredients
pantry staples, 16–17
for pasta dough, 23–26
weighing, 10

K
kale
Any-Greens Filling, 226, *227*
Kale & Arugula Pesto, *273,* 277
White Bean Soup with Parmesan &
Kale, 350, *351*

L
ladle, 15
Lagane, 86, *87*
Lamb, Port-Braised, Ragù with
Shallots & Rosemary, 321–23,
322
lasagne
about, 198–99
Autumn Squash Lasagne, 201
Bolognese-Style Meat Lasagne,
200
Cheesy Spinach Lasagne, *11,* 201
My Favorite Lasagne, 200–201
Portofino-Style Pesto Lasagne, 201
Sorrento-Style Baked Gnocchi
with Tomatoes and Mozzarella
(Gnocchi alla Sorrentina), 203
lemon
Citrus-Scented Pasta Dough, 50
Lemon-Chive Butter, 297
Meyer Lemon & Herb Ricotta
Gnocchi Dough, 64
Pecorino, Pepper & Lemon Sauce,
298, *299*
White Fish Ragù with Lemon &
Capers, *326,* 327
liquids, 24–26

M
Malloreddus, 102–3, *103*
malloreddus paddle, 14
maltagliati, about, 79
meat. *See also* beef; meaty sauces;
sausages
Italian Meat Broth (Brodo di
Carne), *344,* 345
meaty sauces
Casual Bolognese, *311,* 312–13
The Meatiest Meatless Ragù, *316,*
317

Port-Braised Lamb Ragù with
Shallots & Rosemary, 321–23,
322
Roasted Red Pepper & Vegetarian
Sausage Ragù, 318–20, *319*
Sausage, Saffron & Fennel Ragù,
314, *315*
Mezzelune, 155
microplane, 15
mint
Asparagus & Spring Pea Filling
with Mint, 229
Salsa Verde, 357
Miso & Roasted Garlic Sauce, 302,
303
mushrooms
Mushroom, Garlic & Thyme Filling,
216, 231
Wild Mushroom Sauce, *284,* 285

N
nuts
Citrus & Pistachio Pesto, *250,* 275
Kale & Arugula Pesto, *273,* 277
Ligurian Walnut Sauce (Salsa di
Noci), *272,* 279
Red Pesto (Pesto Rosso), *272,* 276
Sage & Hazelnut Pesto, 278
Tomato & Almond Pesto (Pesto alla
Trapanese), *273,* 274

O
oils, 16, 25
olive oil, 16, 25
olives
Salsa Verde, 357
Sweet & Sour Eggplant Sauce with
Burrata, 286, *287*
Tomato Sauce with Olives & Fried
Capers, 264, *265*
onions
Anchovy & Onion Sauce with
Breadcrumbs, *330,* 331
Autumn Squash Lasagne, 201
Braised Onion Ragù, *288,* 289
Caramelized Onion Cheese Sauce,
308–9, *309*
Smoky Caramelized Onion Filling,
239
oranges
Citrus & Pistachio Pesto, *250,* 275
Citrus-Scented Pasta Dough, 50
Orange Vegetable Purée, 55

Orecchiette, *36*, 108–9
Orecchiette Dough, 37
Ossola-Style Chestnut, Squash &
    Potato Gnocchi Dough, 66

P
pantry staples, 16–17
pappardelle
    how it is served, 128
    Tagliolini, Tagliatelle, Fettuccine &
        Pappardelle, *130*, 131–35
Parmigiano-Reggiano
    Autumn Squash Lasagne, 201
    Bolognese-Style Meat Lasagne,
        200
    Butter & Parmesan Sauce
        (Alfredo's Alfredo), 294, *295*
    buying, for recipes, 17
    Cheesy Spinach Lasagne, *11*, 201
    Four-Cheese Filling, 215
    Four-Cheese Sauce (Quattro
        Formaggi), 306, *307*
    Fried Zucchini Sauce, 282, *283*
    Parmesan Broth, 342–43
    Parmesan-Garlic Butter, 297
    Portofino-Style Pesto Lasagne, 201
    White Bean Soup with Parmesan &
        Kale, 350, *351*
parsley
    Parsley-Speckled Pasta Dough,
        46, *47*
    Salsa Verde, 357
pasta. *See also* pasta dough; pasta
    shapes
    Chickpea Soup with Harissa &
        Rosemary, *348*, 349
    cooking in broths and soups, 206
    draining, note about, 253
    dried, cooking "al dente," 204
    fresh, blanching and air-drying,
        207
    fresh, cooking and storing, 204–7
    pairing with sauce, 251–53
    pantry staples, 16–17
    tools, 13–15
    White Bean Soup with Parmesan &
        Kale, 350, *351*
pasta basket, 15
pasta dough. *See also* egg pasta
    dough; flour and water pasta
    dough; gluten-free pasta dough;
    gnocchi dough
    about, 20

creases in, 33
FAQs, 32–33
freezing, 32
gluten and starch in, 25
ideal texture, 30, 33
ingredients, 23–26
kneading time, 33
making by hand, 27–29
making in a food processor, 30
making in a stand mixer, 30
resting and storing, 30–32
serving sizes, 10
techniques, 27–32
too dry, 33
tools for, 13–14
too sticky, 33
vegetable purées for, 55
pasta machine, 14, 114–16
pasta pan, 15
pasta shapes. *See also* hand-cut
    pastas; hand-formed pastas;
    pasta sheets; short-cut pastas;
    stuffed pastas
    cooking in broths and soups, 206
    FAQs, 79
    leftover scraps, ideas for, 79
    rolling, tip for, 79
    sticky, remedy for, 79
    tools for, 14–15
    before you start, 78–79
pasta sheets
    Herb-Laminated Pasta Sheets, *120*,
        121–23
    Patterned Pasta Sheets, 124–27,
        127
    rolling by hand, 117
    rolling gluten-free dough, 117
    rolling with a pasta machine,
        114–16
    short- and long-term storage, 207
    Two-Toned Pasta Sheets, 125
    Two-Toned Polka Dots, 125
pasta wheel (rotella), 14
pastry bags, 15
Patterned Pasta Sheets, 124–27, *127*
peas
    Asparagus & Spring Pea Filling
        with Mint, 229
    Slow-Roasted Salmon & Crème
        Fraîche Sauce with Peas, 328,
        329
peppers
    Orange Vegetable Purée, 55

Red Pesto (Pesto Rosso), *272*, 276
Roasted Red Pepper & Vegetarian
    Sausage Ragù, 318–20, *319*
pesto
    Basil Pesto, *269*, 270–71
    Citrus & Pistachio Pesto, *250*, 275
    Kale & Arugula Pesto, *273*, 277
    Portofino-Style Pesto Lasagne, 201
    Red Pesto (Pesto Rosso), *272*, 276
    Sage & Hazelnut Pesto, 278
    Tomato & Almond Pesto (Pesto alla
        Trapanese), *273*, 274
Pici, *82*, 83–85
Pici Dough, 37
Pink Vegetable Purée, 55
piping bag, 213
Pistachio & Citrus Pesto, *250*, 275
plant-based meat
    The Meatiest Meatless Ragù, *316*,
        317
    Roasted Red Pepper & Vegetarian
        Sausage Ragù, 318–20, *319*
Port-Braised Lamb Ragù with Shallots
    & Rosemary, 321–23, *322*
Portofino-Style Pesto Lasagne, 201
potatoes
    Gluten-Free Potato Gnocchi
        Dough, 69
    Mashed Potato & Chive Filling, 232
    Ossola-Style Chestnut, Squash &
        Potato Gnocchi Dough, 66
    Potato Gnocchi Dough, 67–69, *68*
    Sweet Potato Gnocchi Dough,
        70–73, *71*
potato ricer, 14
pumpkin
    Pumpkin & Ricotta Gnocchi Dough,
        65
    Smoky Pumpkin Sauce, *304*, 305

R
ravioli
    "Classic" Ravioli, 152–57, *154*
    compared with tortelli, 150
    Corzetti Ravioli, 148–49, *149*
    Double-Stuffed Ravioli (Ravioli
        Doppi), 162–65, *165*
    Egg Yolk Ravioli (Uovo in Ravioli),
        159–61, *292*
ricotta, 17
    Black Pepper & Pecorino Filling, 219
    Braised Shallot & Grana Padano
        Filling, 236–37

Four-Cheese Filling, 215
Homemade Ricotta, 61
Meyer Lemon & Herb Ricotta
   Gnocchi Dough, 64
Mushroom, Garlic & Thyme Filling,
   216, 231
Pumpkin & Ricotta Gnocchi Dough,
   65
Ricotta Gnocchi Dough, 60–63, *63*
Roasted Garlic & Rosemary Filling,
   222
Smoked Salmon Filling, 240
Smoky Caramelized Onion Filling,
   239
Spinach & Ricotta Filling, *217,* 218
Whipped Ricotta Filling, 214, *217*
rolling pin, 14
rosemary
   Chickpea Soup with Harissa &
      Rosemary, *348,* 349
   Port-Braised Lamb Ragù with
      Shallots & Rosemary, 321–23,
      322
   Roasted Garlic & Rosemary Filling,
      222
Rye & Sour Cream Pasta Dough, *48,*
   49

S
saffron
   Golden Saffron Sauce, *300,* 301
   Saffron Pasta Dough, 41
   Sausage, Saffron & Fennel Ragù,
      314, *315*
sage
   Autumn Squash Lasagne, 201
   Butter & Sage Sauce (Burro e
      Salvia), *292,* 293
   Sage & Hazelnut Pesto, 278
   Smoky Pumpkin Sauce, *304,* 305
salmon
   Roasted Salmon & Mascarpone
      Filling, 240
   Slow-Roasted Salmon & Crème
      Fraîche Sauce with Peas, 328,
      329
   Smoked Salmon Filling, 240
Salsa Verde, 357
salt, 16, 32, 205–6
sauces. *See also* butter, cream, and
   cheese sauces; fish sauces;
   meaty sauces; tomato sauces;
   vegetable and herb sauces

Besciamella, 202
   pairing with fillings, 213
   pairing with pasta, 251–53
   Salsa Verde, 357
   serving sizes, 10
   tools for, 15
sausages
   Roasted Red Pepper & Vegetarian
      Sausage Ragù, 318–20, *319*
   Sausage, Saffron & Fennel Ragù,
      314, *315*
   Sausage & Spinach Filling, 245
scale, 13
Scarpinocc, 166–67, *167*
semola rimacinata
   about, 23, 26
   Almost All-Yolk Pasta Dough, *44,*
      45
   Basil Pasta Dough, 38
   Black Pepper Pasta Dough, 46,
      47
   brands used, 16
   Citrus-Scented Pasta Dough, 50
   Colorful Egg Pasta Dough, 54
   Colorful Flour & Water Pasta
      Dough, *53,* 54
   Durum Wheat & Water Pasta
      Dough, 37
   Parsley-Speckled Pasta Dough,
      46, *47*
   Saffron Pasta Dough, 41
   Standard Egg Pasta Dough, 45
   substituting semolina for, 23
   Vegan "Egg" Pasta Dough, 45
   Whole Wheat & Water Pasta
      Dough, 38
semolina. *See also* semola rimacinata
   about, 23, 26
   brand used, 16
   substitute, note about, 32
   using in place of semola
      rimacinata, 23
shaker, 14
shallots
   Braised Shallot & Grana Padano
      Filling, 236–37
   Port-Braised Lamb Ragù with
      Shallots & Rosemary, 321–23,
      322
sheet pan, 14
short-cut pastas
   Corzetti Ravioli, 148–49, *149*
   Corzetti Stampati, 146–47, *147*

Farfalle, 140–41, *141*
   Garganelli, 142–44, *145*
   short- and long-term storage, 207
   Sorpresine, *137,* 138–39
slotted spoon, 15
soft wheat. *See also* all-purpose flour;
   00 (double-zero) flour
   about, 23–24, 26
Sorpresine, *137,* 138–39
Sorrento-Style Baked Gnocchi with
   Tomatoes and Mozzarella
   (Gnocchi alla Sorrentina), 203
soups
   Chickpea Soup with Harissa &
      Rosemary, *348,* 349
   Grandma Ruthe's Chicken Soup,
      346, *347*
   White Bean Soup with Parmesan &
      Kale, 350, *351*
Sour Cream & Rye Pasta Dough, *48,*
   49
spices, flavoring dough with, 26
spider sieve, 15
spinach
   Any-Greens Filling, 226, *227*
   Cheesy Spinach Lasagne, *11,* 201
   Green Vegetable Purée, 55
   Sausage & Spinach Filling, 245
   Spinach & Ricotta Filling, *217,* 218
Spizzulus, 104–5, *105*
spray bottle, 14
squash
   Autumn Squash Lasagne, 201
   Fried Zucchini Sauce, 282, *283*
   Ossola-Style Chestnut, Squash &
      Potato Gnocchi Dough, 66
   Pumpkin & Ricotta Gnocchi Dough,
      65
   Smoky Pumpkin Sauce, *304,* 305
   Winter Squash & Brown Butter
      Filling, *216,* 234–35
stand mixer, 30
starch, in wheat flour, 25
stockpot, 15
Strozzapreti, 88–90, *91*
stuffed pastas
   about, 150–51
   Agnolotti & Agnolotti del Plin, *176,*
      177–81, *179*
   Cappelletti, 168–71, *171*
   Caramelle, 182–85, *185*
   "Classic" Ravioli, 152–57, *154*
   cooking, note about, 206

stuffed pastas (*cont.*)
  cooking in broths and soups, 206
  Double-Stuffed Ravioli (Ravioli Doppi), 162–65, *165*
  Egg Yolk Ravioli (Uovo in Ravioli), 159–61, *292*
  lasagne, about, 198–99
  Mezzelune, 155
  My Favorite Lasagne, 200–201
  Scarpinocc, 166–67, *167*
  short- and long-term storage, 207
  Sorrento-Style Baked Gnocchi with Tomatoes and Mozzarella (Gnocchi alla Sorrentina), 203
  Stuffed Gnocchi (Gnocchi Ripieni), 196, *197*
  Tortelloni & Tortellini, 172–75, *175*
  Triangoli, 155
Sweet Potato Gnocchi Dough, 70–73, *71*

T
tagliatelle
  how it is served, 128
  Tagliolini, Tagliatelle, Fettuccine & Pappardelle, *130,* 131–35
tagliolini
  how it is served, 128
  Tagliolini, Tagliatelle, Fettuccine & Pappardelle, *130,* 131–35
Thyme, Mushroom & Garlic Filling, *216,* 231
tomatoes. *See also* tomato sauces
  canned, buying, 17, 254
  Pantry Tuna & Tomato Sauce, 332, *333*
  passata di pomodoro, about, 254
  Red Pesto (Pesto Rosso), *272,* 276
  San Marzano, buying, 254

Sausage, Saffron & Fennel Ragù, 314, *315*
Sorrento-Style Baked Gnocchi with Tomatoes and Mozzarella (Gnocchi alla Sorrentina), 203
Spicy Tomato–Anchovy Butter, 297
Sweet & Sour Eggplant Sauce with Burrata, 286, *287*
Tomato & Almond Pesto (Pesto alla Trapanese), *273,* 274
Tomato Broth, 338, *339*
White Fish Ragù with Lemon & Capers, *326,* 327
tomato sauces
  All-Purpose Tomato Sauce, Three Ways, *255,* 256–57
  choosing tomatoes for, 254
  Fiery Calabrian Chili Sauce, *266,* 267
  No-Cook Tomato & Basil Sauce, *258,* 259
  Slow-Roasted Tomato & Garlic Sauce, *262,* 263
  Tomato-Cream Sauce (No-Vodka Vodka Sauce), 260, *261*
  Tomato Sauce with Olives & Fried Capers, 264, *265*
tongs, 15
tools, 13–15
tortelli, compared with ravioli, 150
Tortelloni & Tortellini, 172–75, *175*
Triangoli, 155
Tuna & Tomato Sauce, Pantry, 332, *333*
Two-Toned Pasta Sheets, 125
Two-Toned Polka Dots, 125

V
Vegan Besciamella, 202
Vegan "Egg" Pasta Dough, 45

vegetable and herb sauces. *See also* pesto
  about, 268
  Braised Onion Ragù, *288,* 289
  Broccoli Sauce, *280,* 281
  Fried Zucchini Sauce, 282, *283*
  Ligurian Walnut Sauce (Salsa di Noci), *272,* 279
  Sweet & Sour Eggplant Sauce with Burrata, 286, *287*
  Wild Mushroom Sauce, *284,* 285
vegetables. *See also* vegetable and herb sauces; *specific vegetables*
  adding to pasta dough, 25
  vegetable purées for dough, 55

W
walnuts
  Kale & Arugula Pesto, *273,* 277
  Ligurian Walnut Sauce (Salsa di Noci), *272,* 279
water, for dough, 24
wheat flour, gluten and starch in, 25
whole-grain flour
  about, 26
  brands used, 16
  storing, 16
  types of, 26
  Whole Wheat Egg Pasta Dough, 45
  Whole Wheat & Water Pasta Dough, 38
  working with, 24
wine
  for pasta dough, 26
  Red Wine Pasta Dough, 50
  White Wine Pasta Dough, 50, *51*
wooden board, 13

Z
Zucchini, Fried, Sauce, 282, *283*

about the author

MERYL FEINSTEIN is a chef, pasta maker, and food writer who left the corporate world for the food industry in 2018. After graduating from the Institute of Culinary Education, Meryl got her start at the renowned New York establishments Lilia and Misi, where she was part of the pasta production team. During her time in New York, she founded Pasta Social Club, a platform that brings people together over a shared love of food, learning, and making connections both on- and offline. She was also a chef-in-residence for the experiential dining program Resident and hosted a supper club in Brooklyn.

Meryl lives with her husband, Adam, in Washington, DC, where she develops recipes and teaches pasta-making workshops. Her writing and recipes have been featured in *Food & Wine* and Food52, for which she was the website's Resident Pasta Maker. She has been quoted as an expert in pasta making for BBC Travel, *La Cucina Italiana,* and Martha Stewart websites and for *New York* magazine, and more. Her dishes draw on her travels in Italy, ongoing research into the rich history of traditional pasta making, and her Jewish heritage, which is at the heart of her love of eating, sharing, and laughing around a communal table.

pastasocialclub.com   @pastasocialclub